HINDU SCR

Hymns from tl

Five Upan

The Bhagavadgītā

EDITED BY NICOL MACNICOL

LONDON: J. M. DENT & SONS LTD.
NEW YORK: E. P. DUTTON & CO. INC.

Printed in Great Britain
by
Hazell, Watson & Viney, Ltd.
London and Aylesbury
for
J. M. Dent & Sons, Ltd.
Aldine House Bedford St London
First Published in this Edition 1938

FOREWORD

THAT Religion, though not infrequently administered as opiate to the people, did not always originate as such, is often ignored by thinkers whose intellectual bias inclines them to purely economic interpretations of social phenomena. A publication therefore which is likely to provide an insight into the inspiration and development of one of the oldest of the living religions, should be welcomed by all intelligent and impartial readers.

Perhaps the most significant thing that strikes the reader as he goes through some of the Vedic Hymns collected here is that they read, not like so many commandments, enjoined by priests or prophets, which in the European mind are identified with Oriental religions, including Christianity, but as a poetic testament of a people's collective reaction to the wonder and awe of existence. A people of vigorous and unsophisticated imagination awakened at the very dawn of civilization to a sense of the inexhaustible mystery that is implicit in Life. It was a simple faith of theirs that attributed divinity to every element and force of Nature, but it was a brave and joyous one, in which fear of the gods was balanced by trust in them, in which the sense of mystery only gave enchantment to life, without weighing it down with bafflement—the faith of a race unburdened with intellectual brooding on the conflicting diversity of the objective universe, though now and again illumined by such flashes of intuitive experience as 'Truth is one: (though) the wise call it by various names' (Ṛigveda I, 164, 46).

It is this brooding on the meaning of existence that chiefly distinguishes the spirit of the Hymns from that of the Upanishads. The same wonder and poetry are there, but deepened and widened by the calm of meditation. Keener spiritual longing shifts the emphasis from the wonder of the outside universe to the significance of the self within. The quest for Reality rebukes the emotional exuberance of the early poet, and compels him inwards to explore the infinite depths of the Soul in which the central principle of creation is reflected.

The early authors were childlike in their reaction, fascinated by what they beheld and naïvely seeking to adjust to it their hopes and fears; but as when children grow they gather an increasing awareness of their selves, the later authors sought more and more a centre of reference in their own consciousness, a subjective counterpart to the objective majesty that had so long held them enthralled in awe, an answer in their own being to the cosmic challenge of the visible universe.

A transcendental spirit of enquiry challenges the old gods, and their mechanical propitiation prescribed by the sacred texts. Says Nārada: 'I know the Ṛigveda, the Yajur, the Sāma-veda, with all these I know only the Mantras and the sacred books, I do not know the Self.'[1] The eternal, the unchanging, the one without a second, is proclaimed, for fear of whom fire burns, for fear of whom the sun shines, and for fear of whom the winds, the clouds, and death perform their offices. And if this Supreme Self is unknowable and incomprehensible, it is yet realizable through self-discipline and knowledge by the Self in man, for the two are ultimately one. Thus man is delivered from the fear of the Cosmic Forces and is made part of the Divine Will.

But the Upanishads, though they measured the highest reaches of the philosophic imagination of our people, were yet incomplete in their answer to the complex longing of the human soul. Their emphasis was too intellectual, and did not sufficiently explore the approach to Reality through love and devotion. Man can never be fully and wholly fulfilled through self-discipline and knowledge, though that self-discipline be superhuman and knowledge transcendental. A more human approach lies through love, which easily withdraws most of the obstacles that the Self interposes between the contemplator and the contemplated, though love too needs self-discipline for its disinterested expression.

This lesson was duly emphasized by the Bhagavadgītā, which finally expounded the harmony between diverse approaches to the Reality that is one, through knowledge, through love, through righteous and detached living, and developed the thesis, that any means that helped the individual to rise above the demands of the ego to his identity with the Supreme Self that is in all being, were the truly legitimate means of that individual's spiritual fulfilment. Thus was rounded up the entire range of Indian spiritual and philosophic speculation and practice, and were reconciled the paths of dispassionate contemplation of the Impersonal, of ecstatic devotion to the Personal, of disinterested

1 *Chhāndogya Upanishad*, VII, *i*, 2, 3.

living in the world of the actual. Sacrifice of desire and not of the object, renunciation of the Self, not of the world, were made the keynote of this harmony of spiritual endeavours.

Such, in brief, is the impression left on the mind of an Indian as he surveys the many many centuries that stretch between the Hymns of the Vedas and the arguments of the Bhagavadgītā.

RABINDRANATH TAGORE.

Thanks are due to the Clarendon Press, Oxford, for permission to use the Upanishads from Max Müller's translation of the *Sacred Books of the East*; E. J. Lazarus & Co. for permission to reprint from *Hymns of the Ṛigveda*; and to Messrs. Dent for *Bhagavadgītā*.

The Introductions in these volumes have not been included in this reprint. A few of the notes to the translations, however, have been included; in the case of the *Bhagavadgītā*, the Summaries given in the notes have been printed at the beginning of each 'Lesson.'

CONTENTS

PAGE

FOREWORD vii

INTRODUCTION xiii

PART I

HYMNS FROM THE ṚIGVEDA

I. TO AGNI: I. 1 3

II. TO VARUṆA: I. 25 4

III. TO INDRA: I. 32 6

IV. TO SŪRYA (THE SUN): I. 50 8

V. TO DAWN: I. 113 9

VI. TO VISHṆU: I. 154 12

VII. TO INDRA: II. 12 13

VIII. TO BRAHMAṆASPATI: II. 25 14

IX. TO VARUṆA: II. 28 15

X. TO INDRA AND OTHERS: III. 62 16

XI. TO VARUṆA: V. 85 18

XII. TO THE WATERS: VII. 49 19

XIII. TO DAWN: VII. 77 20

XIV. TO VARUṆA: VII. 88 21

XV. TO VARUṆA: VIII. 41 22

XVI. TO SOMA PAVAMĀNA: IX. 15 23

XVII. TO THE FATHERS (FUNERAL HYMN): X. 15 . 24

PAGE

XVIII. To Viśvakarman: x. 81 26

XIX. To Viśvakarman: x. 82 27

XX. The Purusha Sūkta (Hymn of Man): x. 90. 28

XXI. To Liberality: x. 117 30

XXII. To Indra: x. 119 31

XXIII. To Prajāpati: x. 121. 32

XXIV. To Agni and Others: x. 124 . . . 33

XXV. To Speech: x. 125 35

XXVI. To Night: x. 127 36

XXVII. The Song of Creation: x. 129 . . . 36

XXVIII. To Faith: x. 151 37

XXIX. Funeral Hymn: x. 154 38

XXX. To Vāyu: x. 168 39

PART II

Bṛihadāraṇyaka Upanishad 43

Chhāndogya Upanishad 117

Kaṭha Upanishad 195

Īśā Upanishad 207

Śvetāśvatara Upanishad 210

PART III

Bhagavadgītā 225

Glossary 291

INTRODUCTION

THE documents included in this volume have been chosen as representative of three successive stages in the history of ancient Hinduism. The fact that they date from so early a period—none of them, probably, being as late as the beginning of the Christian era—must not suggest that they have only an antiquarian interest. These Scriptures are among the main roots of the Hindu religion, which is alive and powerful in contemporary India, and indeed to them, with a single exception, is still attributed an authority equivalent to what is signified by the word 'revelation.' The exception is the last document in the collection, the Bhagavadgītā, which is the latest in time and, in consequence, possesses a less august authority. At the same time it is accorded a place practically on a level with the Upanishads, and is the Scripture that exercises the widest and deepest influence in the India of to-day.

The language in which all these books were originally composed and in which they are still chanted and studied is Sanscrit. The periods to which they belong cannot be determined with any certainty. They have come to us from the midst of a darkness which it is difficult to penetrate. The obscurity which surrounds the origin and early development of the religion of which these are the earliest written records has been increased in recent years by what the excavations at Harappa and Mohenjodaro have revealed. Its beginnings seem to recede farther and farther into the dark backward of time. At the same time the researches that have been pursued during the last hundred years into this religion and its sacred language have been immensely fruitful. From them may be said to have issued the sciences of comparative philology and of comparative religion. Certainly the documents included in this collection have a profound significance in the history of religious aspiration. They furnish evidence of the wrestlings of men's minds with the problem of life and destiny through a period that must have covered at least 1,500 years. The three periods to which these Scriptures belong are separated in time by centuries, and each bears distinctive characteristics of the stage of reflection and discovery which had then been reached. To the first period belong the Vedic Hymns, to the second the Upanishads, and to the third the Bhagavadgītā.

I. The Hymns of the Ṛigveda

Scholars in the West incline to suggest for the composition of the earliest of these hymns a date ranging between 1500 B.C. and 1200 B.C. Indian tradition, on the other hand, claims for them a much earlier antiquity. Any judgment on this matter has to be based entirely, it must be remembered, on internal evidence derived from the Hymns themselves, and is, in consequence, uncertain. It is, however, obvious that this literature is earlier than that of either Greece or Israel, and reveals a high level of civilization among those who found in it the expression of their worship. The view may be said still to hold the field that the Hymns represent the experiences of Aryan tribes as they establish themselves among hostile aborigines in the north-west of India. They are not primitive productions nor are the deities worshipped the creations of human terror. It may be said that the gods are in the main of the order that in Greek religion is termed Olympian. Just as the phallic stone-post was unsuitable to the dignity of Homer, and the Pelasgian Hermes, whose symbol that was, was on that account excluded from the Iliad, so the Aryans also turned away with scorn from the similar worships which they found among the dark-skinned 'dāsas' whom they subdued. 'The Ṛigveda,' Professor Berriedale Keith writes, 'does not present us with any naïve outpouring of the primitive religious consciousness, but with a state of belief which must have been the product of much priestly effort and the outcome of wholesale syncretism.'[1] Accordingly, while there are clinging to the skirts of the Ṛigveda elements belonging to lower conceptions, its worship is in the main directed to sky-gods, and the hymns which are gathered within it are of an aristocratic type and have been selected and approved by a priesthood.

The collection comprises ten books and a total of 1,017 hymns. These grew into their present form, it is surmised, during a long period—perhaps eight centuries—and it is possible to see some indications of change and development when we consider the characteristics of the deities worshipped and the

[1] *Cambridge History of India*, I, 103.

ideas that are associated with one god or another. We cannot do more than glance at one or two among these deities. The most popular god in the pantheon would seem to have been Indra, to whom more than one-fourth of the hymns are directed. He is a warrior god, boastful and gross, but a fit leader of tribes fighting their way through mountain storms and in the midst of enemies. He is hardly, however, a god such as would long satisfy the growing mind of this people, and in one hymn, included in this collection (p. 13), there is a suggestion that some had already begun to turn away from him and say, 'He is not.' It is not surprising, therefore, to find that Indra has no future in India, while Iran goes farther and declares him, in the Avesta, to be a demon. The history of Varuṇa is strangely different. This is a god of the wide sky, who has a pre-eminence among the Vedic gods as, more than any other, identified with the moral order as its guardian. It is agreed by scholars that he is to be identified with Ahura Mazda, the 'Wise Lord' of Zarathustra, one of the loftiest figures that men have ever worshipped; but while he retained his moral eminence in Iran, in India he soon disappears altogether from sight. It is not Varuṇa, any more than Indra, that represents the true direction of the Indian religious mind. It was not an order of righteousness and the Guardian of that order that that mind was really seeking, nor could it find satisfaction in a god who has seemed to many to be more Semitic than Vedic. Not until the tenth book of the Ṛig, when we begin to exchange the too hot blood of Indra for symbols and abstractions, when the imperatives of the ethical order give place to ambiguous speculations as to the cosmic order and its meaning, are we aware that the Indian spirit is finding its natural element and the direction of its future travail. The name Veda signifies 'knowledge,' and already it is becoming evident that the road by which these ancient sages will journey will be rather the road of those who seek to understand than the road of those who are ready to obey or to love.

It is therefore to the hymns of the tenth book that we turn with deepest interest. Those from this book that have been included in the present selection give some indication of the questions that at that time began to occupy attention. The worshippers do not now approach the gods with prayers for cattle or saying, 'Promise us gifts, O Savitar.' The questions they ask are, 'What god shall we adore with our oblation?'

(x, 121, see p. 32). 'Who verily knows and who can here declare it, where it was born and whence comes this creation? The gods are later than this world's production. Who knows, then, whence it first came into being?' (x, 129, see p. 37). The hymn which has as its refrain the first of those questions was given by Max Müller the appropriate title, 'To the Unknown God.' The other hymn quoted, which is generally called 'The Hymn of Creation,' might equally have borne that designation, seeing that it answers its own question in its final stanza, 'Whose eye controls this world in highest heaven, he verily knows, or perhaps he knows not.' The pale cast of thought lies over many of these late hymns, transforming the deities who had once been so full of elemental energy into shadows. 'O Faith, endow us with belief,' one cries, as though not Fear but Faith created the gods, while 'Speech' and 'the Wind' seem to others to be fit symbols of that ultimate essence which they would fain discover. The last words of the concluding hymn in this selection (p. 39) are appropriate to represent the aspirations of these Vedic seers, as they reach behind the powers of nature, seeking some final truth in which their minds can rest.

Germ of the world, the deities' vital spirit, this god moves ever as his will inclines him.
His voice is heard, his shape is ever viewless. Let us adore this Wind with our oblation.

The interest of these ancient hymns lies not so much in their poetical value, though their close contact with nature gives them at times a glow and rapture that are of the very stuff of poetry. It lies rather in the brave adventures, made so long ago and recorded here, of those who seek to discover the significance of our world and of man's life within it. In one direction and another those ancient sages have sought answers to their questions, and in the selections that follow from later Scriptures, this pursuit and its discoveries are carried forward. India here sets out on a quest which she has never ceased to follow. What could be more interesting than to watch these ancient corsairs of the spirit setting forth upon that quest and to listen, after so long a time, to what Max Müller calls 'the first word spoken by the Aryan man?'

II. The Upanishads

We pass to the next stage in this journey of the Indian spirit, and find ourselves breathing a very different air. The subject that engrosses the attention of the seers of the Upanishads is the same that moved the Vedic singers. Their questions are those that recur so often in the hymns with which the Ṛigveda ends, but the Vedic deities are no longer the centre of their hopes. Not the mountain passes only are left behind and forgotten; Indra and Rudra and the gifts that were once sought from them are forgotten also. It is in a spirit of irony that the words are used, 'May the divine Varuṇa, Prajāpati, Savitṛi bring us food!'[1] 'Husband, wife, sons, wealth, cattle are not dear, that one may love them, but that one may love the Ātman, therefore are they dear.'[2] This new vision that has dawned upon them, that of the Ātman, the Ultimate Self, and its significance, has swallowed up all the gods and all the lesser gifts they bring to men. Now in the jungles of a different India, one of wide spaces and slowly flowing rivers, they meditate on the essence of man within and the essence of the world without until there dawns upon them what seems to them to be the final truth of their identity and, in consequence, of the way of escape. Much argument and much reflection must have preceded that discovery, for it comes to them with inward rapture as the supreme attainment, the crown of all their toil. The word 'Upanishad' is derived, we are told, from a root that means 'to sit.' These debates were sessions of those who, 'their hair grown white and having seen their son's son,' the duties of life accomplished, had gone forth from among their fellows to the quietude and release that the forest gave. And there, in 'the sessions of sweet, silent thought,' 'all losses are restored and sorrows end.' If Shakespeare's first adjective is scarcely appropriate to this kind of thinking, his second is altogether so. There is much discussion in the Upanishads, but one is aware that sometimes between question and answer came long silences. The truth they are striving after is beyond speech and indeed beyond knowing. When questions arise that are of very grave consequence for man, their answers are not to be proclaimed aloud. Thus when it comes to the matter of man's final destiny Yājñavalkya takes his pupil aside where no one else can hear. Hand in hand they whisper together, and 'after that Jāratkārava Ārtabhāga held his peace.'[3]

It is not for the systems that they build or for the truths that

[1] *Chhāndogya Upanishad*, I, xii, 5.
[2] *Bṛihadāraṇyaka Upanishad*, IV, v, 6 ff. See pp. 99 f.
[3] *Bṛihadāraṇyaka Upanishad*, III, ii, 13. See p. 71.

they can be said to have discovered that these Scriptures are to be so greatly prized, but rather for the simplicity and earnestness with which great problems are approached. As Professor F. W. Thomas has recently pointed out, 'What gives to the Upanishads their unique quality and unfailing human appeal is an earnest sincerity of tone, as of friends conferring upon matters of deep concern.'[1] We have seen what were some of the perplexing questions to which already in the early Vedic period answers were being sought. Many centuries had passed since then. The Punjab has been left behind, and some of the most remarkable intuitions of these Scriptures seem to have had their origin as far east as Bihār. This is the centre, it will be remembered, from which Buddha's teaching first issued, and it is generally agreed that the chief Upanishads—probably all or nearly all those included in the present collection—are earlier than the rise of Buddhism. Thus we may accept the view that these Upanishads are older then 500 B.C. It follows, if the judgment of Western scholars is well grounded, that a period of, perhaps, four centuries separates the theosophical speculations of these Scriptures from the baffled questionings with which the Ṛigveda ends. Cities have now arisen, taking the place of the uncertain and temporary locations of tribes fighting their way to the possession of a new land, and a stable civilization has come into being and has even begun to feel tired and grown old.

By that time the questions that the Vedic poet had begun to ask had multiplied many times. We get a glimpse, in the early literature of Buddhism, of the Babel of debate that then bewildered men. A Buddhist Scripture names sixty-three philosophical schools that are said to have existed in the days of Buddha. One cannot doubt that a similar condition of intellectual anarchy had prevailed for a considerable time before then. It was indeed a sense of the vanity of much of the speculation that was abroad that drove Buddha to break loose from it all and find a new and different way. He turned from the over-subtlety of much of these speculations as being unprofitable: 'the matter,' he would say, 'does not tend to advantage, to the principle of the religious life.'[2] No doubt there were many charlatans among those who put on the robe of the mendicant and became wanderers and forest-dwellers. The Upanishads are themselves witnesses how foolish and how futile their

1 *The Legacy of India*, p. 62.
2 *Majjima Nikaya*, LXIII, 431.

thinking often was as well as sometimes so wise and so discerning. The name of these Scriptures itself comes to convey the significance of a mystery, a secret disclosure that—sometimes, it would appear, because it was so daring—must be revealed in forest solitudes and there only to a fit disciple.

Such adventurous thinkers must inevitably have been in some cases in antagonism to the priestly classes and the priestly ritual. There are indications of this, though these should not be unduly stressed. There is one passage, for example, in the Chhāndogya where this antagonism finds frank expression. A procession of dogs is described, marching like priests, each dog holding the tail of the dog in front, and crying, 'Om, let us eat! Om, let us drink!'[1] The fact that non-Brāhmans take part in these discussions as well as Brāhmans may mean no more than that the period was one of widespread questioning and that there were sceptic kings as well as sceptic priests. At the same time there are no more daring speculations in all these Scriptures than those of two Brāhmans, Yājñavalkya and the father of Śvetaketu.

The main theme of the Upanishads, involved though it is in so much that is trivial and wholly irrelevant to it, centres round the two words, 'brahman' and 'ātman.' The crowning discovery that they have made is that these two are the same, that is to say, that the reality of the world without is identical with the reality of the self within. This is the final secret that solves all problems. On the way towards that attainment, many alternative suggestions are made and rejected. One such, for example, is that food is brahman, and the conclusion, 'I am the eater of food,' seems for a moment at least to foreshadow the profounder discovery that was to come. 'I overcome the world, I, endowed with golden light.'[2] When the revelation has been more fully grasped and more worthily expressed, as by Uddālaka Āruṇi to his son, it can only be repeated again and again in rapture. 'It is the True. It is the Self, and thou, O Śvetaketu, art it.'[3] 'I am brahman' and 'Thou art that' are the two key-words of the Upanishad secret which unlock felicity.

What is it that they attain by this means? There is no question but that shadows lay in that day upon life that made the

[1] *Chhāndogya Upanishad*, I, xii, 4–5. See p. 127.
[2] *Taittirīya Upanishad*, III, x, 6.
[3] *Chhāndogya Upanishad*, VI, viii ff.

desire to escape from it imperative. The vista of unending rebirths (or, as the Brāhmaṇas say, 're-deaths'), determined inevitably by the deeds men do, had caused thoughtful men to despair of existence and to desire to flee from it. This is the prospect that led Buddha himself later to pronounce existence itself to be misery. If then this secret, this 'upanishad,' was a way of escape, how great was the relief. 'He that knows it, after having become quiet, subdued, satisfied, patient, and collected, sees self in Self, sees all as Self. . . . This great, unborn Self, undecaying, undying, immortal, fearless, is indeed Brahman.'[1] It was as though they said, 'Time ends, eternity's begun.'

But what 'eternity' is this? Yājñavalkya's wife Maitreyi, wishing to enquire further of her husband, asked him to tell her clearly of immortality. He replied, 'That Self is to be described by No, No! He is incomprehensible, for he cannot be comprehended. . . . How, O beloved, should he know the Knower? Thus far goes immortality.' These deep waters would seem to have been too deep for Maitreyī. 'Here, sir,' she says, 'thou hast landed me in utter bewilderment.'[2] The Indian thinker has reached a region, which, whether or not it be the region of the ultimately true, is a place where few can breathe and where the mystics themselves are dumb. 'It is in truth unspeakable,' says Plotinus, 'for if you say anything of it you make it a particular thing.'

Whether or not to Yājñavalkya brahman was conceived as having some shadowy personality, whether, indeed, we should write the name with a capital letter or not, one cannot say with confidence, and Indian interpreters of the Upanishads have on this question always been divided. The coming together of religious longings and philosophical speculations gives to these writings, as to those of such a kindred spirit as Plotinus, that 'troubled intensity,' as it has been called, in which, more than in any positive results they reach, consist their value and their attraction.

The last three Upanishads included in the present collection are probably the latest in date, and may be placed between 500 and 400 B.C. In them the Self is no longer such a purely impersonal goal as had dismayed Maitreyī. Both the Muṇḍaka and the Kaṭha describe the means by which the soul is prepared

[1] *Bṛihadāraṇyaka Upanishad*, IV, iv, 23–25. See p. 99.
[2] *Bṛihadāraṇyaka Upanishad*, IV, v. See p. 101.

to 'see the majesty of the Self' as a moral discipline, and even declare that 'he whom the Self chooses, by him the Self can be gained.' [1] With these Upanishads we approach the standpoint of the next Scripture with which this selection appropriately closes, since it furnishes a notable attempt to bring together some of the varying streams that have flowed down to it through the centuries and to give them a new power and a new direction.

III. The Bhagavadgītā

When we turn to this Scripture, we find ourselves in what is unmistakably a new religious milieu. Its relation with the ancient tradition is maintained through the fact that always behind it looms the Vedic deity Vishṇu. But the fact that with Vishṇu has come to be associated the doctrine of 'avatārs' or descents has made it possible for various newer and more popular worships to be linked up with him and to share in his prestige. One of these was associated with a hero-god called Kṛishṇa, who had drawn to himself many followers and who evoked from them a fervent devotion which was known as 'bhakti.' Thus, while other Vedic deities were fading from the scene, these worships obtained for Vishṇu new vigour and a wider range of influence. In this way there were brought together within Vaishṇavism—each strengthening the other—two movements superficially so diverse as that which centred round the human personality of the warrior Kṛishṇa and that which was concerned with the lonely speculations of the forest-sages.

One of the products of this confluence of various religious streams was the Bhagavadgītā. At some time, probably in or about the second century before the beginning of the Christian era, the genius of an individual or, perhaps, the successive insights of several individuals, succeeded in producing in this document a remarkable eirenicon. The Indian religious spirit and the Indian syncretistic genius united to create what has proved through the centuries a spring of living religious emotion. To those who study this poem from outside, as the foreign student does, it scarcely reveals its entire secret. It certainly seems probable that more than one hand has been at work on its production in its present form, and that that explains why, while its teaching is undoubtedly theistic, its theism must be

[1] *Kaṭha Upanishad*, I, ii, 20, 23, 24 (see pp. 199–200), and *Muṇḍaka Upanishad*, III, ii, 3, 4.

described as half-hearted. It is a garland of many-coloured beauties rather than a well-knit harmony of truth.

The value of the Gītā is accordingly to be estimated, not by the inconsistencies of its theory, but by the experiences of good that well up in it, testifying to springs that reach down deeper than theory. Among these experiences, central to them all, and giving the whole message its value, is bhakti. The word signifies something new, perhaps, in respect of the authority with which it was then uttered, but something which must have had a long history in many hearts in India. The word has been interpreted by one of the greatest of modern 'bhaktas,' who was also a great Sanscrit scholar, Sir Ramkrishna Bhandarkar, as 'loving faith,' and it is, something that has proved itself a precious element in living religion far beyond the bounds of India.

According to Rāmānuja, one of the great system-builders of a later century, the Gītā ends with the words of Kṛishṇa (xviii, 66) which sum up the whole lesson of bhakti: 'Surrendering all the laws, come for refuge to me alone. I will deliver thee from all sins; grieve not.' 'The laws' comprise all that religious custom and tradition might require, sacrifice and works and yogic practice. These ways of attainment have been transcended. 'Whatever be thy work, thine eating, thy sacrifice, thy gift, thy mortification, make thou it an offering to me, O son of Kuntī' (ix, 27).

With 'loving faith' in this central position, a new orientation was given to the religion, and the range of its appeal was greatly widened. Thus it became democratic as the older Brāhmanism could hardly be. The door of hope was not, indeed, opened to all humanity, but it is a great advance to find the Gītā declaring that 'even they that be born of sin,' that is, women and the two lowest classes of the 'sacred order,' Vaiśyas and Śūdras, may by devotion to Kṛishṇa 'come to the supreme path' (ix, 32). And further—a transformation recognized as full of significance by the Hindu of to-day—'action' (karma) ceases to be something always to be shunned as an inevitable means of bondage. Deeds done in the spirit of devotion, 'action that is free from desire,' service, we may say, that is rendered for unselfish ends, no longer enchains, but on the contrary sets men free. 'Casting off all thy works upon me,' Kṛishṇa can say to Arjuna, even on the battlefield, 'put away thy fever and fight.' This is a summons that has found many echoes in the heart of the Indian of to-day.

It is from the governing conception of bhakti that the new life and power of the Gītā issue forth. When we turn to consider who it is to whom this warmth of devotion is to be directed, it may well seem strange to us that the Kṛishṇa who claims it and who is so wise a teacher of religious truth appears elsewhere in the Mahābhārata, of which this poem is a part, as a far from estimable character, as one indeed who is more of a Ulysses than a Nestor. It may also appear incongruous to us that such a message should be conveyed by a charioteer on a battle-field, and should have for its immediate aim the encouragement of a warrior to slay his kinsmen. But perhaps what seems to the Occidental most startling is the theophany that is granted to Arjuna in Lesson XI. Some scholars would resolve the difficulty by separating this section and the opening passage of the poem, in which Arjuna is urged to fight, from the rest as the product of an earlier and cruder religion. Perhaps, however, one has to take into account the religious forms that Hinduism has inherited and believe that this is what appears 'numinous' to it. 'Looking upon thy mighty form,' says Arjuna, 'of many mouths and eyes . . . the worlds and I quake' (xi, 23). Archbishop Söderblom's comment deserves our attention. 'The Vedic gods,' he says, 'have become harmless. This god has a property which is essential to religion. He can terrify.'[1]

The central teaching of the poem is a bhakti theism directed to a god who has 'descended' to human level, but who possesses at the same time a form of terror. There is other teaching as well which is not easy to harmonize with this. There is what is called in Dr. Barnett's translation the School of the Count (Sāṃkhya), which can dispense with a personal deity, and there is the School of the Rule (Yoga) which is theistic. The former seeks by knowledge that end of deliverance from rebirth which engrosses all Indian religion; the latter seeks it by ascetic practice. In neither of them has the worship of a personal god the place that it has in bhakti, to which in the poem they are definitely reckoned as inferior. By both these ways men may journey to 'extinction in Brahma' (v. 24). Between that goal and what Kṛishṇa calls 'coming to me,' there seems to be a deep gulf of difference, and yet to Indian readers the contradictions may not present a difficulty. This aspect of the poem may be stated in the words of Dr. Surendra Das Gupta, the Principal of the Sanscrit College, Calcutta. 'Sometimes,' he writes,

[1] *The Living God*, p. 118.

'in the same passage, and sometimes in passages of the same context the Gītā takes a pantheistic view, reverting in the same breath to a transcendental view, or to a theistic view, and thus seeming to imply that no contradiction was felt in the different aspects of God as preserver and controller of the world, as the substance of the world, life and soul, and as the transcendent substratum underlying them all.'[1]

From the time of its first appearance down through the centuries until to-day, this poem has exercised a remarkable influence. It holds a place alongside of the Upanishads as one of the great sources of the later theological constructions, and every system-builder had to prove his work to be in agreement with the Gītā's message. In Sanscrit and in the vernaculars it has been repeatedly expounded and translated, and it has deeply affected Buddhism as well as Hinduism. Even more remarkable is the evidence of the renewal of its power over men that we find in modern India. Whatever the reasons that may account for this—and one of them certainly is that the Gītā preaches a gospel of action and promises deliverance, in consequence, from the baneful tradition of inaction—the facts are unmistakable and significant. Some of the most distinguished figures in the Indian political field have actually published expositions of its teaching. 'The central sum of the whole system of the Gītā,' writes one of these, Lala Lajpat Rai, 'is the truth that everyone must do his own duty, be true to his own Dharma, at any risk and at any sacrifice.'[2] By all of them this Scripture is exalted as containing a message for their people such as, they believe, the present time urgently demands, what another political leader, Bal Gangadhar Tilak, calls Energism. They hear in it a summons to action. We may well accept the judgment of Dr. Barnett: 'If the greatness of a book be measured by its power over the souls of men, then assuredly the Gītā is a great book.'[3]

N. MACNICOL.

1938.

[1] *Indian Idealism*, p. 59.
[2] *The Message of the Gītā*, p. 33.
[3] *Bhagavadgītā or The Lord's Song.* Translated by L. D. Barnett (The Temple Classics), p. 79.

PART I

HYMNS FROM THE ṚIGVEDA

I

1. 1. To Agni

1\. I LAUD Agni,[1] the chosen priest, god, minister of sacrifice,
The hotar, lavishest of wealth.

2\. Worthy is Agni to be praised by living as by ancient seers:
He shall bring hitherward the gods.

3\. Through Agni man obtaineth wealth, yea, plenty, waxing day by day,
Most rich in heroes, glorious.

4\. Agni, the perfect sacrifice which thou encompassest about
Verily goeth to the gods.

5\. May Agni, sapient-minded priest, truthful, most gloriously great,
The god, come hither with the gods.

6\. Whatever blessing, Agni, thou wilt grant unto thy worshipper,
That, Angiras, is indeed thy truth.

7\. To thee, dispeller of the night, O Agni, day by day with prayer
Bringing thee reverence, we come;

8\. Ruler of sacrifices, guard of law eternal, radiant one,
Increasing in thine own abode.

9\. Be to us easy of approach, even as a father to his son;
Agni, be with us for our weal.

[1] The deity to whom this hymn is addressed is Agni, the god of fire, the most prominent, next to Indra, of the deities of the Ṛigveda. Agni is the messenger and mediator between earth and heaven, announcing to the gods the hymns, and conveying to them the oblations of their worshippers, inviting them with the sound of his crackling flames and bringing them down to the place of sacrifice.

II

I. 25.

To Varuṇa

1. Whatever law of thine, O god, O Varuṇa,[1] as we are men,
Day after day we violate,

2. Give us not as a prey to death, to be destroyed by thee in wrath,
To thy fierce anger when displeased.

3. To gain thy mercy, Varuṇa, with hymns we bind thy heart, as binds
The charioteer his tethered horse.

4. They flee from me dispirited, bent only on obtaining wealth,
As to their nests the birds of air.

5. When shall we bring, to be appeased, the hero, lord of warrior might,
Him, the far-seeing Varuṇa?

6. This—this with joy they both[2] accept in common: never do they fail
The ever-faithful worshipper.

7. He knows the path of birds that fly through heaven, and, sovran of the sea,
He knows the ships that are thereon.

8. True to his holy law, he knows the twelve moons with their progeny;
He knows the moon of later birth.

9. He knows the pathway of the wind, the spreading, high, and mighty wind;
He knows the gods who dwell above.

10. Varuṇa, true to holy law, sits down among his people; he,
Most wise, sits there to govern all.

[1] Varuṇa is king of the air and of the sea, the latter being often regarded as identical with the former. See Introduction, p. xv.
[2] Varuṇa and Mitra. They are both Ādityas, sons of Aditi.

11. From thence perceiving, he beholds all wondrous things, both what hath been
And what hereafter will be done.

12. May that Āditya, very wise, make fair paths for us all our days;
May he prolong our lives for us.

13. Varuṇa, wearing golden mail, hath clad him in a shining robe;
His spies are seated round about.

14. The god whom enemies threaten not, nor those who tyrannize o'er men,
Nor those whose minds are bent on wrong.

15. He who gives glory to mankind, not glory that is incomplete,
To our own bodies giving it.

16. Yearning for the wide-seeing one, my thoughts move onward unto him
As kine unto their pastures move.

17. Once more together let us speak, because my meath[1] is brought; priest-like
Thou eatest what is dear to thee.

18. Now saw I him whom all may see; I saw his car above the earth;
He hath accepted these my songs.

19. Varuṇa, hear this call of mine: be gracious unto us this day,
Longing for help I cry to thee.

20. Thou, O wise god, art lord of all, thou art the king of earth and heaven;
Hear, as thou goest on thy way.

21. Release us from the upper bond, untie the bond between, and loose
The bonds below, that I may live.

[1] *My meath:* or honey (*mádhu*), the libation of soma-juice.

III[1]

I. 32.

To Indra

1. I WILL declare the manly deeds of Indra, the first that he achieved, the thunder-wielder.
He slew the dragon, then disclosed the waters, and cleft the channels of the mountain torrents.

2. He slew the dragon lying on the mountain: his heavenly bolt of thunder Tvashṭar fashioned.
Like lowing kine in rapid flow descending, the waters glided downward to the ocean.

3. Impetuous as a bull, he chose the soma, and in three sacred beakers drank the juices.
Maghavan grasped the thunder for his weapon, and smote to death this firstborn of the dragons.

4. When, Indra, thou hadst slain the dragon's firstborn, and overcome the charms of the enchanters,
Then, giving life to Sun and Dawn and Heaven, thou foundest not one foe to stand against thee.

5. Indra, with his own great and deadly thunder, smote into pieces Vṛitra, worst of Vṛitras.
As trunks of trees, what time the axe hath felled them low on the earth, so lies the prostrate dragon.

6. He, like a mad, weak warrior, challenged Indra, the great, impetuous, many-slaying hero.
He, brooking not the clashing of the weapons, crushed—Indra's foe—the shattered forts in falling.

7. Footless and handless still, he challenged Indra, who smote him with his bolt between the shoulders.
Emasculate yet claiming manly vigour, thus Vṛitra lay with scattered limbs dissevered.

1 'In this we have an ample elucidation of the original purport of the legend of Indra slaying Vṛitra. . . . Vṛitra is nothing more than the accumulation of vapour, condensed or figuratively shut up in, or obstructed by, a cloud. Indra, with his thunderbolt, or atmospheric or electrical influence, divides the aggregated mass, and vent is given to the rain which then descends upon the earth' (Wilson).

8. There, as he lies like a bank-bursting river, the waters taking courage flow above him.
The dragon lies beneath the feet of torrents which Vṛitra with his greatness had encompassed.

9. Then humbled was the strength of Vṛitra's mother: Indra hath cast his deadly bolt against her.
The mother was above, the son was under, and like a cow beside her calf lay Dānu.

10. Rolled in the midst of never-ceasing currents flowing without a rest for ever onward,
The waters bear off Vṛitra's nameless body: the foe of Indra sank to during darkness.

11. Guarded by Ahi stood the thralls of Dāsas, the waters stayed like kine held by the robber.
But he, when he had smitten Vṛitra, opened the cave wherein the floods had been imprisoned.

12. A horse's tail wast thou when he, O Indra, smote on thy bolt; thou, god without a second,
Thou has won back the kine, hast won the soma; thou hast let loose to flow the seven rivers.

13. Nothing availed him lightning, nothing thunder, hailstorm of mist which he had spread around him:
When Indra and the dragon strove in battle, Maghavan gained the victory for ever.

14. Whom sawest thou to avenge the dragon, Indra, that fear possessed thy heart when thou hadst slain him;
That, like a hawk affrighted through the regions, thou crossedst nine-and-ninety flowing rivers?

15. Indra is king of all that moves and moves not, of creatures tame and horned, the thunder-wielder.
Over all living men he rules as sovran, containing all as spokes within the felly.

IV

I. 50. **To Sūrya (the Sun)**

1. His bright rays bear him up aloft, the god who knoweth all that lives,
Sūrya, that all may look on him.

2. The constellations pass away, like thieves, together with their beams,
Before the all-beholding Sun.

3. His herald rays are seen afar refulgent o'er the world of men,
Like flames of fire that burn and blaze.

4. Swift and all beautiful art thou, O Sūrya, maker of the light,
Illuming all the radiant realm.

5. Thou goest to the hosts of gods, thou comest hither to mankind,
Hither all light to behold.

6. With that same eye of thine wherewith thou lookest, brilliant Varuṇa,
Upon the busy race of men,

7. Traversing sky and wide mid-air, thou metest with thy beams our days,
Sun, seeing all things that have birth.

8. Seven bay steeds harnessed to thy car bear thee, O thou far-seeing one,
God, Sūrya with the radiant hair.

9. Sūrya hath yoked the pure bright seven, the daughters of the car ; with these,
His own dear team, he goeth forth.

10. Looking upon the loftier light above the darkness, we have come
To Sūrya, god among the gods, the light that is most excellent.

11. Rising this day, O rich in friends, ascending to the loftier heaven,
Sūrya, remove my heart's disease, take from me this my yellow hue.

12. To parrots and to starlings let us give away my yellowness
Or this my yellowness let us transfer to haritāla trees.

13. With all his conquering vigour, this Āditya hath gone up on high,
Giving my foe into mine hand: let me not be my foeman's prey.

V

I. 113.

To Dawn

1. This light is come, amid all lights the fairest; born is the brilliant, far-extending brightness.
Night, sent away for Savitar's[1] uprising, hath yielded up a birthplace for the morning.

2. The fair, the bright is come with her white offspring; to her the dark one hath resigned her dwelling.
Akin, immortal, following each other, changing their colours, both the heavens move onward.

3. Common, unending is the sisters' pathway: taught by the gods, alternately they travel.
Fair-formed, of different hues and yet one-minded, Night and Dawn clash not, neither do they tarry.

4. Bright leader of glad sounds, our eyes behold her: splendid in hue she hath unclosed the portals.
She, stirring up the world, hath shown us riches: Dawn hath awakened every living creature.

5. Rich Dawn, she sets afoot the coiled-up sleeper, one for enjoyment, one for wealth or worship,
Those who saw little for extended vision: all living creatures hath the Dawn awakened.

[1] *Savitar:* the sun.

6. One to high sway, one to exalted glory, one to pursue his gain and one his labour;
All to regard their different vocations, all moving creatures hath the Dawn awakened.

7. We see her there, the child of heaven, apparent, the young maid, flushing in her shining raiment.
Thou sovran lady of all earthly treasure, flush on us here, auspicious Dawn, this morning.

8. She, first of endless morns to come hereafter, follows the path of morns that have departed.
Dawn, at her rising, urges forth the living: him who is dead she wakes not from his slumber.

9. As thou, Dawn, hast caused Agni to be kindled, and with the sun's eye hast revealed creation,
And hast awakened men to offer worship, thou hast performed, for gods, a noble service.

10. How long a time, and they shall be together.—Dawns that have shone and dawns to shine hereafter?[1]
She yearns for former dawns with eager longing, and goes forth gladly shining with the others.

11. Gone are the men who in the days before us looked on the rising of the earlier morning.
We, we the living, now behold her brightness, and they come nigh who shall hereafter see her.

12. Foe-chaser, born of Law, the law's protectress, joy-giver, waker of all pleasant voices,
Auspicious, bringing food for gods' enjoyment, shine on us here, most bright, O Dawn, this morning.

13. From days eternal hath Dawn shone, the goddess, and shows this light to-day, endowed with riches.
So will she shine on days to come; immortal she moves on in her own strength, undecaying.

[1] The meaning appears to be: How long have we to live? When will all our future dawns be with those that have passed away? Wilson, following Sāyana, translates: 'For how long a period is it that the dawns have risen? For how long a period will they rise?'

14. In the sky's borders hath she shone in spendour : the goddess hath thrown off the veil of darkness.
Awakening the world with purple horses, on her well-harnessed chariot Dawn approaches.

15. Bringing all life-sustaining blessings with her, showing herself, she sends forth brilliant lustre.
Last of the countless mornings that have vanished, first of bright morns to come hath Dawn arisen.

16. Arise ! the breath, the life, again hath reached us : darkness hath passed away, and light approacheth.
She for the sun hath left a path to travel : we have arrived where men prolong existence.

17. Singing the praises of refulgent mornings with his hymn's web, the priest, the poet, rises.
Shine then to-day, rich maid, on him who lauds thee, shine down on us the gift of life and offspring.

18. Dawns giving sons all heroes, kine and horses, shining upon the man who brings oblations,—
These let the soma-presser gain when ending his glad songs louder than the voice of Vāyu.

19. Mother of gods, Aditi's form of glory, ensign of sacrifice, shine forth exalted.
Rise up, bestowing praise on our devotion : all-bounteous, make us chief among the people.

20. Whatever splendid wealth the dawns bring with them to bless the man who offers praise and worship,
Even that may Mitra, Varuṇa vouchsafe us, and Aditi and Sindhu, earth and heaven.

VI

I. 154.

To Vishṇu

1. I WILL declare the mighty deeds of Vishṇu,[1] of him who measured out the earthly regions,
Who propped the highest place of congregation,[2] thrice setting down his footstep, widely striding.

2. For this his mighty deed is Vishṇu lauded, like some wild beast, dread, prowling, mountain roaming;
He within whose three wide-extended paces all living creatures have their habitation.

3. Let the hymn lift itself as strength to Vishṇu, the bull, far-striding, dwelling on the mountains,
Him who alone with triple step hath measured this common dwelling-place, long, far extended,

4. Him whose three places that are filled with sweetness, imperishable, joy as it may list them,
Who verily alone upholds the threefold, the earth, the heaven, and all living creatures.

5. May I attain to that his well-loved mansion where men devoted to the gods are happy.
For there springs, close akin to the wide-strider, the well of meath in Vishṇu's highest footstep.

6. Fain would we go unto your dwelling-places where there are many horned and nimble oxen,
For mightily, there, shineth down upon us the widely-striding Bull's sublimest mansion.

[1] That which distinguishes Vishṇu from the other Vedic deities is chiefly his striding over the heavens, which he is said to do in three paces, explained as denoting the threefold manifestation of light in the form of fire, lightning, and the sun, or as designating the three daily stations of the sun, in his rising, culminating, and setting.

[2] *The highest place of congregation:* heaven, where the gods are assembled.

VII

II. 12. **To Indra**

1. He who, just born, chief god of lofty spirit by power and might became the gods' protector,
Before whose breath through greatness of his valour the two worlds trembled, he, O men, is Indra.

2. He who fixed fast and firm the earth that staggered, and set at rest the agitated mountains,
Who measured out the air's wide middle region and gave the heaven support, he, men, is Indra.

3. Who slew the dragon, freed the seven rivers, and drove the kine forth from the cave of Vala,
Begat the fire between two stones, the spoiler in warrior's battle, he, O men, is Indra.

4. By whom this universe was made to tremble, who chased away the humbled brood of demons,
Who, like a gambler gathering his winnings, seized the foe's riches, he, O men, is Indra.

5. Of whom, the terrible, they ask, Where is he? or verily they say of him, He is not.
He sweeps away, like birds, the foe's possessions. Have faith in him, for he, O men, is Indra.

6. Stirrer to action of the poor and lowly, of priest, of suppliant who sings his praises;
Who, fair-faced, favours him who presses soma with stones made ready, he, O men, is Indra.

7. He under whose supreme control are horses, all chariots, and the villages, and cattle;
He who gave being to the sun and morning, who leads the waters, he, O men, is Indra.

8. To whom two armies cry in close encounter, both enemies the stronger and the weaker;
Whom two invoke upon one chariot mounted, each for himself, he, O ye men, is Indra.

9. Without whose help our people never conquer; whom, battling, they invoke to give them succour;
He of whom all this world is but the copy, who shakes things moveless, he, O men, is Indra.

10. He who hath smitten, ere they knew their danger, with his hurled weapon many grievous sinners;
Who pardons not his boldness who provokes him, who slays the Dasyu, he, O men, is Indra.

11. He who discovered in the fortieth autumn Śambara as he dwelt among the mountains;
Who slew the dragon putting forth his vigour, the demon lying there, he, men, is Indra.

12. Who with seven guiding reins, the bull, the mighty, set free the seven great floods to flow at pleasure;
Who, thunder-armed, rent Rauhiṇa in pieces when scaling heaven, he, O ye men, is Indra.

13. Even the heaven and earth bow down before him, before his very breath the mountains tremble.
Known as the soma-drinker, armed with thunder, who wields the bolt, he, O ye men, is Indra.

14. Who aids with favour him who pours the soma and him who brews it, sacrificer, singer,
Whom prayer exalts, and pouring forth of soma, and this our gift, he, O ye men, is Indra.

15. Thou verily art fierce and true who sendest strength to the man who brews and pours libation.
So may we evermore, thy friends, O Indra, speak loudly to the synod with our heroes.

VIII

II. 25. TO BRAHMAṆASPATI[1]

1. HE, lighting up the flame, shall conquer enemies: strong shall he be who offers prayer and brings his gift.
He with his seed spreads forth beyond another's seed, whomever Brahmaṇaspati takes for his friend.

1 *Brahmaṇaspati:* alternating with Bṛihaspati, the deity in whom the action of the worshipper upon the gods is personified. A comparatively recent god, as the representative of the hierarchy, he is gradually encroaching on the jurisdiction of Indra, the warrior god of the Kshatriyas, claiming his achievements as his own and assuming his attributes.

2. With heroes he shall overcome his hero foes, and spread his wealth by kine: wise by himself is he.
His children and his children's children grow in strength, whomever Brahmaṇaspati takes for his friend.

3. He, mighty like a raving river's billowy flood, as a bull conquers oxen, overcomes with strength.
Like Agni's blazing rush he may not be restrained, whomever Brahmaṇaspati takes for his friend.

4. For him the floods of heaven flow never-failing down: first with the heroes he goes forth to war for kine.
He slays in unabated vigour with great might, whomever Brahmaṇaspati takes for his friend.

5. All roaring rivers pour their waters down for him, and many a flawless shelter hath been granted him.
Blest with the happiness of gods he prospers well, whomever Brahmaṇaspati takes for his friend.

IX

II. 28.

To Varuṇa

1. This laud of the self-radiant wise Āditya[1] shall be supreme o'er all that is in greatness.
I beg renown of Varuṇa the mighty, the god exceeding kind to him who worships.

2. Having extolled thee, Varuṇa, with thoughtful care may we have high fortune in thy service.
Singing thy praises like the fires at coming, day after day, of mornings rich in cattle.

3. May we be in thy keeping, O thou leader, wide ruling Varuṇa, Lord of many heroes.
O sons of Aditi, for ever faithful, pardon us, gods, admit us to your friendship.

4. He made them flow, the Āditya, the sustainer: the rivers run by Varuṇa's commandment.
These feel no weariness, nor cease from flowing: swift have they flown like birds in air around us.

[1] *This laud:* the poet magnifies the importance of the worship which he offers to the Āditya Varuṇa, the great king over all, the god of natural, peaceful, moral order as contrasted with Indra, the god of battles.

5. Loose me from sin as from a band that binds me: may we swell, Varuṇa, thy spring of order.
Let not my thread, while I weave song, be severed, nor my work's sum, before the time, be shattered.

6. Far from me, Varuṇa, remove all danger: accept me graciously, thou holy sovran.
Cast off, like cords that hold a calf, my troubles: I am not even mine eyelid's lord without thee.

7. Strike us not, Varuṇa, with those dread weapons which, Asura, at thy bidding wound the sinner.
Let us not pass away from light to exile. Scatter, that we may live, the men who hate us.

8. O mighty Varuṇa, now and hereafter, even as of old, will we speak forth our worship.
For in thyself, invincible god, thy statutes ne'er to be moved are fixed as on a mountain.

9. Move far from me what sins I have committed: let me not suffer, King, for guilt of others.
Full many a morn remains to dawn upon us: in these, O Varuṇa, while we live direct us.

10. O king, whoever, be he friend or kinsman, hath threatened me affrighted in my slumber—
If any wolf or robber fain would harm us, therefrom, O Varuṇa, give thou us protection.

11. May I not live, O Varuṇa, to witness my wealthy, liberal, dear friend's destitution.
King, may I never lack well-ordered riches. Loud may we speak with heroes in assembly.

X

III. 62. To Indra and Others[1]

1. Your well-known prompt activities aforetime needed no impulse from your faithful servant.
Where, Indra-Varuṇa, is now that glory wherewith ye brought support to those who loved you?

[1] The hymn consists of six *trichas* or triplets, the deities of which are severally (1) Indra and Varuṇa, (2) Bṛihaspati, (3) Pūshan, (4) Savitar, (5) Soma, (6) Mitra and Varuṇa.

2. This man, most diligent, seeking after riches, incessantly invokes you for your favour.
Accordant, Indra-Varuṇa, with Maruts, with heaven and earth, hear ye mine invocation.

3. O Indra-Varuṇa, ours be this treasure, ours be wealth, Maruts, with full store of heroes.
May the Varūtrīs with their shelter aid us, and Bhāratī and Hotrā with the mornings.

4. Be pleased with our oblations, thou loved of all gods, Bṛihaspati:
Give wealth to him who brings thee gifts.

5. At sacrifices, with your hymns worship the pure Bṛihaspati—
I pray for power which none may bend—

6. The bull of men, whom none deceive, the wearer of each shape at will,
Bṛihaspati most excellent.

7. Divine, resplendent Pūshan, this our newest hymn of eulogy
By us is chanted forth to thee.

8. Accept with favour this my song, be gracious to the earnest thought,
Even as a bridegroom to his bride.

9. May he who sees all living things, sees them together at a glance—
May he, may Pūshan be our help.

10. May we attain that excellent glory of Savitar the god:
So may he stimulate our prayers.[1]

11. With understanding, earnestly, of Savitar the god we crave
Our portion of prosperity.

[1] This stanza is the Sāvitrī, the Gāyatrī *par excellence*, 'the celebrated verse of the Vedas which forms part of the daily devotions of the Brāhmans and was first made known to English readers by Sir W. Jones's translation of a paraphrastic interpretation; he renders it, Let us adore the supremacy of that divine sun, the god-head, who illuminates all, from whom all proceed, to whom all must return, whom we invoke to direct our understandings aright in our progress towards his holy seat.'

12. Men, singers worship Savitar the god with hymn and holy rites,
Urged by the impulse of their thoughts.

13. Soma, who gives success, goes forth, goes to the gathering-place of gods,
To seat him at the seat of Law.

14. To us and to our cattle may Soma give salutary food,
To biped and to quadruped.

15. May Soma, strengthening our power of life, and conquering our foes,
In our assembly take his seat.

16. May Mitra-Varuṇa, sapient pair, bedew our pasturage with oil,
With meath the regions of the air.

17. Far-ruling, joyful when adored, ye reign through majesty of might,
With pure laws everlastingly.

18. Lauded by Jamadagni's song, sit in the place of holy Law:
Drink soma, ye who strengthen Law.

XI

v. 85. To Varuṇa

1. Sing forth a hymn sublime and solemn, grateful to glorious Varuṇa, imperial ruler,
Who hath struck out, like one who slays the victim, earth as a skin to spread in front of Sūrya.

2. In the tree-tops the air he hath extended, put milk in kine and vigorous speed in horses,
Set intellect in hearts, fire in the waters, Sūrya in heaven and Soma on the mountain.

3. Varuṇa lets the big cask, opening downward, flow through the heaven and earth and air's mid-region.
Therewith the universe's sovran waters earth as the shower of rain bedews the barley.

4. When Varuṇa is fain for milk, he moistens the sky, the land, and earth to her foundation.
Then straight the mountains clothe them in the rain-cloud: the heroes, putting forth their vigour, loose them.

5. I will declare this mighty deed of magic, of glorious Varuṇa, the lord immortal,
Who, standing in the firmament, hath meted the earth out with the sun as with a measure.

6. None, verily, hath ever let or hindered this the most wise god's mighty deed of magic,
Whereby with all their flood, the lucid rivers fill not one sea wherein they pour their waters.

7. If we have sinned against the man who loves us, have ever wronged a brother, friend, or comrade,
The neighbour ever with us, or a stranger, O Varuṇa, remove from us the trespass.

8. If we, as gamesters cheat at play, have cheated, done wrong unwittingly or sinned of purpose,
Cast all these sins away like loosened fetters, and, Varuṇa, let us be thine own beloved.

XII

VII. 49. **To the Waters**

1. Forth from the middle of the flood the Waters—their chief the sea—flow cleansing, never sleeping.
Indra, the bull, the thunderer, dug their channels; here let those Waters, goddesses, protect me.

2. Waters which come from heaven, or those that wander dug from the earth, or flowing free by nature,
Bright, purifying, speeding to the ocean; here let those Waters, goddesses, protect me.

3. Those amid whom goes Varuṇa the sovran, he who discriminates men's truth and falsehood—
Distilling meath, the bright, the purifying; here let those Waters, goddesses, protect me.

4. They from whom Varuṇa the king, and Soma, and all the deities drink strength and vigour,
They into whom Vaiśvānara Agni entered; here let those Waters, goddesses, protect me.

XIII

VII. 77. To Dawn

1. She hath shone brightly like a youthful woman, stirring to motion every living creature.
Agni hath come to feed on mortals' fuel. She hath made light and chased away the darkness.

2. Turned to this all, far-spreading, she hath risen and shone in brightness with white robes about her.
She hath beamed forth lovely with golden colours, mother of kine, guide of the days she bringeth.

3. Bearing the gods' own eye, auspicious lady, leading her courser white and fair to look on,
Distinguished by her beams, Dawn shines apparent, come forth to all the world with wondrous treasure.

4. Draw nigh with wealth and dawn away the foeman: prepare for us wide pasture free from danger.
Drive away those who hate us, bring us riches: pour bounty, opulent lady, on the singer.

5. Send thy most excellent beams to shine and light us, giving us lengthened days, O Dawn, O goddess,
Granting us food, thou who hast all things precious, and bounty rich in chariots, kine, and horses.

6. O Ushas, nobly-born, daughter of heaven, whom the Vasishṭhas with their hymns make mighty,
Bestow thou on us vast and glorious riches. Preserve us evermore, ye gods, with blessings.

XIV

VII. 88. **To Varuṇa**

1. Present to Varuṇa thine hymn, Vasishṭha, bright, most delightful to the bounteous giver,
Who bringeth on to us the Bull,[1] the lofty, the holy, laden with a thousand treasures.

2. And now, as I am come before his presence, I take the face of Varuṇa for Agni's.
So might he bring—lord also of the darkness—the light in heaven that I may see its beauty!

3. When Varuṇa and I embark together and urge our boat into the midst of ocean,
We, when we ride o'er ridges of the waters, will swing within that swing and there be happy.[2]

4. Varuṇa placed Vasishṭha in the vessel, and deftly with his might made him a Ṛishi.
When days shone bright, the sage made him a singer, while the heavens broadened and the dawns were lengthened.

5. What hath become of those our ancient friendships, when without enmity we walked together?
I, Varuṇa, thou glorious lord, have entered thy lofty home, thine house with thousand portals.

6. If he, thy true ally, hath sinned against thee, still, Varuṇa, he is the friend thou lovedst.
Let us not, Living One, as sinners, know thee: give shelter, as a sage, to him who lauds thee.

[1] *The Bull:* the sun.

[2] 'The kernel of the hymn lies in verses 3–6. The singer believes that he has been forsaken by his helper Varuṇa; with anguish he remembers his communion with the god in former times. In a vision he sees himself translated into Varuṇa's realm, he goes sailing with the god, is called to be Ṛishi or holy singer to the god, and is in his palace with him. Now, Varuṇa has withdrawn his favour, yet let him have mercy on his singer, and not punish him so grievously for his sin. The hymn perhaps originally closed with verse 6.'—Prof. von Roth's note in the *Siebenzig Lieder*, translated by Prof. Peterson.

7. While we abide in these fixed habitations, and from the lap of Aditi win favour,
May Varuṇa untie the bond that binds us. Preserve us, evermore, ye gods, with blessings.

XV

VIII. 41.

To Varuṇa

1. To make this Varuṇa come forth, sing thou a song unto the band of Maruts wiser than thyself—
This Varuṇa who guardeth well the thoughts of men like herds of kine.
Let all the others die away.

2. Him altogether praise I with the song and hymns our fathers sang, and with Nābhāka's eulogies—
Him dwelling at the rivers' source, surrounded by his sisters seven.

3. The night he hath encompassed, and stablished the morns with magic art: visible over all is he.
His dear ones, following his law, have prospered the three dawns for him.

4. He, visible o'er all the earth, stablished the quarters of the sky:
He measured out the eastern place, that is the fold of Varuṇa: like a strong herdsman is the god.

5. He who supports the worlds of life, he who well knows the hidden names mysterious of the morning beams,
He cherishes much wisdom, sage, as heaven brings forth each varied form,

6. In whom all wisdom centres, as the nave is set within the wheel.
Haste ye to honour Trita, as kine haste to gather in the fold, even as they muster steeds to yoke.

7. He wraps these regions as a robe; he contemplates the tribes of gods and all the works of mortal men.
Before the home of Varuṇa all the gods follow his decree.

8. He is an ocean far-removed, yet through the heaven to him ascends the worship which these realms possess.
With his bright foot he overthrew their magic, and went up to heaven,

9. Ruler, whose bright, far-seeing rays, pervading all three earths, have filled the three superior realms of heaven.
Firm is the seat of Varuṇa: over the seven he rules as king.

10. Who, after his decree, o'erspread the dark ones with a robe of light;
Who measured out the ancient seat, who pillared both the worlds apart as the unborn supported heaven.
Let all the others die away.

XVI

IX. 15.

To Soma Pavamāna [1]

1. THROUGH the fine fingers, with the song, this hero comes with rapid cars,
Going to Indra's special place.

2. In holy thought he ponders much for the great worship of the gods,
Where the immortals have their seat.

3. Like a good horse is he led out, when on the path that shines with light
The mettled steeds exert their strength.

4. He brandishes his horns on high, and whets them, bull who leads the herd,
Doing with might heroic deeds.

5. He moves, a vigorous steed, adorned with beauteous rays of shining gold,
Becoming sovran of the streams.

[1] Nearly all the hymns of Book IX are addressed to the deified soma-juice, or to Soma, or Indu, the moon, who, as containing the celestial nectar, the drink of the gods, is identified with the soma-plant and its exhilarating juice. As the moon-god pours down his ambrosial rain through the sieve of heaven, he is addressed and worshipped as Pavamāna (self-purifying), represented by the soma-juice as it undergoes purification by flowing through the wool which is used as a filter or strainer.

6. He, over places rough to pass, bringing rich treasures closely packed,
Descends into the reservoirs.

7. Men beautify him in the vats, him worthy to be beautified,
Him who brings forth abundant food.

8. Him, even him, the fingers ten and the seven songs make beautiful,
Well-weaponed, best of gladdeners.

XVII

x. 15. To the Fathers (Funeral Hymn)

1. May they ascend, the lowest, highest, midmost, the fathers who deserve a share of soma.
May they who have attained the life of spirits, gentle and righteous, aid us when we call them.

2. Now let us pay this homage to the Fathers, to those who passed of old and those who followed,
Those who have rested in the earthly region, and those who dwell among the mighty races.

3. I have attained the gracious-minded Fathers, I have gained son and progeny from Vishṇu.
They who enjoy pressed juices with oblation, seated on sacred grass, come oftenest hither.

4. Fathers who sit on sacred grass, come, help us: these offerings have we made for you; accept them.
So come to us with most auspicious favour, and give us health and strength without a trouble.

5. May they, the Fathers, worthy of the soma, invited to their favourite oblations
Laid on the sacred grass, come nigh and listen: may they be gracious unto us and bless us.

6. Bowing your bended knees and seated southward, accept this sacrifice of ours with favour.
Punish us not for any sin, O Fathers, which we through human frailty have committed.

7. Lapped in the bosom of the purple mornings, give riches to the man who brings oblations.
Grant to your sons a portion of that treasure, and, present, give them energy, ye Fathers.

8. Our ancient Fathers who deserve the soma, who came, most noble, to our soma banquet—
With these let Yama, yearning with the yearning, rejoicing eat our offerings at his pleasure.

9. Come to us, Agni, with the gracious Fathers who dwell in glowing light, the very Kavyas,
Who thirsted 'mid the gods, who hasten hither, oblation-winners, theme of singers' praises.

10. Come, Agni, come with countless ancient Fathers, dwellers in light, primeval, God-adorers,
Eaters and drinkers of oblations, truthful, who travel with the deities and Indra.

11. Fathers whom Agni's flames have tasted, come ye nigh: ye kindly leaders, take ye each your proper place.
Eat sacrificial food presented on the grass: grant riches with a multitude of hero sons.

12. Thou, Agni Jātavedas, when entreated, didst bear the offerings which thou madest fragrant,
And give them to the Fathers who did eat them with Svadhā. Eat, thou god, the gifts we bring thee.

13. Thou, Jātavedas, knowest well the number of Fathers who are here and who are absent,
Of Fathers whom we know and whom we know not: accept the sacrifice well-prepared with portions.

14. They who, consumed by fire or not cremated, joy in their offering in the midst of heaven—
Grant them, O sovran lord, the world of spirits and their own body, as thy pleasure wills it.

XVIII

x. 81. To Viśvakarman [1]

1. He who sate down as Hotar-priest, the Ṛishi, our father, offering up all things existing—
He, seeking through his wish a great possession, came among men on earth as archetypal.

2. What was the place whereon he took his station? What was it that supported him? How was it?
Whence Viśvakarman, seeing all, producing the earth, with mighty power disclosed the heavens.

3. He who hath eyes on all sides round about him, a mouth on all sides, arms and feet on all sides,
He, the sole god, producing earth and heaven, weldeth them, with his arms as wings, together.

4. What was the tree, what wood in sooth produced it, from which they fashioned out the earth and heaven?
Ye thoughtful men inquire within your spirit whereon he stood when he established all things.

5. Thine highest, lowest, sacrificial natures and these thy midmost here, O Viśvakarman,
Teach thou thy friends at sacrifice, O Blessed, and come thyself, exalted, to our worship.

6. Bring thou thyself, exalted with oblation, O Viśvakarman, earth and heaven to worship.
Let other men around us live in folly: here let us have a rich and liberal patron.

7. Let us invoke to-day, to aid our labour, the lord of speech, the thought-swift Viśvakarman.
May he hear kindly all our invocations who gives all bliss for aid, whose works are righteous.

[1] Viśvakarman is represented in this hymn as the universal father and generator, the creator of all things and architect of the worlds.

XIX

x. 82. To Viśvakarman

1. The father of the eye, the wise in spirit, created both these worlds submerged in fatness.
Then when the eastern ends were firmly fastened, the heavens and the earth were far extended.

2. Mighty in mind and power is Viśvakarman, maker, disposer, and most lofty presence.
Their offerings joy in rich juice where they value one, only one, beyond the seven Ṛishis.

3. Father who made us, he who, as disposer, knoweth all races and all things existing,
Even he alone, the deities' name-giver—him other beings seek for information.

4. To him in sacrifice they offered treasures—Ṛishis of old, in numerous troops, as singers,
Who, in the distant, near, and lower region, made ready all these things that have existence.

5. That which is earlier than this earth and heaven, before the Asuras and gods had being—
What was the germ primeval which the waters received where all the gods were seen together?

6. The waters, they received that germ primeval wherein the gods were gathered all together.
It rested set upon the unborn's navel, that one wherein abide all things existing.

7. Ye will not find him who produced these creatures: another thing hath risen up among you.
Enwrapt in misty cloud, with lips that stammer, hymn-chanters wander and are discontented.

XX

x. 90. The Purusha Sūkta (Hymn of Man)

1. A thousand heads hath Purusha,[1] a thousand eyes, a thousand feet.
On every side pervading earth he fills a space ten fingers wide.

2. This Purusha is all that yet hath been and all that is to be,
The lord of immortality which waxes greater still by food.

3. So mighty is his greatness; yea, greater than this is Purusha.
All creatures are one-fourth of him, three-fourths eternal life in heaven.

4. With three-fourths Purusha went up: one-fourth of him again was here.
Thence he strode out to every side over what eats not and what eats.

5. From him Virāj was born; again Purusha from Virāj was born.
As soon as he was born he spread eastward and westward o'er the earth.

6. When gods prepared the sacrifice with Purusha as their offering,
Its oil was spring; the holy gift was autumn; summer was the wood.

7. They balmed as victim on the grass Purusha born in earliest time.
With him the deities and all Sādhyas and Ṛishis sacrificed.

[1] *Purusha*, embodied spirit, or man personified and regarded as the soul and original source of the universe, the personal and life-giving principle in all animated beings, is said to have a *thousand*, that is innumerable, *heads, eyes, and feet*, as being one with all created life. *A space ten fingers wide:* the region of the heart of man, wherein the soul was supposed to reside. Although as the universal soul he pervades the universe, as the individual soul he is enclosed in a space of narrow dimensions.

8. From that great general sacrifice the dripping fat was gathered up.
He formed the creatures of the air, and animals both wild and tame.

9. From that great general sacrifice Ṛichas and Sāma-hymns were born:
Therefrom were spells and charms produced; the Yajus had its birth from it.

10. From it were horses born, from it all cattle with two rows of teeth:
From it were generated kine, from it the goats and sheep were born.

11. When they divided Purusha, how many portions did they make?
What do they call his mouth, his arms? What do they call his thighs and feet?

12. The Brāhman was his mouth, of both his arms was the Rājanya made.
His thighs became the Vaiśya, from his feet the Śūdra was produced.

13. The moon was gendered from his mind, and from his eye the sun had birth;
Indra and Agni from his mouth were born, and Vāyu from his breath.

14. Forth from his navel came mid-air; the sky was fashioned from his head;
Earth from his feet, and from his ear the regions. Thus they formed the worlds.

15. Seven fencing-sticks had he, thrice seven layers of fuel were prepared,
When the gods, offering sacrifice, bound, as their victim, Purusha.

16. Gods, sacrificing, sacrificed the victim: these were the earliest holy ordinances.
The mighty ones attained the height of heaven, there where the Sādhyas, gods of old, are dwelling.

XXI

X. 117. **To Liberality**

1. The gods have not ordained hunger to be our death: even to the well-fed man comes death in varied shape.
The riches of the liberal never waste away, while he who will not give finds none to comfort him.

2. The man with food in store who, when the needy comes in miserable case begging for bread to eat,
Hardens his heart against him—even when of old he did him service—finds not one to comfort him.

3. Bounteous is he who gives unto the beggar who comes to him in want of food and feeble.
Success attends him in the shout of battle. He makes a friend of him in future troubles.

4. No friend is he who to his friend and comrade who comes imploring food, will offer nothing.
Let him depart—no home is that to rest in—and rather seek a stranger to support him.

5. Let the rich satisfy the poor implorer, and bend his eye upon a longer pathway.
Riches come now to one, now to another, and like the wheels of cars are ever rolling.

6. The foolish man wins food with fruitless labour: that food —I speak the truth—shall be his ruin.
He feeds no trusty friend, no man to love him. All guilt is he who eats with no partaker.

7. The ploughshares ploughing makes the food that feeds us, and with its feet cuts through the path it follows.
Better the speaking than the silent Brāhman: the liberal friend outvalues him who gives not.

8. He with one foot hath far outrun the biped, and the two-footed catches the three-footed.
Four-footed creatures come when bipeds call them, and stand and look where five are met together.

9. The hands are both alike: their labour differs. The yield of sister milch-kine is unequal.
Twins even differ in their strength and vigour: two, even kinsmen, differ in their bounty.

XXII

X. 119. **To Indra**

1. This, even this was my resolve, to win a cow, to win a steed:
Have I not drunk of soma-juice?

2. Like violent gusts of wind the draughts that I have drunk have lifted me:
Have I not drunk of soma-juice?

3. The draughts I drank have borne me up, as fleet-foot horses draw a car:
Have I not drunk of soma-juice?

4. The hymn hath reached me, like a cow who lows to meet her darling calf:
Have I not drunk of soma-juice?

5. As a wright bends a chariot-seat, so round my heart I bend the hymn:
Have I not drunk of soma-juice?

6. Not as a mote within the eye count the five tribes of men with me:
Have I not drunk of soma-juice?

7. The heavens and earth themselves have not grown equal to one half of me:
Have I not drunk of soma-juice?

8. I in my grandeur have surpassed the heavens and all this spacious earth:
Have I not drunk of soma-juice?

9. Aha! this spacious earth will I deposit either here or there:
Have I not drunk of soma-juice?

10. In one short moment will I smite the earth in fury here or there:
Have I not drunk of soma-juice?

11. One of my flanks is in the sky; I let the other trail below:
Have I not drunk of soma-juice?

12. I, greatest of the mighty ones, am lifted to the firmament:
Have I not drunk of soma-juice?

13. I seek the worshipper's abode; oblation-bearer to the gods:
Have I not drunk of soma-juice?

XXIII

X. 121. **To Prajāpati**

1. In the beginning rose Hiraṇyagarbha,[1] born only lord of all created beings.
He fixed and holdeth up this earth and heaven. What god shall we adore with our oblation?

2. Giver of vital breath, of power and vigour, he whose commandments all the gods acknowledge:
The lord of death, whose shade is life immortal. What god shall we adore with our oblation?

3. Who by his grandeur hath become sole ruler of all the moving world that breathes and slumbers:
He who is lord of men and lord of cattle. What god shall we adore with our oblation?

4. His, through his might, are these snow-covered mountains, and men call sea and Rasā[2] his possession:
His arms are these, his are these heavenly regions. What god shall we adore with our oblation?

[1] *Hiraṇyagarbha:* literally 'the gold-germ'; 'source of golden-light'; the Sun-god, 'as the great power of the universe, from which all other powers and existences, divine and earthly, are derived, a conception which is the nearest approach to the later mystical conception of Brahmā, the creator of the world.'—Wallis.

[2] *Rasā*, the mythical river of the firmament.

5. By him the heavens are strong and earth is stedfast, by him light's realm and sky-vault are supported:
By him the regions in mid-air were measured. What god shall we adore with our oblation?

6. To him, supported by his help, two armies embattled look with trembling in their spirit,
When over them the risen sun is shining. What god shall we adore with our oblation?

7. What time the mighty waters came, containing the universal germ, producing Agni,
Thence sprang the gods' one spirit into being. What god shall we adore with our oblation?

8. He in his might surveyed the floods containing productive force and generating worship.
He is the god of gods, and none beside him. What god shall we adore with our oblation?

9. Ne'er may he harm us who is earth's begetter, nor he whose laws are sure, the heavens' creator,
He who brought forth the great and lucid waters. What god shall we adore with our oblation?

10. Prajāpati! thou only comprehendest all these created things, and none beside thee.
Grant us our hearts' desire when we invoke thee: may we have store of riches in possession.

XXIV

X. 124. **To Agni and Others**

1. Come to this sacrifice of ours,[1] O Agni, threefold, with seven threads and five divisions.
Be our oblation-bearer and preceder: thou hast lain long enough in during darkness.

2. I come a god foreseeing from the godless to immortality by secret pathways.[2]
While I, ungracious one, desert the gracious, leave mine own friends and seek the kin of strangers.

[1] Indra speaks.

[2] Agni speaks. He has left Varuṇa, originally the supreme deity whose power was waning, and associated himself with Indra, who has

3. I, looking to the guest of other lineage, have founded many a rule of law and order.
I bid farewell to the great god, the father, and, for neglect, obtain my share of worship.

4. I tarried many a year within this altar: I leave the father, for my choice is Indra.
Away pass Agni, Varuṇa, and Soma. Rule ever changes: this I come to favour.

5. These Asuras have lost their powers of magic.[1] But thou, O Varuṇa, if thou dost love me,
O king, discerning truth and right from falsehood, come and be lord and ruler of my kingdom.

6. Here is the light of heaven, here all is lovely; here there is radiance, here is air's wide region.
Let us two slaughter Vṛitra.[2] Forth, O Soma! Thou art oblation: we therewith will serve thee.

7. The sage hath fixed his form by wisdom in the heavens: Varuṇa with no violence let the waters flow.
Like women-folk, the floods that bring prosperity have caught his hue and colour as they gleamed and shone.

8. These wait upon his loftiest power and vigour: he dwells in these who triumph in their godhead;
And they, like people who elect their ruler, have in abhorrence turned away from Vṛitra.

9. They call him swan, the abhorrent floods' companion, moving in friendship with celestial waters.
The poets in their thought have looked on Indra swiftly approaching when Anushṭup calls him.

superseded that god. *From the godless:* from Varuṇa, who in the decline of his supremacy has neglected Agni and sacrifice.

1 Indra speaks. *These Asuras:* Agni, Varuṇa, and Soma. *Come and be lord:* Indra offers Varuṇa spiritual and moral sovereignty as compensation for his loss of general supremacy.

2 *Let us two:* the exhortation is addressed by Indra to Soma. *Vṛitra:* regarded as in league with Varuṇa, the fiendish enemy in the shape of Varuṇa.

XXV

X. 125. **To Speech**

1. I TRAVEL with the Rudras and the Vasus, with the Ādityas and all-gods I wander.[1]
I hold aloft both Varuṇa and Mitra, Indra and Agni, and the Pair of Aśvins.

2. I cherish and sustain high-swelling Soma, and Tvashṭar I support, Pūshan, and Bhaga.
I load with wealth the zealous sacrificer who pours the juice and offers his oblation.

3. I am the queen, the gatherer-up of treasures, most thoughtful, first of those who merit worship.
Thus gods have stablished me in many places with many homes to enter and abide in.

4. Through me alone all eat the food that feeds them—each man who sees, breathes, hears the word outspoken.
They know it not, but yet they dwell beside me. Hear, one and all, the truth as I declare it.

5. I, verily, myself announce and utter the word that gods and men alike shall welcome.
I make the man I love exceeding mighty, make him a sage, a Ṛishi, and a Brāhman.

6. I bind the bow for Rudra that his arrow may strike and slay the hater of devotion.
I rouse and order battle for the people, and I have penetrated earth and heaven.

7. On the world's summit I bring forth the father: my home is in the waters, in the ocean.
Thence I extend o'er all existing creatures, and touch even yonder heaven with my forehead.

8. I breathe a strong breath like the wind and tempest, the while I hold together all existence.
Beyond this wide earth and beyond the heavens I have become so mighty in my grandeur.

[1] Speech is personified, the Word, the first creation and representative of spirit, and the means of communication between men and gods.

XXVI

X. 127.

To Night

1. With all her eyes the goddess Night looks forth approaching many a spot:
She hath put all her glories on.

2. Immortal, she hath filled the waste, the goddess hath filled height and depth:
She conquers darkness with her light.

3. The goddess as she comes hath set the Dawn her sister in her place:
And then the darkness vanishes.

4. So favour us this night, O thou whose pathways we have visited
As birds their nest upon the tree.

5. The villagers have sought their homes, and all that walks and all that flies,
Even the falcons fain for prey.

6. Keep off the she-wolf and the wolf; O Ūrmyā, keep the thief away:
Easy be thou for us to pass.

7. Clearly hath she come nigh to me who decks the dark with richest hues:
O morning, cancel it like debts.

8. These have I brought to thee like kine. O Night, thou child of heaven, accept
This laud as for a conqueror.

XXVII

X. 129.

The Song of Creation

1. Then was not non-existent nor existent: there was no realm of air, no sky beyond it.
What covered in, and where? and what gave shelter? Was water there, unfathomed depth of water?

2. Death was not then, nor was there aught immortal: no sign was there, the day's and night's divider.
That one thing, breathless, breathed by its own nature: apart from it was nothing whatsoever.

3. Darkness there was: at first concealed in darkness, this All was indiscriminated chaos.
All that existed then was void and formless: by the great power of warmth was born that unit.

4. Thereafter rose desire in the beginning, Desire, the primal seed and germ of spirit.
Sages who searched with their heart's thought discovered the existent's kinship in the non-existent.

5. Transversely was their severing line extended: what was above it then, and what below it?
There were begetters, there were mighty forces, free action here and energy up yonder.

6. Who verily knows and who can here declare it, whence it was born and whence comes this creation?
The gods are later than this world's production. Who knows, then, whence it first came into being?

7. He, the first origin of this creation, whether he formed it all or did not form it,
Whose eye controls this world in highest heaven, he verily knows it, or perhaps he knows not.

XXVIII

X. 151. **To Faith**

1. By faith is Agni kindled, through faith is oblation offered up.
We celebrate with praises faith upon the height of happiness.

2. Bless thou the man who gives, O Faith; Faith, bless the man who fain would give.
Bless thou the liberal worshippers; bless thou the word that I have said.

3. Even as the deities maintained faith in the mighty Asuras,[1]
So make this uttered wish of mine true for the liberal worshippers.

4. Guarded by Vāyu, gods and men who sacrifice draw near to faith.
Man winneth faith by yearnings of the heart, and opulence by faith.

5. Faith in the early morning, Faith at noonday will we invocate,
Faith at the setting of the sun. O Faith, endow us with belief.

XXIX

X. 154. FUNERAL HYMN

1. FOR some is soma purified, some sit by sacrificial oil:
To those for whom the meath flows forth, even to those let him depart.

2. Invincible through fervour,[2] those whom fervour hath advanced to heaven,
Who showed great fervour in their lives—even to those let him depart.

3. The heroes who contend in war and boldly cast their lives away,
Or who give guerdon thousandfold—even to those let him depart.

4. Yea, the first followers of Law, law's pure and holy strengtheners,
The fathers, Yama, fervour-moved—even to those let him depart.

5. Skilled in a thousand ways and means, the sages who protect the sun,
The Ṛishis, Yama, fervour-moved—even to those let him depart.

[1] *Asuras:* the primeval Āṛyan gods, Dyaus, Varuṇa, and some others, who were venerated by Indra and other Indo-Āryan deities of a later creation.

[2] *Fervour: tápas:* literally, warmth, heat; religious fervour, asceticism, austerity, self-denial, and abstracted meditation.

XXX

x. 168. **To Vāyu**

1. O THE Wind's chariot, O its power and glory! Crashing it goes and hath a voice of thunder.
It makes the regions red and touches heaven, and as it moves the dust of earth is scattered.

2. Along the traces of the Wind they hurry, they come to him as dames to an assembly.
Borne on his car with these for his attendants, the god speeds forth, the universe's monarch.

3. Travelling on the paths of air's mid-region, no single day doth he take rest or slumber.
Holy and earliest-born, friend of the waters, where did he spring and from what region came he?

4. Germ of the world, the deities' vital spirit, this god moves ever as his will inclines him.
His voice is heard, his shape is ever viewless. Let us adore this Wind with our oblation.

PART II

BṚIHADĀRAṆYAKA UPANISHAD

First Adhyāya

FIRST BRĀHMAṆA

1. Verily the dawn is the head of the horse which is fit for sacrifice, the sun its eye, the wind its breath, the mouth the Vaiśvānara fire, the year the body of the sacrificial horse. Heaven is the back, the sky the belly, the earth the chest, the quarters the two sides, the intermediate quarters the ribs, the members the seasons, the joints the months and half-months, the feet days and nights, the bones the stars, the flesh the clouds. The half-digested food is the sand, the rivers the bowels, the liver and the lungs the mountains, the hairs the herbs and trees. As the sun rises it is the forepart, as it sets the hindpart of the horse. When the horse shakes itself, then it lightens; when it kicks, it thunders; when it makes water, it rains; voice is its voice.

2. Verily day arose after the horse as the (golden) vessel, called Mahiman (greatness), which (at the sacrifice) is placed before the horse. Its place is in the eastern sea. The night arose after the horse as the (silver) vessel, called Mahiman, which (at the sacrifice) is placed behind the horse. Its place is in the western sea. Verily, these two vessels (or greatnesses) arose to be on each side of the horse.

As a racer he carried the Devas, as a stallion the Gandharvas, as a runner the Asuras, as a horse men. The sea is its kin, the sea is its birthplace.

SECOND BRĀHMAṆA

1. In the beginning there was nothing (to be perceived) here whatsoever. By death indeed all this was concealed—by hunger; for death is hunger. Death (the first being) thought, 'Let me have a body.' Then he moved about, worshipping. From him thus worshipping water was produced. And he said: 'Verily, there appeared to me, while I worshipped (archate), water (ka).' This is why water is called ar-ka. Surely there is water (or pleasure) for him who thus knows the reason why water is called arka.

2. Verily water is arka. And what was there as the froth of the water, that was hardened, and became the earth. On that earth he (death) rested, and from him, thus resting and heated, Agni (Virāj) proceeded, full of light.

3. That being divided itself threefold, Āditya (the sun) as the third, and Vāyu (the air) as the third. That spirit (prāṇa) became threefold. The head was the eastern quarter, and the arms this and that quarter (i.e. the north-eastern and south-eastern, on the left and right sides). Then the tail was the western quarter, and the two legs this and that quarter (i.e. the north-western and south-western). The sides were the southern and northern quarters, the back heaven, the belly the sky, the dust the earth. Thus he (Mṛityu, as arka) stands firm in the water, and he who knows this stands firm wherever he goes.

4. He desired, 'Let a second body be born of me,' and he (death or hunger) embraced speech in his mind. Then the seed became the year. Before that time there was no year. Speech bore him so long as a year, and after that time sent him forth. Then when he was born, he (death) opened his mouth, as if to swallow him. He cried, Bhāṇ! and that became speech.

5. He thought, 'If I kill him, I shall have but little food.' He therefore brought forth by that speech and by that body (the year) all whatsoever exists, the Ṛich, the Yajus, the Sāman, the metres, the sacrifices, men, and animals.

And whatever he (death) brought forth, that he resolved to eat (ad). Verily because he eats everything, therefore is Aditi (death) called Aditi. He who thus knows why Aditi is called Aditi becomes an eater of everything, and everything becomes his food.

6. He desired to sacrifice again with a greater sacrifice. He toiled and performed penance. And while he toiled and performed penance, glorious power went out of him. Verily glorious power means the senses (prāṇa). Then when the senses had gone out, the body took to swelling (śva-yitum), and mind was in the body.

7. He desired that this body should be fit for sacrifice (medhya), and that he should be embodied by it. Then he became a horse (aśva), because it swelled (aśvat), and was fit for sacrifice (medhya); and this is why the horse-sacrifice is called Aśva-medha.

Verily he who knows him thus, knows the Aśva-medha.

Then, letting the horse free, he thought, and at the end of a year he offered it up for himself, while he gave up the (other) animals to the deities. Therefore the sacrificers offered up the purified horse belonging to Prajāpati (as dedicated) to all the deities.

Verily the shining sun is the Aśvamedha-sacrifice, and his body is the year; Agni is the sacrificial fire (arka), and these worlds are his bodies. These two are the sacrificial fire and the Aśvamedha-sacrifice, and they are again one deity, viz. death. He (who knows this) overcomes another death, death does not reach him, death is his Self, he becomes one of those deities.

THIRD BRĀHMAṆA

1. There were two kinds of descendants of Prajāpati, the Devas and the Asuras. Now the Devas were indeed the younger, the Asuras the elder ones. The Devas, who were struggling in these worlds, said: 'Well, let us overcome the Asuras at the sacrifices (the Jyotishṭoma) by means of the udgītha.'

2. They said to speech (Vāch): 'Do thou sing out for us (the udgītha).' 'Yes,' said speech, and sang (the udgītha). Whatever delight there is in speech, that she obtained for the Devas by singing (the three pavamānas); but that she pronounced well (in the other nine pavamānas), that was for herself. The Asuras knew: 'Verily, through this singer they will overcome us.' They therefore rushed at the singer and pierced her with evil. That evil which consists in saying what is bad, that is that evil.

3. Then they (the Devas) said to breath (scent): 'Do thou sing out for us.' 'Yes,' said breath, and sang. Whatever delight there is in breath (smell), that he obtained for the Devas by singing; but that he smelled well, that was for himself. The Asuras knew: 'Verily, through this singer they will overcome us.' They therefore rushed at the singer, and pierced him with evil. That evil which consists in smelling what is bad, that is that evil.

4. Then they said to the eye: 'Do thou sing out for us.' 'Yes,' said the eye, and sang. Whatever delight there is in the eye, that he obtained for the Devas by singing; but that he saw well, that was for himself. The Asuras knew: 'Verily, through this singer they will overcome us.' They therefore rushed at the singer, and pierced him with evil. That evil which consists in seeing what is bad, that is that evil.

5. Then they said to the ear: 'Do thou sing out for us.' 'Yes,' said the ear, and sang. Whatever delight there is in the ear, that he obtained for the Devas by singing; but that he heard well, that was for himself. The Asuras knew: 'Verily, through this singer they will overcome us.' They therefore rushed at the singer, and pierced him with evil. That evil which consists in hearing what is bad, that is that evil.

6. Then they said to the mind: 'Do thou sing out for us.' 'Yes,' said the mind, and sang. Whatever delight there is in the mind, that he obtained for the Devas by singing; but that he thought well, that was for himself. The Asuras knew: 'Verily, through this singer they will overcome us.' They therefore rushed at the singer, and pierced him with evil. That evil which consists in thinking what is bad, that is that evil.

Thus they overwhelmed these deities with evils, thus they pierced them with evil.

7. Then they said to the breath in the mouth: 'Do thou sing for us.' 'Yes,' said the breath, and sang. The Asuras knew: 'Verily, through this singer they will overcome us.' They therefore rushed at him and pierced him with evil. Now as a ball of earth will be scattered when hitting a stone, thus they perished, scattered in all directions. Hence the Devas rose, the Asuras fell. He who knows this, rises by his Self, and the enemy who hates him falls.

8. Then they (the Devas) said: 'Where was he then who thus stuck to us?' It was (the breath) within the mouth (āsye 'ntar), and therefore called Ayāsya; he was the sap (rasa) of the limbs (aṅga), and therefore called Āṅgirasa.

9. That deity was called Dūr, because death was far (dūran) from it. From him who knows this, death is far off.

10. That deity, after having taken away the evil of those deities, viz. death, sent it to where the end of the quarters of the earth is. There he deposited their sins. Therefore let no one go to a man, let no one go to the end (of the quarters of the earth), that he may not meet there with evil, with death.

11. That deity, after having taken away the evil of those deities, viz. death, carried them beyond death.

12. He carried speech across first. When speech had become freed from death, it became (what it had been before) Agni (fire). That Agni, after having stepped beyond death, shines.

13. Then he carried breath (scent) across. When breath had

become freed from death, it became Vāyu (air). That Vāyu, after having stepped beyond death, blows.

14. Then he carried the eye across. When the eye had become freed from death, it became Āditya (the sun). That Āditya, after having stepped beyond death, burns.

15. Then he carried the ear across. When the ear had become freed from death, it became the quarters (space). These are our quarters (space), which have stepped beyond death.

16. Then he carried the mind across. When the mind had become freed from death, it became the moon (Chandramas). That moon, after having stepped beyond death, shines. Thus does that deity carry him, who knows this, across death.

17. Then breath (vital), by singing, obtained for himself eatable food. For whatever food is eaten, is eaten by breath alone, and in it breath rests.

The Devas said: 'Verily, thus far, whatever food there is, thou hast by singing acquired it for thyself. Now therefore give us a share in that food.' He said: 'You, there, enter into me.' They said 'Yes,' and entered all into him. Therefore whatever food is eaten by breath, by it the other senses are satisfied.

18. If a man knows this, then his own relations come to him in the same manner; he becomes their supporter, their chief leader, their strong ruler. And if ever anyone tries to oppose one who is possessed of such knowledge among his own relatives, then he will not be able to support his own belongings. But he who follows the man who is possessed of such knowledge, and who with his permission wishes to support those whom he has to support, he indeed will be able to support his own belongings.

19. He was called Ayāsya Āṅgirasa, for he is the sap (rasa) of the limbs (aṅga). Verily, breath is the sap of the limbs. Yes, breath is the sap of the limbs. Therefore from whatever limb breath goes away, that limb withers, for breath verily is the sap of the limbs.

20. He (breath) is also Bṛihaspati, for speech is Bṛihatī (Ṛigveda), and he is her lord; therefore he is Bṛihaspati.

21. He (breath) is also Brahmaṇaspati, for speech is Brahman (Yajur-veda), and he is her lord; therefore he is Brahmaṇaspati.

He (breath) is also Sāman (the Udgītha), for speech is Sāman (Sāma-veda), and that is both speech (sā) and breath (ama). This is why Sāman is called Sāman.

22. Or because he is equal (sama) to a grub, equal to a gnat, equal to an elephant, equal to these three worlds, nay, equal to

this universe, therefore he is Sāman. He who thus knows this Sāman, obtains union and oneness with Sāman.

23. He (breath) is Udgītha. Breath verily is Ut, for by breath this universe is upheld (uttabdha); and speech is Gīthā, song. And because he is ut and gīthā, therefore he (breath) is Udgītha.

24. And thus Brahmadatta Chaikitāneya (the grandson of Chikitāna), while taking Soma (rājan), said: 'May this Soma strike my head off, if Ayāsya Āṅgirasa sang another Udgītha than this. He sang it indeed as speech and breath.'

25. He who knows what is the property of this Sāman, obtains property. Now verily its property is tone only. Therefore let a priest, who is going to perform the sacrificial work of a Sāma-singer, desire that his voice may have a good tone, and let him perform the sacrifice with a voice that is in good tone. Therefore people (who want a priest) for a sacrifice, look out for one who possesses a good voice, as for one who possesses property. He who thus knows what is the property of that Sāman, obtains property.

26. He who knows what is the gold of that Sāman, obtains gold. Now verily its gold is tone only. He who thus knows what is the gold of that Sāman, obtains gold.

27. He who knows what is the support of that Sāman, he is supported. Now verily its support is speech only. For, as supported in speech, that breath is sung as that Sāman. Some say the support is in food.

Next follows the Abhyāroha (the ascension) of the Pavamāna verses. Verily the Prastotṛi begins to sing the Sāman, and when he begins, then let him (the sacrificer) recite these (three Yajus-verses):

'Lead me from the unreal to the real! Lead me from darkness to light! Lead me from death to immortality!'

Now when he says, 'Lead me from the unreal to the real,' the unreal is verily death, the real immortality. He therefore says, 'Lead me from death to immortality, make me immortal.'

When he says, 'Lead me from darkness to light,' darkness is verily death, light immortality. He therefore says, 'Lead me from death to immortality, make me immortal.'

When he says, 'Lead me from death to immortality,' there is nothing there, as it were, hidden (obscure, requiring explanation).

28. Next come the other Stotras with which the priest may obtain food for himself by singing them. Therefore let the

sacrificer, while these Stotras are being sung, ask for a boon, whatever desire he may desire. An Udgātṛi priest who knows this obtains by his singing whatever desire he may desire either for himself or for the sacrificer. This (knowledge) indeed is called the conqueror of the worlds. He who thus knows this Sāman, for him there is no fear of his not being admitted to the worlds.

FOURTH BRĀHMAṆA

1. In the beginning this was Self alone, in the shape of a person (purusha). He looking round saw nothing but his Self. He first said, 'This is I'; therefore he became I by name. Therefore even now, if a man is asked, he first says, 'This is I,' and then pronounces the other name which he may have. And because before (pūrva) all this, he (the Self) burnt down (ush) all evils, therefore he was a person (pur-usha). Verily he who knows this, burns down everyone who tries to be before him.

2. He feared, and therefore anyone who is lonely fears. He thought, 'As there is nothing but myself, why should I fear?' Thence his fear passed away. For what should he have feared? Verily fear arises from a second only.

3. But he felt no delight. Therefore a man who is lonely feels no delight. He wished for a second. He was so large as man and wife together. He then made this his Self to fall in two (pat), and thence arose husband (pati) and wife (patnī). Therefore Yājñavalkya said: 'We two are thus (each of us) like half a shell.' Therefore the void which was there, is filled by the wife. He embraced her, and men were born.

4. She thought, 'How can he embrace me, after having produced me from himself? I shall hide myself.'

She then became a cow, the other became a bull and embraced her, and hence cows were born. The one became a mare, the other a stallion; the one a male ass, the other a female ass. He embraced her, and hence one-hoofed animals were born. The one became a she-goat, the other a he-goat; the one became a ewe, the other a ram. He embraced her, and hence goats and sheep were born. And thus he created everything that exists in pairs, down to the ants.

5. He knew, 'I indeed am this creation, for I created all this.' Hence he became the creation, and he who knows this lives in this his creation.

6. Next he thus produced fire by rubbing. From the mouth,

as from the fire-hole, and from the hands he created fire. Therefore both the mouth and the hands are inside without hair, for the fire-hole is inside without hair.

And when they say, 'Sacrifice to this or sacrifice to that god,' each god is but his manifestation, for he is all gods.

Now, whatever there is moist, that he created from seed; this is Soma. So far verily is this universe either food or eater. Soma indeed is food, Agni eater. This is the highest creation of Brahman, when he created the gods from his better part, and when he, who was (then) mortal, created the immortals. Therefore it was the highest creation. And he who knows this, lives in this his highest creation.

7. Now all this was then undeveloped. It became developed by form and name, so that one could say, 'He, called so and so, is such a one.' Therefore at present also all this is developed by name and form, so that one can say, 'He, called so and so, is such a one.'

He (Brahman or the Self) entered thither, to the very tips of the finger-nails, as a razor might be fitted in a razor-case, or as fire in a fire-place.

He cannot be seen, for, in part only, when breathing, he is breath by name; when speaking, speech by name; when seeing, eye by name; when hearing, ear by name; when thinking, mind by name. All these are but the names of his acts. And he who worships (regards) him as the one or the other, does not know him, for he is apart from this (when qualified) by the one or the other (predicate). Let men worship him as Self, for in the Self all these are one. This Self is the footstep of everything, for through it one knows everything. And as one can find again by footsteps what was lost, thus he who knows this finds glory and praise.

8. This, which is nearer to us than anything, this Self, is dearer than a son, dearer than wealth, dearer than all else.

And if one were to say to one who declares another than the Self dear, that he will lose what is dear to him, very likely it would be so. Let him worship the Self alone as dear. He who worships the Self alone as dear, the object of his love will never perish.

9. Here they say: 'If men think that by knowledge of Brahman they will become everything, what then did that Brahman know, from whence all this sprang?'

10. Verily in the beginning this was Brahman, that Brahman

knew (its) Self only, saying, 'I am Brahman.' From it all this sprang. Thus, whatever Deva was awakened (so as to know Brahman), he indeed became that (Brahman); and the same with Ṛishis and men. The Ṛishi Vāmadeva saw and understood it, singing, 'I was Manu (moon), I was the sun.' Therefore now also he who thus knows that he is Brahman, becomes all this, and even the Devas cannot prevent it, for he himself is their Self.

Now if a man worships another deity, thinking the deity is one and he another, he does not know. He is like a beast for the Devas. For verily, as many beasts nourish a man, thus does every man nourish the Devas. If only one beast is taken away, it is not pleasant; how much more when many are taken! Therefore it is not pleasant to the Devas that men should know this.

11. Verily in the beginning this was Brahman, one only. That being one, was not strong enough. It created still further the most excellent Kshatra (power), viz. those Kshatras (powers) among the Devas—Indra, Varuṇa, Soma, Rudra, Parjanya, Yama, Mṛityu, Īśāna. Therefore there is nothing beyond the Kshatra, and therefore at the Rājasūya sacrifice the Brāhmaṇa sits down below the Kshatriya. He confers that glory on the Kshatra alone. But Brahman is (nevertheless) the birthplace of the Kshatra. Therefore though a king is exalted, he sits down at the end (of the sacrifice) below the Brahman, as his birthplace. He who injures him, injures his own birthplace. He becomes worse, because he has injured one better than himself.

12. He was not strong enough. He created the Viś (people), the classes of Devas which in their different orders are called Vasus, Rudras, Ādityas, Viśve Devas, Maruts.

13. He was not strong enough. He created the Śūdra colour (caste), as Pūshan (as nourisher). This earth verily is Pūshan (the nourisher); for the earth nourishes all this whatsoever.

14. He was not strong enough. He created still further the most excellent Law (dharma). Law is the Kshatra (power) of the Kshatra, therefore there is nothing higher than the Law. Thenceforth even a weak man rules a stronger with the help of the Law, as with the help of a king. Thus the Law is what is called the true. And if a man declares what is true, they say he declares the Law; and if he declares the Law, they say he declares what is true. Thus both are the same.

15. There are then this Brahman, Kshatra, Viś, and Śūdra. Among the Devas that Brahman existed as Agni (fire) only, among men as Brāhmaṇa, as Kshatriya through the (divine) Kshatriya, as Vaiśya through the (divine) Vaiśya, as Śūdra through the (divine) Śūdra. Therefore people wish for their future state among the Devas through Agni (the sacrificial fire) only; and among men through the Brāhmaṇa, for in these two forms did Brahman exist.

Now if a man departs this life without having seen his true future life (in the Self), then that Self, not being known, does not receive and bless him, as if the Veda had not been read, or as if a good work had not been done. Nay, even if one who does not know that (Self), should perform here on earth some great holy work, it will perish for him in the end. Let a man worship the Self only as his true state. If a man worships the Self only as his true state, his work does not perish, for whatever he desires that he gets from that Self.

16. Now verily this Self (of the ignorant man) is the world of all creatures. In so far as man sacrifices and pours out libations, he is the world of the Devas; in so far as he repeats the hymns, etc., he is the world of the Ṛishis; in so far as he offers cakes to the fathers and tries to obtain offspring, he is the world of the fathers; in so far as he gives shelter and food to men, he is the world of men; in so far as he finds fodder and water for the animals, he is the world of the animals; in so far as quadrupeds, birds, and even ants live in his houses, he is their world. And as everyone wishes his own world not to be injured, thus all beings wish that he who knows this should not be injured. Verily this is known and has been well reasoned.

17. In the beginning this was Self alone, one only. He desired, 'Let there be a wife for me that I may have offspring, and let there be wealth for me that I may offer sacrifices.' Verily this is the whole desire, and, even if wishing for more, he would not find it. Therefore now also a lonely person desires, 'Let there be a wife for me that I may have offspring, and let there be wealth for me that I may offer sacrifices.' And so long as he does not obtain either of these things, he thinks he is incomplete. Now his completeness (is made up as follows): mind is his Self (husband); speech the wife; breath the child; the eye all worldly wealth, for he finds it with the eye; the ear his divine wealth, for he hears it with the ear. The body (ātman) is his work, for with the body he works. This is the fivefold sacrifice, for

fivefold is the animal, fivefold man, fivefold all this whatsoever. He who knows this, obtains all this.

FIFTH BRĀHMAṆA

1. 'When the father (of creation) had produced by knowledge and penance (work) the seven kinds of food, one of his (foods) was common to all beings, two he assigned to the Devas. (1)

'Three he made for himself, one he gave to the animals. In it all rests, whatsoever breathes and breathes not. (2)

'Why then do these not perish, though they are always eaten? He who knows this imperishable one, he eats food with his face. (3)

'He goes even to the Devas, he lives on strength.' (4)

2. When it is said, that 'the father produced by knowledge and penance the seven kinds of food,' it is clear that (it was he who) did so. When it is said, that 'one of his (foods) was common,' then that is that common food of his which is eaten. He who worships (eats) that (common food), is not removed from evil, for verily that food is mixed (property). When it is said, that 'two he assigned to the Devas,' that is the huta, which is sacrificed in fire, and the prahuta, which is given away at a sacrifice. But they also say, the new-moon and full-moon sacrifices are here intended, and therefore one should not offer them as an ishṭi or with a wish.

When it is said, that 'one he gave to animals,' that is milk. For in the beginning (in their infancy) both men and animals live on milk. And therefore they either make a new-born child lick ghṛita (butter), or they make it take the breast. And they call a new-born creature 'atṛiṇâda,' i.e. not eating herbs. When it is said, that 'in it all rests, whatsoever breathes and breathes not,' we see that all this, whatsoever breathes and breathes not, rests and depends on milk.

And when it is said (in another Brāhmaṇa), that a man who sacrifices with milk a whole year, overcomes death again, let him not think so. No, on the very day on which he sacrifices, on that day he overcomes death again; for he who knows this, offers to the gods the entire food (viz. milk).

When it is said, 'Why do these not perish, though they are always eaten?' we answer, Verily, the Person is the imperishable, and he produces that food again and again.

When it is said, 'He who knows this imperishable one,' then, verily, the Person is the imperishable one, for he produces this food by repeated thought, and whatever he does not work by his works, that perishes.

When it is said, that 'he eats food with his face,' then face means the mouth, he eats it with his mouth.

When it is said, that 'he goes even to the Devas, he lives on strength,' that is meant as praise.

3. When it is said, that 'he made three for himself,' that means that he made mind, speech, and breath for himself. As people say, 'My mind was elsewhere, I did not see; my mind was elsewhere, I did not hear,' it is clear that a man sees with his mind and hears with his mind. Desire, representation, doubt, faith, want of faith, memory, forgetfulness, shame, reflexion, fear, all this is mind. Therefore even if a man is touched on the back, he knows it through the mind.

Whatever sound there is, that is speech. Speech indeed is intended for an end or object, it is nothing by itself.

The up-breathing, the down-breathing, the back-breathing, the out-breathing, the on-breathing, all that is breathing is breath (prāṇa) only. Verily that Self consists of it; that Self consists of speech, mind, and breath.

4. These are the three worlds: earth is speech, sky mind, heaven breath.

5. These are the three Vedas: the Ṛigveda is speech, the Yajur-veda mind, the Sāma-veda breath.

6. These are the Devas, Fathers, and men: the Devas are speech, the Fathers mind, men breath.

7. These are father, mother, and child: the father is mind, the mother speech, the child breath.

8. These are what is known, what is to be known, and what is unknown.

What is known has the form of speech, for speech is known. Speech, having become this, protects man.

9. What is to be known has the form of mind, for mind is what is to be known. Mind, having become this, protects man.

10. What is unknown has the form of breath, for breath is unknown. Breath, having become this, protects man.

11. Of that speech (which is the food of Prajāpati) earth is the body, light the form, viz. this fire. And so far as speech extends, so far extends the earth, so far extends fire.

12. Next, of this mind heaven is the body, light the form, viz.

this sun. And so far as this mind extends, so far extends heaven, so far extends the sun. If they (fire and sun) embrace each other, then wind is born, and that is Indra, and he is without a rival. Verily a second is a rival, and he who knows this, has no rival.

13. Next, of this breath water is the body, light the form, viz. this moon. And so far as this breath extends, so far extends water, so far extends the moon.

These are all alike, all endless. And he who worships them as finite, obtains a finite world, but he who worships them as infinite, obtains an infinite world.

14. That Prajāpati is the year, and he consists of sixteen digits. The nights indeed are his fifteen digits, the fixed point his sixteenth digit. He is increased and decreased by the nights. Having on the new-moon night entered with the sixteenth part into everything that has life, he is thence born again in the morning. Therefore let no one cut off the life of any living thing on that night, not even of a lizard, in honour (pūjārtham) of that deity.

15. Now verily that Prajāpati, consisting of sixteen digits, who is the year, is the same as a man who knows this. His wealth constitutes the fifteen digits, his Self the sixteenth digit. He is increased and decreased by that wealth. His Self is the nave, his wealth the felly. Therefore even if he loses everything, if he lives but with his Self, people say, he lost the felly (which can be restored again).

16. Next there are verily three worlds, the world of men, the world of the Fathers, the world of the Devas. The world of men can be gained by a son only, not by any other work. By sacrifice the world of the fathers, by knowledge the world of the Devas is gained. The world of the Devas is the best of worlds, therefore they praise knowledge.

17. Next follows the handing over. When a man thinks he is going to depart, he says to his son: 'Thou art Brahman (the Veda, so far as acquired by the father); thou art the sacrifice (so far as performed by the father); thou art the world.' The son answers: 'I am Brahman, I am the sacrifice, I am the world.' Whatever has been learnt (by the father) that, taken as one, is Brahman. Whatever sacrifices there are, they, taken as one, are the sacrifice. Whatever worlds there are, they, taken as one, are the world. Verily here ends this (what has to be done by a father, viz. study, sacrifice, etc.). 'He (the son),

being all this, preserved me from this world,' thus he thinks. Therefore they call a son who is instructed (to do all this), a world-son (lokya), and therefore they instruct him.

When a father who knows this departs this world, then he enters into his son together with his own spirits (with speech, mind, and breath). If there is anything done amiss by the father, of all that the son delivers him, and therefore he is called Putra, son. By help of his son the father stands firm in this world. Then these divine immortal spirits (speech, mind, and breath) enter into him.

18. From the earth and from fire, divine speech enters into him. And verily that is divine speech whereby, whatever he says, comes to be.

19. From heaven and the sun, divine mind enters into him. And verily that is divine mind whereby he becomes joyful, and grieves no more.

20. From water and the moon, divine breath (spirit) enters into him. And verily that is divine breath which, whether moving or not moving, does not tire, and therefore does not perish. He who knows this, becomes the Self of all beings. As that deity (Hiraṇyagarbha) is, so does he become. And as all beings honour that deity (with sacrifice, etc.), so do all beings honour him who knows this.

Whatever grief these creatures suffer, that is all one (and therefore disappears). Only what is good approaches him; verily, evil does not approach the Devas.

21. Next follows the consideration of the observances (acts). Prajāpati created the actions (active senses). When they had been created, they strove among themselves. Voice held, I shall speak; the eye held, I shall see; the ear held, I shall hear; and thus the other actions too, each according to its own act. Death, having become weariness, took them and seized them. Having seized them, death held them back (from their work). Therefore speech grows weary, the eye grows weary, the ear grows weary. But death did not seize the central breath. Then the others tried to know him, and said: 'Verily, he is the best of us, he who, whether moving or not, does not tire and does not perish. Well, let all of us assume his form.' Thereupon they all assumed his form, and therefore they are called after him 'breaths' (spirits).

In whatever family there is a man who knows this, they call that family after his name. And he who strives with one who knows this, withers away and finally dies. So far with regard to the body.

22. Now with regard to the deities.

Agni (fire) held, I shall burn; Āditya (the sun) held, I shall warm; Chandramas (the moon) held, I shall shine; and thus also the other deities, each according to the deity. And as it was with the central breath among the breaths, so it was with Vāyu, the wind among those deities. The other deities fade, not Vāyu. Vāyu is the deity that never sets.

23. And here there is this Śloka:

'He from whom the sun rises, and into whom it sets' (he verily rises from the breath, and sets in the breath).

'Him the Devas made the law, he only is to-day, and he to-morrow also' (whatever these Devas determined then, that they perform to-day also).

Therefore let a man perform one observance only, let him breathe up and let him breathe down, that the evil death may not reach him. And when he performs it, let him try to finish it. Then he obtains through it union and oneness with that deity (with prāṇa).

SIXTH BRĀHMAṆA

1. Verily this is a triad, name, form, and work. Of these names, that which is called speech is the Uktha (hymn, supposed to mean also origin), for from it all names arise. It is their Sāman (song, supposed to mean also sameness), for it is the same as all names. It is their Brahman (prayer, supposed to mean also support), for it supports all names.

2. Next, of the forms, that which is called eye is the Uktha (hymn), for from it all forms arise. It is their Sāman (song), for it is the same as all forms. It is their Brahman (prayer), for it supports all forms.

3. Next, of the works, that which is called body is the Uktha (hymn), for from it all works arise. It is their Sāman (song), for it is the same as all works. It is their Brahman (prayer), for it supports all works.

That being a triad is one, viz. this Self: and the Self, being one, is that triad. This is the immortal, covered by the true. Verily breath is the immortal, name and form are the true, and by them the immortal is covered.

Second Adhyāya

First Brāhmaṇa[1]

1. There was formerly the proud Gārgya Bālāki, a man of great reading. He said to Ajātaśatru of Kāśi, 'Shall I tell you Brahman?' Ajātaśatru said: 'We give a thousand (cows) for that speech (of yours), for verily all people run away, saying, Janaka (the king of Mithilā) is our father (patron).'

2. Gārgya said: 'The person that is in the sun, that I adore as Brahman.' Ajātaśatru said to him: 'No, no! Do not speak to me on this. I adore him verily as the supreme, the head of all beings, the king. Whoso adores him thus, becomes supreme, the head of all beings, a king.'

3. Gārgya said: 'The person that is in the moon (and in the mind) that I adore as Brahman.' Ajātaśatru said to him: 'No, no! Do not speak to me on this. I adore him verily as the great, clad in white raiment, as Soma, the king. Whoso adores him thus, Soma is poured out and poured forth for him day by day, and his food does not fail.'

4. Gārgya said: 'The person that is in the lightning (and in the heart), that I adore as Brahman.' Ajātaśatru said to him: 'No, no! Do not speak to me on this. I adore him verily as the luminous. Whoso adores him thus, becomes luminous, and his offspring becomes luminous.'

5. Gārgya said: 'The person that is in the ether (and in the ether of the heart), that I adore as Brahman.' Ajātaśatru said to him: 'No, no! Do not speak to me on this. I adore him as what is full, and quiescent. Whoso adores him thus, becomes filled with offspring and cattle, and his offspring does not cease from this world.'

6. Gārgya said: 'The person that is in the wind (and in the breath), that I adore as Brahman.' Ajātaśatru said to him: 'No, no! Do not speak to me on this. I adore him as Indra Vaikuṇṭha, as the unconquerable arm (of the Maruts). Whoso adores him thus, becomes victorious, unconquerable, conquering his enemies.'

[1] Whatever has been taught up to this point refers to avidyā, ignorance. Now, however, vidyā, the highest knowledge, is to be taught, and this is done, first of all, by a dialogue between Gārgya Dṛiptabālāki and king Ajātaśatru, the former, though a Brāhmaṇa, representing the imperfect, the latter, though a Kshatriya, the perfect knowledge of Brahman. While Gārgya worships the Brahman as the sun, the moon, etc., as limited, as active and passive, Ajātaśatru knows the Brahman as the Self.

7. Gārgya said: 'The person that is in the fire (and in the heart), that I adore as Brahman.' Ajātaśatru said to him: 'No, no! Do not speak to me on this. I adore him as powerful. Whoso adores him thus, becomes powerful, and his offspring becomes powerful.'

8. Gārgya said: 'The person that is in the water (in seed, and in the heart), that I adore as Brahman.' Ajātaśatru said to him: 'No, no! Do not speak to me on this. I adore him as likeness. Whoso adores him thus, to him comes what is likely (or proper), not what is improper; what is born from him is like unto him.'

9. Gārgya said: 'The person that is in the mirror, that I adore as Brahman.' Ajātaśatru said to him: 'No, no! Do not speak to me on this. I adore him verily as the brilliant. Whoso adores him thus, he becomes brilliant, his offspring becomes brilliant, and with whomsoever he comes together, he outshines them.'

10. Gārgya said: 'The sound that follows a man while he moves, that I adore as Brahman.' Ajātaśatru said to him: 'No, no! Do not speak to me on this. I adore him verily as life. Whoso adores him thus, he reaches his full age in this world, breath does not leave him before the time.'

11. Gārgya said: 'The person that is in space, that I adore as Brahman.' Ajātaśatru said to him: 'No, no! Do not speak to me on this. I adore him verily as the second who never leaves us. Whoso adores him thus, becomes possessed of a second, his party is not cut off from him.'

12. Gārgya said: 'The person that consists of the shadow, that I adore as Brahman.' Ajātaśatru said to him: 'No, no! Do not speak to me on this. I adore him verily as death. Whoso adores him thus, he reaches his whole age in this world, death does not approach him before the time.'

13. Gārgya said: 'The person that is in the body, that I adore as Brahman.' Ajātaśatru said to him: 'No, no! Do not speak to me on this. I adore him verily as embodied. Whoso adores him thus, becomes embodied, and his offspring becomes embodied.'

Then Gārgya became silent.

14. Ajātaśatru said: 'Thus far only?' 'Thus far only,' he replied. Ajātaśatru said: 'This does not suffice to know it (the true Brahman).' Gārgya replied: 'Then let me come to you, as a pupil.'

15. Ajātaśatru said: 'Verily, it is unnatural that a Brāhmaṇa should come to a Kshatriya, hoping that he should tell him the Brahman. However, I shall make you know him clearly'; thus saying, he took him by the hand and rose.

And the two together came to a person who was asleep. He called him by these names, 'Thou, great one, clad in white raiment, Soma, king.' He did not rise. Then rubbing him with his hand, he woke him, and he arose.

16. Ajātaśatru said: 'When this man was thus asleep, where was then the person (purusha), the intelligent? and from whence did he thus come back?' Gārgya did not know this.

17. Ajātaśatru said: 'When this man was thus asleep, then the intelligent person (purusha), having through the intelligence of the senses (prāṇas) absorbed within himself all intelligence, lies in the ether, which is in the heart. When he takes in these different kinds of intelligence, then it is said that the man sleeps (svapiti). Then the breath is kept in, speech is kept in, the ear is kept in, the eye is kept in, the mind is kept in.

18. 'But when he moves about in sleep (and dream), then these are his worlds. He is, as it were, a great king; he is, as it were, a great Brāhmaṇa; he rises, as it were, and he falls. And as a great king might keep in his own subjects, and move about, according to his pleasure, within his own domain, thus does that person (who is endowed with intelligence) keep in the various senses (prāṇas) and move about, according to his pleasure, within his own body (while dreaming).

19. 'Next, when he is in profound sleep, and knows nothing, there are the seventy-two thousand arteries called Hita, which from the heart spread through the body. Through them he moves forth and rests in the surrounding body. And as a young man, or a great king, or a great Brāhmaṇa, having reached the summit of happiness, might rest, so does he then rest.

20. 'As the spider comes out with its thread, or as small sparks come forth from fire, thus do all senses, all worlds, all Devas, all beings come forth from that Self. The Upanishad (the true name and doctrine) of that Self is "the True of the True." Verily the senses are the True, and he is the True of the True.'

SECOND BRĀHMAṆA

1. Verily he who knows the babe with his place, his chamber, his post, and his rope, he keeps off the seven relatives who hate him. Verily by the young is meant the inner life, by his place

this (body), by his chamber this (head), by his post the vital breath, by his rope the food.

2. Then the seven imperishable ones approach him. There are the red lines in the eye, and by them Rudra clings to him. There is the water in the eye, and by it Parjanya clings to him. There is the pupil, and by it Āditya (sun) clings to him. There is the dark iris, and by it Agni clings to him. There is the white eye-ball, and by it Indra clings to him. With the lower eye-lash the earth, with the upper eye-lash the heaven clings to him. He who knows this, his food does never perish.

3. On this there is this Śloka:

'There is a cup having its mouth below and its bottom above. Manifold glory has been placed into it. On its lip sit the seven Ṛishis, the tongue as the eighth communicates with Brahman.' What is called the cup having its mouth below and its bottom above is this head, for its mouth (the mouth) is below, its bottom (the skull) is above. When it is said that manifold glory has been placed into it, the senses verily are manifold glory, and he therefore means the senses. When he says that the seven Ṛishis sit on its lip, the Ṛishis are verily the (active) senses, and he means the senses. And when he says that the tongue as the eighth communicates with Brahman, it is because the tongue, as the eighth, does communicate with Brahman.

4. These two (the two ears) are the Ṛishis Gautama and Bharadvāja; the right Gautama, the left Bharadvāja. These two (the eyes) are the Ṛishis Viśvāmitra and Jamadagni; the right Viśvāmitra, the left Jamadagni. These two (the nostrils) are the Ṛishis Vasishṭha and Kaśyapa; the right Vasishṭha, the left Kaśyapa. The tongue is Atri, for with the tongue food is eaten, and Atri is meant for Atti, eating. He who knows this becomes an eater of everything, and everything becomes his food.

THIRD BRĀHMAṆA

1. There are two forms of Brahman, the material and the immaterial, the mortal and the immortal, the solid and the fluid, sat (being) and tya (that) (i.e. sat-tya, true).

2. Everything except air and sky is material, is mortal, is solid, is definite. The essence of that which is material, which is mortal, which is solid, which is definite is the sun that shines, for he is the essence of sat (the definite).

3. But air and sky are immaterial, are immortal, are fluid, are indefinite. The essence of that which is immaterial, which is

immortal, which is fluid, which is indefinite is the person in the disk of the sun, for he is the essence of tyad (the indefinite). So far with regard to the Devas.

4. Now with regard to the body. Everything except the breath and the ether within the body is material, is mortal, is solid, is definite. The essence of that which is material, which is mortal, which is solid, which is definite is the eye, for it is the essence of sat (the definite).

5. But breath and the ether within the body are immaterial, are immortal, are fluid, are indefinite. The essence of that which is immaterial, which is immortal, which is fluid, which is indefinite is the person in the right eye, for he is the essence of tyad (the indefinite).

6. And what is the appearance of that person? Like a saffron-coloured raiment, like white wool, like cochineal, like the flame of fire, like the white lotus, like sudden lightning. He who knows this, his glory is like unto sudden lightning.

Next follows the teaching (of Brahman) by No, no! for there is nothing else higher than this (if one says): 'It is not so.' Then comes the name 'the True of the True,' the senses being the True, and he (the Brahman) the True of them.

FOURTH BRĀHMAṆA [1]

1. Now when Yājñavalkya was going to enter upon another state, he said: 'Maitreyī, verily I am going away from this my house (into the forest). Forsooth, let me make a settlement between thee and that Kātyāyanī (my other wife).'

2. Maitreyī said: 'My lord, if this whole earth, full of wealth, belonged to me, tell me, should I be immortal by it?'

'No,' replied Yājñavalkya; 'like the life of rich people will be thy life. But there is no hope of immortality by wealth.'

3. And Maitreyī said: 'What should I do with that by which I do not become immortal? What my lord knoweth (of immortality), tell that to me.'

4. Yājñavalkya replied: 'Thou who art truly dear to me, thou speakest dear words. Come, sit down, I will explain it to thee, and mark well what I say.'

[1] To the end of the third Brāhmaṇa of the second Adhyāya, all that has been taught does not yet impart the highest knowledge, the identity of the personal and the true Self, the Brahman. In the fourth Brāhmaṇa, in which the knowledge of the true Brahman is to be set forth, the Sannyāsa, the retiring from the world, is enjoined, when all desires cease, and no duties are to be performed.

5. And he said: 'Verily, a husband is not dear, that you may ove the husband; but that you may love the Self, therefore a ιusband is dear.

'Verily, a wife is not dear, that you may love the wife; but hat you may love the Self, therefore a wife is dear.

'Verily, sons are not dear, that you may love the sons; but hat you may love the Self, therefore sons are dear.

'Verily, wealth is not dear, that you may love wealth; but hat you may love the Self, therefore wealth is dear.

'Verily, the Brāhman-class is not dear, that you may love he Brāhman-class; but that you may love the Self, therefore he Brāhman-class is dear.

'Verily, the Kshatra-class is not dear, that you may love the Kshatra-class; but that you may love the Self, therefore the Kshatra-class is dear.

'Verily, the worlds are not dear, that you may love the vorlds; but that you may love the Self, therefore the worlds re dear.

'Verily, the Devas are not dear, that you may love the Devas; but that you may love the Self, therefore the Devas are ear.

'Verily, creatures are not dear, that you may love the reatures; but that you may love the Self, therefore are creatures ear.

'Verily, everything is not dear, that you may love everything; ut that you may love the Self, therefore everything is dear.

'Verily, the Self is to be seen, to be heard, to be perceived, to e marked, O Maitreyī! When we see, hear, perceive, and know ıe Self, then all this is known.

6. 'Whosoever looks for the Brāhman-class elsewhere than the Self, was abandoned by the Brāhman-class. Whosoever oks for the Kshatra-class elsewhere than in the Self, was bandoned by the Kshatra-class. Whosoever looks for the orlds elsewhere than in the Self, was abandoned by the worlds. Vhosoever looks for the Devas elsewhere than in the Self, was bandoned by the Devas. Whosoever looks for creatures elsehere than in the Self, was abandoned by the creatures. Whoever looks for anything elsewhere than in the Self, was abanned by everything. This Brāhman-class, this Kshatra-class, ese worlds, these Devas, these creatures, this everything, all is at Self.

7. 'Now as the sounds of a drum, when beaten, cannot be

seized externally (by themselves), but the sound is seized, when the drum is seized or the beater of the drum;

8. 'And as the sounds of a conch-shell, when blown, cannot be seized externally (by themselves), but the sound is seized, when the shell is seized or the blower of the shell;

9. 'And as the sounds of a lute, when played, cannot be seized externally (by themselves), but the sound is seized, when the lute is seized or the player of the lute;

10. 'As clouds of smoke proceed by themselves out of a lighted fire kindled with damp fuel, thus, verily, O Maitreyī, has been breathed forth from this great Being what we have as Ṛigveda, Yajur-veda, Sāma-veda, Atharvāṇgirasas, Itihāsa (legends), Purāṇa (cosmogonies), Vidyā (knowledge), the Upanishads, Ślokas (verses), Sūtras (prose rules), Anuvyākhyānas (glosses), Vyākhyānas (commentaries). From him alone all these were breathed forth.

11. 'As all waters find their centre in the sea, all touches in the skin, all tastes in the tongue, all smells in the nose, all colours in the eye, all sounds in the ear, all percepts in the mind, all knowledge in the heart, all actions in the hands, all movements in the feet, and all the Vedas in speech—

12. 'As a lump of salt, when thrown into water, becomes dissolved into water, and could not be taken out again, but wherever we taste (the water) it is salt—thus verily, O Maitreyī, does this great Being, endless, unlimited, consisting of nothing but knowledge, rise from out these elements, and vanish again in them. When he has departed, there is no more knowledge (name), I say, O Maitreyī.' Thus spoke Yājñavalkya.

13. Then Maitreyī said: 'Here thou has bewildered me, Sir when thou sayest that having departed, there is no more knowledge.'

But Yājñavalkya replied: 'O Maitreyī, I say nothing that is bewildering. This is enough, O beloved, for wisdom.

'For when there is as it were duality, then one sees the other one smells the other, one hears the other, one salutes the other one perceives the other, one knows the other; but when the Self only is all this, how should he smell another, how should he see another, how should he hear another, how should he salute another, how should he perceive another, how should he know another? How should he know him by whom he knows all this? How, O beloved, should he know (himself), the Knower?'

FIFTH BRĀHMAṆA

1. This earth is the honey (madhu, the effect) of all beings, and all beings are the honey (madhu, the effect) of this earth. Likewise this bright, immortal person in this earth, and that bright immortal person incorporated in the body (both are madhu). He indeed is the same as that Self, that Immortal, that Brahman, that All.

2. This water is the honey of all beings, and all beings are the honey of this water. Likewise this bright, immortal person in this water, and that bright, immortal person, existing as seed in the body (both are madhu). He indeed is the same as that Self, that Immortal, that Brahman, that All.

3. This fire is the honey of all beings, and all beings are the honey of this fire. Likewise this bright, immortal person in this fire, and that bright, immortal person, existing as speech in the body (both are madhu). He indeed is the same as that Self, that Immortal, that Brahman, that All.

4. This air is the honey of all beings, and all beings are the honey of this air. Likewise this bright, immortal person in this air, and that bright, immortal person existing as breath in the body (both are madhu). He indeed is the same as that Self, that Immortal, that Brahman, that All.

5. This sun is the honey of all beings, and all beings are the honey of this sun. Likewise this bright, immortal person in this sun, and that bright, immortal person existing as the eye in the body (both are madhu). He indeed is the same as that Self, that Immortal, that Brahman, that All.

6. This space (diśah, the quarters) is the honey of all beings, and all beings are the honey of this space. Likewise this bright, immortal person in this space, and that bright, immortal person existing as the ear in the body (both are madhu). He indeed is the same as that Self, that Immortal, that Brahman, that All.

7. This moon is the honey of all beings, and all beings are the honey of this moon. Likewise this bright, immortal person in this moon, and that bright, immortal person existing as mind in the body (both are madhu). He indeed is the same as that Self, that Immortal, that Brahman, that All.

8. This lightning is the honey of all beings, and all beings are the honey of this lightning. Likewise this bright, immortal person in this lightning, and that bright, immortal person

existing as light in the body (both are madhu). He indeed is the same as that Self, that Immortal, that Brahman, that All.

9. This thunder is the honey of all beings, and all beings are the honey of this thunder. Likewise this bright, immortal person in this thunder, and that bright, immortal person existing as sound and voice in the body (both are madhu). He indeed is the same as that Self, that Immortal, that Brahman, that All.

10. This ether is the honey of all beings, and all beings are the honey of this ether. Likewise this bright, immortal person in this ether, and that bright, immortal person existing as heart-ether in the body (both are madhu). He indeed is the same as that Self, that Immortal, that Brahman, that All.

11. This law (dharma) is the honey of all beings, and all beings are the honey of this law. Likewise this bright, immortal person in this law, and that bright, immortal person existing as law in the body (both are madhu). He indeed is the same as that Self, that Immortal, that Brahman, that All.

12. This true (satyam) is the honey of all beings, and all beings are the honey of this true. Likewise this bright, immortal person in what is true, and that bright, immortal person existing as the true in the body (both are madhu). He indeed is the same as that Self, that Immortal, that Brahman, that All.

13. This mankind is the honey of all beings, and all beings are the honey of this mankind. Likewise this bright, immortal person in mankind, and that bright, immortal person existing as man in the body (both are madhu). He indeed is the same as that Self, that Immortal, that Brahman, that All.

14. This Self is the honey of all beings, and all beings are the honey of this Self. Likewise this bright, immortal person in this Self, and that bright, immortal person, the Self (both are madhu). He indeed is the same as that Self, that Immortal, that Brahman, that All.

15. And verily this Self is the lord of all beings, the king of all beings. And as all spokes are contained in the axle and in the felly of a wheel, all beings, and all those selfs (of the earth, water, etc.) are contained in that Self.

16. Verily Dadhyach Ātharvaṇa proclaimed this honey (the madhu-vidyā) to the two Aśvins, and a Ṛishi, seeing this, said (Ṛigveda I, 116, 12):

'O ye two heroes (Aśvins), I make manifest that fearful deed of yours (which you performed) for the sake of gain, like as thunder makes manifest the rain. The honey (madhu-vidyā)

which Dadhyach Ātharvaṇa proclaimed to you through the
ead of a horse,' . . .

17. Verily Dadhyach Ātharvaṇa proclaimed this honey to the
wo Aśvins, and a Ṛishi, seeing this, said (Ṛv. I, 117, 22):

'O Aśvins, you fixed a horse's head on Ātharvaṇa Dadhyach,
nd he, wishing to be true (to his promise), proclaimed to you
he honey, both that of Tvashtṛi and that which is to be your
ecret, O ye strong ones.'

18. Verily Dadhyach Ātharvaṇa proclaimed this honey to the
wo Aśvins, and a Ṛishi, seeing this, said:

'He (the Lord) made bodies with two feet, he made bodies
vith four feet. Having first become a bird, he entered the
odies as purusha (as the person).' This very purusha is in all
odies the puriśaya, i.e. he who lies in the body (and is therefore
alled purusha). There is nothing that is not covered by him,
othing that is not filled by him.

19. Verily Dadhyach Ātharvaṇa proclaimed this honey to the
wo Aśvins, and a Ṛishi, seeing this, said (Ṛv. VI, 47, 18):

'He (the Lord) became like unto every form and this is meant
o reveal the (true) form of him (the Ātman). Indra (the Lord)
ppears multiform through the Māyās (appearances), for his
orses (senses) are yoked, hundreds and ten.'

This (Ātman) is the horses, this (Ātman) is the ten, and the
housands, many and endless. This is the Brahman, without
ause and without effect, without anything inside or outside;
his Self is Brahman, omnipresent and omniscient. This is
he teaching (of the Upanishads).

[The SIXTH BRĀHMAṆA is omitted.]

THIRD ADHYĀYA

FIRST BRĀHMAṆA

Adoration to the Highest Self (Paramātman)!

1. Janaka Vaideha (the king of the Videhas) sacrificed with
sacrifice at which many presents were offered to the priests of
he Aśvamedha). Brāhmaṇas of the Kurus and the Pānchālas
ad come thither, and Janaka Vaideha wished to know which
f those Brāhmaṇas was the best read. So he enclosed a
housand cows, and ten pādas (of gold) were fastened to each
air of horns.

2. And Janaka spoke to them: 'Ye venerable Brāhmaṇas, he
ho among you is the wisest, let him drive away these cows.'

Then those Brāhmaṇas durst not, but Yājñavalkya said to his pupil: 'Drive them away, my dear.'

He replied: 'O glory of the Sāman,' and drove them away.

The Brāhmaṇas became angry and said: 'How could he call himself the wisest among us?'

Now there was Aśvala, the Hotṛi priest of Janaka Vaideha. He asked him: 'Are you indeed the wisest among us, O Yājñavalkya?' He replied: 'I bow before the wisest (the best knower of Brahman), but I wish indeed to have these cows.'

Then Aśvala, the Hotṛi priest, undertook to question him.

3. 'Yājñavalkya,' he said, 'everything here (connected with the sacrifice) is reached by death, everything is overcome by death. By what means then is the sacrificer freed beyond the reach of death?'

Yājñavalkya said: 'By the Hotṛi priest, who is Agni (fire), who is speech. For speech is the Hotṛi of the sacrifice (or the sacrificer), and speech is Agni, and he is the Hotṛi. This constitutes freedom, and perfect freedom (from death).'

4. 'Yājñavalkya,' he said, 'everything here is reached by day and night, everything is overcome by day and night. By what means then is the sacrificer freed beyond the reach of day and night?'

Yājñavalkya said: 'By the Adhvaryu priest, who is the eye, who is Āditya (the sun). For the eye is the Adhvaryu of the sacrifice, and the eye is the sun, and he is the Adhvaryu. This constitutes freedom, and perfect freedom.'

5. 'Yājñavalkya,' he said, 'everything here is reached by the waxing and waning of the moon, everything is overcome by the waxing and waning of the moon. By what means then is the sacrificer freed beyond the reach of the waxing and waning of the moon?'

Yājñavalkya said: 'By the Udgātṛi priest, who is Vāyu (the wind), who is the breath. For the breath is the Udgātṛi of the sacrifice, and the breath is the wind, and he is the Udgātṛi. This constitutes freedom, and perfect freedom.'

6. 'Yājñavalkya,' he said, 'this sky is, as it were, without an ascent (staircase). By what approach does the sacrificer approach the Svarga world?'

Yājñavalkya said: 'By the Brahman priest, who is the mind (manas), who is the moon. For the mind is the Brahman of the sacrifice, and the mind is the moon, and he is the Brahman.

This constitutes freedom, and perfect freedom. These are the complete deliverances (from death).'

Next follow the achievements.

7. 'Yājñavalkya,' he said, 'how many Rich verses will the Hotri priest employ to-day at this sacrifice?'

'Three,' replied Yājñavalkya.

'And what are these three?'

'Those which are called Puronuvākyā, Yājyā, and, thirdly, Śasyā.'

'What does he gain by them?'

'All whatsoever has breath.'

8. 'Yājñavalkya,' he said, 'how many oblations (āhuti) will the Adhvaryu priest employ to-day at this sacrifice?'

'Three,' replied Yājñavalkya.

'And what are these three?'

'Those which, when offered, flame up; those which, when offered, make an excessive noise; and those which, when offered, sink down.'

'What does he gain by them?'

'By those which, when offered, flame up, he gains the Deva (god) world, for the Deva world flames up, as it were. By those which, when offered, make an excessive noise, he gains the Pitri (father) world, for the Pitri world is excessively (noisy). By those which, when offered, sink down, he gains the Manushya (man) world, for the Manushya world is, as it were, down below.'

9. 'Yājñavalkya,' he said, 'with how many deities does the Brahman priest on the right protect to-day this sacrifice?'

'By one,' replied Yājñavalkya.

'And which is it?'

'The mind alone; for the mind is endless, and the Viśvedevas are endless, and he thereby gains the endless world.'

10. 'Yājñavalkya,' he said, 'how many Stotriyā hymns will the Udgātri priest employ to-day at this sacrifice?'

'Three,' replied Yājñavalkya.

'And what are these three?'

'Those which are called Puronuvākyā, Yājyā, and, thirdly, Śasyā.'

'And what are these with regard to the body (adhyātmam)?'

'The Puronuvākyā is Prāṇa (up-breathing), the Yājyā the Apāna (down-breathing), the Śasyā the Vyāna (back-breathing).'

'What does he gain by them?'

'He gains the earth by the Puronuvākyā, the sky by the Yājyā, heaven by the Śasyā.'

After that Aśvala held his peace.

SECOND BRĀHMAṆA

1. Then Jāratkārava Ārtabhāga asked. 'Yājñavalkya,' he said, 'how many Grahas are there, and how many Atigrahas?'

'Eight Grahas,' he replied, 'and eight Atigrahas.'

'And what are these eight Grahas and eight Atigrahas?'

2. 'Prāṇa (breath) is one Graha, and that is seized by Apāna (down-breathing) as the Atigrāha, for one smells with the Apāna.

3. 'Speech (vāch) is one Graha, and that is seized by name (nāman) as the Atigrāha, for with speech one pronounces names.

4. 'The tongue is one Graha, and that is seized by taste as the Atigrāha, for with the tongue one perceives tastes.

5. 'The eye is one Graha, and that is seized by form as the Atigrāha, for with the eye one sees forms.

6. 'The ear is one Graha, and that is seized by sound as the Atigrāha, for with the ear one hears sounds.

7. 'The mind is one Graha, and that is seized by desire as the Atigrāha, for with the mind one desires desires.

8. 'The arms are one Graha, and these are seized by work as the Atigrāha, for with the arms one works work.

9. 'The skin is one Graha, and that is seized by touch as the Atigrāha, for with the skin one perceives touch. These are the eight Grahas and the eight Atigrāhas.'

10. 'Yājñavalkya,' he said, 'everything is the food of death. What then is the deity to whom death is food?'

'Fire (agni) is death, and that is the food of water. Death is conquered again.'

11. 'Yājñavalkya,' he said, 'when such a person (a sage) dies, do the vital breaths (prāṇas) move out of him or no?'

'No,' replied Yājñavalkya; 'they are gathered up in him, he swells, he is inflated, and thus inflated the dead lies at rest.'

12. 'Yājñavalkya,' he said, 'when such a man dies, what does not leave him?'

'The name,' he replied; 'for the name is endless, the Viśvedevas are endless, and by it he gains the endless world.'

13. 'Yājñavalkya,' he said, 'when the speech of this dead person enters into the fire, breath into the air, the eye into the

sun, the mind into the moon, the hearing into space, into the earth the body, into the ether the self, into the shrubs the hairs of the body, into the trees the hairs of the head, when the blood and the seed are deposited in the water, where is then that person?'

Yājñavalkya said: 'Take my hand, my friend. We two alone shall know of this; let this question of ours not be (discussed) in public.' Then these two went out and argued, and what they said was karman (work), what they praised was karman, viz. that a man becomes good by good work, and bad by bad work.

After that Jāratkārava Ārtabhāga held his peace.

THIRD BRĀHMAṆA

1. Then Bhujyu Lāhyāyani asked. 'Yājñavalkya,' he said, 'we wandered about as students, and came to the house of Patanchala Kāpya. He had a daughter who was possessed by a Gandharva. We asked him, "Who art thou?" and he (the Gandharva) replied: "I am Sudhanvan, the Aṅgirasa." And when we asked him about the ends of the world, we said to him, "Where were the Pārikshitas?" Where then were the Pārikshitas, I ask thee, Yājñavalkya, where were the Pārikshitas?'

2. Yājñavalkya said: 'He said to thee, I suppose, that they went where those go who have performed a horse-sacrifice.'

He said: 'And where do they go who have performed a horse-sacrifice?'

Yājñavalkya replied: 'Thirty-two journeys of the car of the sun is this world. The earth surrounds it on every side, twice as large, and the ocean surrounds this earth on every side, twice as large. Now there is between them a space as large as the edge of a razor or the wing of a mosquito. Indra, having become a bird, handed them (through the space) to Vāyu (the air), and Vāyu (the air), holding them within himself, conveyed them to where they dwell who have performed a horse-sacrifice. Somewhat in this way did he praise Vāyu indeed. Therefore Vāyu (air) is everything by itself, and Vāyu is all things together. He who knows this, conquers death.'

After that Bhujyu Lāhyāyani held his peace.

FOURTH BRĀHMAṆA

1. Then Ushasta Chākrāyaṇa asked. 'Yājñavalkya,' he said, 'tell me the Brahman which is visible, not invisible, the self (ātman), who is within all.'

Yājñavalkya replied: 'This, thy Self, who is within all.'

'Which Self, O Yājñavalkya, is within all?'

Yājñavalkya replied: 'He who breathes in the up-breathing, he is thy Self, and within all. He who breathes in the down-breathing, he is thy Self, and within all. He who breathes in the on-breathing, he is thy Self, and within all. He who breathes in the out-breathing, he is thy Self, and within all. This is thy Self, who is within all.'

2. Ushasta Chākrāyaṇa said: 'As one might say, this is a cow, this is a horse, thus has this been explained by thee. Tell me the Brahman which is visible, not invisible, the Self, who is within all.'

Yājñavalkya replied: 'This, thy Self, who is within all.'

'Which Self, O Yājñavalkya, is within all?'

Yājñavalkya replied: 'Thou couldst not see the (true) seer of sight, thou couldst not hear the (true) hearer of hearing, nor perceive the perceiver of perception, nor know the knower of knowledge. This is thy Self, who is within all. Everything also is of evil.'

After that Ushasta Chākrāyaṇa held his peace.

FIFTH BRĀHMAṆA

Then Kahola Kaushītakeya asked. 'Yājñavalkya,' he said, 'tell me the Brahman which is visible, not invisible, the Self (ātman), who is within all.'

Yājñavalkya replied: 'This, thy Self, who is within all.'

'Which Self, O Yājñavalkya, is within all?'

Yājñavalkya replied: 'He who overcomes hunger and thirst, sorrow, passion, old age, and death. When Brāhmaṇas know that Self, and have risen above the desire for sons, wealth, and (new) worlds, they wander about as mendicants. For a desire for sons is desire for wealth, a desire for wealth is desire for worlds. Both these are indeed desires. Therefore let a Brāhmaṇa, after he has done with learning, wish to stand by real strength; after he has done with that strength and learning, he becomes a Muni (a Yogin); and after he has done with what is not the knowledge of a Muni, and with what is the knowledge of a Muni, he is a Brāhmaṇa. By whatever means he has become a Brāhmaṇa, he is such indeed. Everything else is of evil.'

After that Kahola Kaushītakeya held his peace.

SIXTH BRĀHMAṆA

Then Gārgī Vāchaknavī asked. 'Yājñavalkya,' she said, 'everything here is woven, like warp and woof, in water.

What then is that in which water is woven, like warp and woof?'

'In air, O Gārgī,' he replied.

'In what then is air woven, like warp and woof?'

'In the worlds of the sky, O Gārgī,' he replied.

'In what then are the worlds of the sky woven, like warp and woof?'

'In the worlds of the Gandharvas, O Gārgī,' he replied.

'In what then are the worlds of the Gandharvas woven, like warp and woof?'

'In the worlds of Āditya (sun), O Gārgī,' he replied.

'In what then are the worlds of Āditya (sun) woven, like warp and woof?'

'In the worlds of Chandra (moon), O Gārgī,' he replied.

'In what then are the worlds of Chandra (moon) woven, like warp and woof?'

'In the worlds of the Nakshatras (stars), O Gārgī,' he replied.

'In what then are the worlds of the Nakshatras (stars) woven, like warp and woof?'

'In the worlds of the Devas (gods), O Gārgī,' he replied.

'In what then are the worlds of the Devas (gods) woven, like warp and woof?'

'In the worlds of Indra, O Gārgī,' he replied.

'In what then are the worlds of Indra woven, like warp and woof?'

'In the worlds of Prajāpati, O Gārgī,' he replied.

'In what then are the worlds of Prajāpati woven, like warp and woof?'

'In the worlds of Brahman, O Gārgī,' he replied.

'In what then are the worlds of Brahman woven, like warp and woof?'

Yājñavalkya said: 'O Gārgī, do not ask too much, lest thy head should fall off. Thou askest too much about a deity about which we are not to ask too much. Do not ask too much, O Gārgī.'

After that Gārgī Vāchaknavī held her peace.

SEVENTH BRĀHMAṆA

1. Then Uddālaka Āruṇi asked. 'Yājñavalkya,' he said, 'we dwelt among the Madras in the houses of Patanchala Kāpya, studying the sacrifice. His wife was possessed of a Gandharva, and we asked him: "Who art thou?" He answered: "I am Kabandha Ātharvaṇa." And he said to Patanchala Kāpya

and to (us) students: "Dost thou know, Kāpya, that thread by which this world and the other world, and all beings are strung together?" And Patanchala Kāpya replied: "I do not know it, Sir." He said again to Patanchala Kâpya and to (us) students: "Dost thou know, Kāpya, that puller (ruler) within (antaryâmin), who within pulls (rules) this world and the other world and all beings?" And Patanchala Kāpya replied: "I do not know it, Sir." He said again to Patanchala Kāpya and to (us) students: "He, O Kāpya, who knows that thread and him who pulls (it) within, he knows Brahman, he knows the worlds, he knows the Devas, he knows the Vedas, he knows the Bhūtas (creatures), he knows the Self, he knows everything." Thus did he (the Gandharva) say to them, and I know it. If thou, O Yājñavalkya, without knowing that string and the puller within, drivest away those Brahma-cows (the cows offered as a prize to him who best knows Brahman), thy head will fall off.'

Yājñavalkya said: 'O Gautama, I believe I know that thread and the puller within.'

The other said: 'Anybody may say, I know, I know. Tell what thou knowest.'

2. Yājñavalkya said: 'Vāyu (air) is that thread, O Gautama. By air, as by a thread, O Gautama, this world and the other world, and all creatures are strung together. Therefore, O Gautama, people say of a dead person that his limbs have become unstrung; for by air, as by a thread, O Gautama, they were strung together.'

The other said: 'So it is, O Yājñavalkya. Tell now (who is) the puller within.'

3. Yājñavalkya said: 'He who dwells in the earth, and within the earth, whom the earth does not know, whose body the earth is, and who pulls (rules) the earth within, he is thy Self, the puller (ruler) within, the immortal.

4. 'He who dwells in the water, and within the water, whom the water does not know, whose body the water is, and who pulls (rules) the water within, he is thy Self, the puller (ruler) within, the immortal.

5. 'He who dwells in the fire, and within the fire, whom the fire does not know, whose body the fire is, and who pulls (rules) the fire within, he is thy Self, the puller (ruler) within, the immortal.'

6. 'He who dwells in the sky, and within the sky, whom the

sky does not know, whose body the sky is, and who pulls (rules) the sky within, he is thy Self, the puller (ruler) within, the immortal.

7. 'He who dwells in the air (vāyu), and within the air, whom the air does not know, whose body the air is, and who pulls (rules) the air within, he is thy Self, the puller (ruler) within, the immortal.

8. 'He who dwells in the heaven (dyu), and within the heaven, whom the heaven does not know, whose body the heaven is, and who pulls (rules) the heaven within, he is thy Self, the puller (ruler) within, the immortal.

9. 'He who dwells in the sun (āditya), and within the sun, whom the sun does not know, whose body the sun is, and who pulls (rules) the sun within, he is thy Self, the puller (ruler) within, the immortal.

10. 'He who dwells in the space (diśah), and within the space, whom the space does not know, whose body the space is, and who pulls (rules) the space within, he is thy Self, the puller (ruler) within, the immortal.

11. 'He who dwells in the moon and stars (chandra-tārakam), and within the moon and stars, whom the moon and stars do not know, whose body the moon and stars are, and who pulls (rules) the moon and stars within, he is thy Self, the puller (ruler) within, the immortal.

12. 'He who dwells in the ether (ākāśa), and within the ether, whom the ether does not know, whose body the ether is, and who pulls (rules) the ether within, he is thy Self, the puller (ruler) within, the immortal.'

13. 'He who dwells in the darkness (tamas), and within the darkness, whom the darkness does not know, whose body the darkness is, and who pulls (rules) the darkness within, he is thy Self, the puller (ruler) within, the immortal.

14. 'He who dwells in the light (tejas), and within the light, whom the light does not know, whose body the light is, and who pulls (rules) the light within, he is thy Self, the puller (ruler) within, the immortal.'

So far with respect to the gods (adhidaivatam); now with respect to beings (adhibhūtam).

15. Yājñavalkya said: 'He who dwells in all beings, and within all beings, whom all beings do not know, whose body all beings are, and who pulls (rules) all beings within, he is thy Self, the puller (ruler) within, the immortal.

16. 'He who dwells in the breath (prāṇa), and within the breath, whom the breath does not know, whose body the breath is, and who pulls (rules) the breath within, he is thy Self, the puller (ruler) within, the immortal.

17. 'He who dwells in the tongue (vāch), and within the tongue, whom the tongue does not know, whose body the tongue is, and who pulls (rules) the tongue within, he is thy Self, the puller (ruler) within, the immortal.

18. 'He who dwells in the eye, and within the eye, whom the eye does not know, whose body the eye is, and who pulls (rules) the eye within, he is thy Self, the puller (ruler) within, the immortal.

19. 'He who dwells in the ear, and within the ear, whom the ear does not know, whose body the ear is, and who pulls (rules) the ear within, he is thy Self, the puller (ruler) within, the immortal.

20. 'He who dwells in the mind, and within the mind, whom the mind does not know, whose body the mind is, and who pulls (rules) the mind within, he is thy Self, the puller (ruler) within, the immortal.

21. 'He who dwells in the skin, and within the skin, whom the skin does not know, whose body the skin is, and who pulls (rules) the skin within, he is thy Self, the puller (ruler) within, the immortal.

22. 'He who dwells in knowledge, and within knowledge, whom knowledge does not know, whose body knowledge is, and who pulls (rules) knowledge within, he is thy Self, the puller (ruler) within, the immortal.

23. 'He who dwells in the seed, and within the seed, whom the seed does not know, whose body the seed is, and who pulls (rules) the seed within, he is thy Self, the puller (ruler) within, the immortal; unseen, but seeing; unheard, but hearing; unperceived, but perceiving; unknown, but knowing. There is no other seer but he, there is no other hearer but he, there is no other perceiver but he, there is no other knower but he. This is thy Self, the ruler within, the immortal. Everything else is of evil.'

After that Uddālaka Āruṇi held his peace.

EIGHTH BRĀHMAṆA

1. Then Vāchaknavī said: 'Venerable Brāhmaṇas, I shall ask him two questions. If he will answer them, none of you, I think, will defeat him in any argument concerning Brahman.'

Yājñavalkya said: 'Ask, O Gārgī.'

2. She said: 'O Yājñavalkya, as the son of a warrior from the Kāśīs or Videhas might string his loosened bow, take two pointed foe-piercing arrows in his hand and rise to do battle, I have risen to fight thee with two questions. Answer me these questions.'

Yājñavalkya said: 'Ask, O Gārgī.'

3. She said: 'O Yājñavalkya, that of which they say that it is above the heavens, beneath the earth, embracing heaven and earth, past, present, and future, tell me in what is it woven, like warp and woof?'

4. Yājñavalkya said: 'That of which they say that it is above the heavens, beneath the earth, embracing heaven and earth, past, present, and future, that is woven, like warp and woof, in the ether (ākāśa).'

5. She said: 'I bow to thee, O Yājñavalkya, who hast solved me that question. Get thee ready for the second.'

Yājñavalkya said: 'Ask, O Gārgī.'

6. She said: 'O Yājñavalkya, that of which they say that it is above the heavens, beneath the earth, embracing heaven and earth, past, present, and future, tell me in what is it woven, like warp and woof?'

7. Yājñavalkya said: 'That of which they say that it is above the heavens, beneath the earth, embracing heaven and earth, past, present, and future, that is woven, like warp and woof, in the ether.'

Gārgī said: 'In what then is the ether woven, like warp and woof?'

8. He said: 'O Gārgī, the Brāhmaṇas call this the Akshara (the imperishable). It is neither coarse nor fine, neither short nor long, neither red (like fire) nor fluid (like water); it is without shadow, without darkness, without air, without ether, without attachment, without taste, without smell, without eyes, without ears, without speech, without mind, without light (vigour), without breath, without a mouth (or door), without measure, having no within and no without, it devours nothing, and no one devours it.

9. 'By the command of that Akshara (the imperishable), O Gārgī, sun and moon stand apart. By the command of that Akshara, O Gārgī, heaven and earth stand apart. By the command of that Akshara, O Gārgī, what are called moments (nimesha), hours (muhūrta), days and nights, half-months, months, seasons, years, all stand apart. By the command of that Akshara, O

Gārgī, some rivers flow to the east from the white mountains, others to the west, or to any other quarter. By the command of that Akshara, O Gārgī, men praise those who give, the gods follow the sacrificer, the fathers the Darvī-offering.

10. 'Whosoever, O Gārgi, without knowing that Akshara (the imperishable), offers oblations in this world, sacrifices, and performs penance for a thousand years, his work will have an end. Whosoever, O Gārgī, without knowing this Akshara, departs this world, he is miserable (like a slave). But he, O Gārgī, who departs this world, knowing this Akshara, he is a Brāhmaṇa.

11. 'That Brahman, O Gārgī, is unseen, but seeing; unheard, but hearing; unperceived, but perceiving; unknown, but knowing. There is nothing that sees but it, nothing that hears but it, nothing that perceives but it, nothing that knows but it. In that Akshara, then, O Gārgī, the ether is woven, like warp and woof.'

12. Then said Gārgī: 'Venerable Brāhmans, you may consider it a great thing, if you get off by bowing before him. No one, I believe, will defeat him in any argument concerning Brahman.'

After that Vāchaknavī held her peace.

NINTH BRĀHMAṆA

1. Then Vidagdha Śākalya asked him: 'How many gods are there, O Yājñavalkya?' He replied with this very Nivid: 'As many as are mentioned in the Nivid of the hymn of praise addressed to the Viśvedevas, viz. three and three hundred, three and three thousand.'

'Yes,' he said, and asked again: 'How many gods are there really, O Yājñavalkya?'

'Thirty-three,' he said.

'Yes,' he said, and asked again: 'How many gods are there really, O Yājñavalkya?'

'Six,' he said.

'Yes,' he said, and asked again: 'How many gods are there really, O Yājñavalkya?'

'Three,' he said.

'Yes,' he said, and asked again: 'How many gods are there really, O Yājñavalkya?'

'Two,' he said.

'Yes,' he said, and asked again: 'How many gods are there really, O Yājñavalkya?'

'One and a half (adhyardha),' he said.

'Yes,' he said, and asked again: 'How many gods are there really, O Yājñavalkya?'

'One,' he said.

'Yes,' he said, and asked: 'Who are these three and three hundred, three and three thousand?'

2. Yājñavalkya replied: 'They are only the various powers of them, in reality there are only thirty-three gods.'

He asked: 'Who are those thirty-three?'

Yājñavalkya replied: 'The eight Vasus, the eleven Rudras, the twelve Ādityas. They make thirty-one, and Indra and Prajāpati make the thirty-three.'

3. He asked: 'Who are the Vasus?'

Yājñavalkya replied: 'Agni (fire), Pṛithivī (earth), Vāyu (air), Antariksha (sky), Āditya (sun), Dyu (heaven), Chandramas (moon), the Nakshatras (stars), these are the Vasus, for in them all that dwells (this world) rests; and therefore they are called Vasus.'

4. He asked: 'Who are the Rudras?'

Yājñavalkya replied: 'These ten vital breaths (prāṇas, the senses, i.e. the five jñānendriyas, and the five karmendriyas), and Ātman, as the eleventh. When they depart from this mortal body, they make us cry (rodayanti), and because they make us cry, they are called Rudras.'

5. He asked: 'Who are the Ādityas?'

Yājñavalkya replied: 'The twelve months of the year, and they are Ādityas, because they move along (yanti), taking up everything (ādadānā). Because they move along, taking up everything, therefore they are called Ādityas.'

6. He asked: 'And who is Indra, and who is Prajāpati?'

Yājñavalkya replied: 'Indra is thunder, Prajāpati is the sacrifice.'

He asked: 'And what is the thunder?'

Yājñavalkya replied: 'The thunderbolt.'

He asked: 'And what is the sacrifice?'

Yājñavalkya replied: 'The (sacrificial) animals.'

7. He asked: 'Who are the six?'

Yājñavalkya replied: 'Agni (fire), Pṛithivī (earth), Vāyu (air), Antariksha (sky), Āditya (sun), Dyu (heaven), they are the six, for they are all this, the six.'

8. He asked: 'Who are the three gods?'

Yājñavalkya replied: 'These three worlds, for in them all these gods exist.'

He asked: 'Who are the two gods?'

Yājñavalkya replied: 'Food and breath.'

He asked: 'Who is the one god and a half?'

Yājñavalkya replied: 'He that blows.'

9. Here they say: 'How is it that he who blows like one only, should be called one and a half (adhyardha)?' And the answer is: 'Because, when the wind was blowing, everything grew (adhyardhnot).'

He asked: 'Who is the one god?'

Yājñavalkya replied: 'Breath (prāṇa), and he is Brahman (the Sūtrātman), and they call him That (tyad).'

10. Śākalya said: 'Whosoever knows that person (or god) whose dwelling (body) is the earth, whose sight (world) is fire, whose mind is light—the principle of every (living) self, he indeed is a teacher, O Yājñavalkya.'

Yājñavalkya said: 'I know that person, the principle of every self, of whom thou speakest. This corporeal (material, earthy) person, "he is he." But tell me, Śākalya, who is his devatā (deity)?'

Śākalya replied: 'The Immortal.'

11. Śākalya said: 'Whosoever knows that person whose dwelling is love (a body capable of sensual love), whose sight is the heart, whose mind is light—the principle of every self, he indeed is a teacher, O Yājñavalkya.'

Yājñavalkya replied: 'I know that person, the principle of every self, of whom thou speakest. This love-made (loving) person, "he is he." But tell me, Śākalya, who is his devatā?'

Śākalya replied: 'The women.'

12. Śākalya said: 'Whosoever knows that person whose dwelling are the colours, whose sight is the eye, whose mind is light—the principle of every self, he indeed is a teacher, O Yājñavalkya.'

Yājñavalkya replied: 'I know that person, the principle of every self, of whom thou speakest. That person in the sun, "he is he." But tell me, Śākalya, who is his devatā?'

Śākalya replied: 'The True.'

13. Śākalya said: 'Whosoever knows that person whose dwelling is ether, whose sight is the ear, whose mind is light—the principle of every self, he indeed is a teacher, O Yājñavalkya.'

Yājñavalkya replied: 'I know that person, the principle of every self, of whom thou speakest. The person who hears and answers, " he is he." But tell me, Śākalya, who is his devatā ?'

Śākalya replied: ' Space.'

14. Śākalya said: ' Whosoever knows that person whose dwelling is darkness, whose sight is the heart, whose mind is light—the principle of every self, he indeed is a teacher, O Yājñavalkya.'

Yājñavalkya replied: ' I know that person, the principle of every self, of whom thou speakest. The shadowy person, " he is he." But tell me, Śākalya, who is his devatā ?'

Śākalya replied: ' Death.'

15. Śākalya said: ' Whosoever knows that person whose dwelling is (bright) colours, whose sight is the eye, whose mind is light—the principle of every self, he indeed is a teacher, O Yājñavalkya.'

Yājñavalkya replied: ' I know that person, the principle of every self, of whom thou speakest. The person in the looking-glass, " he is he." But tell me, Śākalya, who is his devatā ?'

Śākalya replied: ' Vital breath (asu).'

16. Śākalya said: ' Whosoever knows that person whose dwelling is water, whose sight is the heart, whose mind is light—the principle of every self, he indeed is a teacher, O Yājñavalkya.'

Yājñavalkya replied: ' I know that person, the principle of every self, of whom thou speakest. The person in the water, " he is he." But tell me, Śākalya, who is his devatā ?'

Śākalya replied: ' Varuṇa.'

17. Śākalya said: ' Whosoever knows that person whose dwelling is seed, whose sight is the heart, whose mind is light—the principle of every self, he indeed is a teacher, O Yājñavalkya.'

Yājñavalkya replied: ' I know that person, the principle of every self, of whom thou speakest. The filial person, " he is he." But tell me, Śākalya, who is his devatā ?'

Śākalya replied: ' Prajāpati.'

18. Yājñavalkya said: ' Śākalya, did those Brāhmaṇas (who themselves shrank from the contest) make thee the victim ?'

Śākalya said: ' Yājñavalkya, because thou hast decried the Brāhmaṇas of the Kuru-Panchālas, what Brahman dost thou know ?'

19. Yājñavalkya said: ' I know the quarters with their deities and their abodes.'

Śākalya said: 'If thou knowest the quarters with their deities and their abodes,

20. 'Which is thy deity in the eastern quarter?'

Yājñavalkya said: 'Āditya (the sun).'

Śākalya said: 'In what does that Āditya abide?'

Yājñavalkya said: 'In the eye.'

Śākalya said: 'In what does the eye abide?'

Yājñavalkya said: 'In the colours, for with the eye he sees the colours.'

Śākalya said: 'And in what then do the colours abide?'

Yājñavalkya said: 'In the heart, for we know colours by the heart, for colours abide in the heart.'

Śākalya said: 'So it is indeed, O Yājñavalkya.'

21. Śākalya said: 'Which is thy deity in the southern quarter?'

Yājñavalkya said: 'Yama.'

Śākalya said: 'In what does that Yama abide?'

Yājñavalkya said: 'In the sacrifice.'

Śākalya said: 'In what does the sacrifice abide?'

Yājñavalkya said: 'In the Dakshiṇā (the gifts to be given to the priests).'

Śākalya said: 'In what does the Dakshiṇā abide?'

Yājñavalkya said: 'In Śraddhā (faith), for if a man believes, then he gives Dakshiṇā, and Dakshiṇā truly abides in faith.'

Śākalya said: 'And in what then does faith abide?'

Yājñavalkya said: 'In the heart, for by the heart faith knows, and therefore faith abides in the heart.'

Śākalya said: 'So it is indeed, O Yājñavalkya.'

22. Śākalya said: 'Which is thy deity in the western quarter?'

Yājñavalkya said: 'Varuṇa.'

Śākalya said: 'In what does that Varuṇa abide?'

Yājñavalkya said: 'In the water.'

Śākalya said: 'In what does the water abide?'

Yājñavalkya said: 'In the seed.'

Śākalya said: 'And in what does the seed abide?'

Yājñavalkya said: 'In the heart. And therefore also they say of a son who is like his father, that he seems as if slipt from his heart, or made from his heart; for the seed abides in the heart.'

Śākalya said: 'So it is indeed, O Yājñavalkya.'

23. Śākalya said: 'Which is thy deity in the northern quarter?'

Yājñavalkya said: 'Soma.'

Śākalya said: 'In what does that Soma abide?'

Yājñavalkya said: 'In the Dīkshā.'

Śākalya said: 'In what does the Dīkshā abide?'

Yājñavalkya said: 'In the True; and therefore they say to one who has performed the Dīkshā, Speak what is true, for in the True indeed the Dīkshā abides.'

Śākalya said: 'And in what does the True abide?'

Yājñavalkya said: 'In the heart, for with the heart do we know what is true, and in the heart indeed the True abides.'

Śākalya said: 'So it is indeed, O Yājñavalkya.'

24. Śākalya said: 'Which is thy deity in the zenith?'

Yājñavalkya said: 'Agni.'

Śākalya said: 'In what does that Agni abide?'

Yājñavalkya said: 'In speech.'

Śākalya said: 'And in what does speech abide?'

Yājñavalkya said: 'In the heart.'

Śākalya said: 'And in what does the heart abide?'

25. Yājñavalkya said: 'O Ahallika, when you think the heart could be anywhere else away from us, if it were away from us, the dogs might eat it, or the birds tear it.'

26. Śākalya said: 'And in what dost thou (thy body) and the Self (thy heart) abide?'

Yājñavalkya said: 'In the Prāṇa (breath).'

Śākalya said: 'In what does the Prāṇa abide?'

Yājñavalkya said: 'In the Apāna (down-breathing).'

Śākalya said: 'In what does the Apāna abide?'

Yājñavalkya said: 'In the Vyāna (back-breathing).'

Śākalya said: 'In what does the Vyāna abide?'

Yājñavalkya said: 'In the Udāna (the out-breathing).'

Śākalya said: 'In what does the Udāna abide?'

Yājñavalkya said: 'In the Samāna. That Self (ātman) is to be described by No, no! He is incomprehensible, for he cannot be (is not) comprehended; he is imperishable, for he cannot perish; he is unattached, for he does not attach himself; unfettered, he does not suffer, he does not fail.

'These are the eight abodes (the earth, etc.), the eight worlds (fire, etc.), the eight gods (the immortal food, etc.), the eight persons (the corporeal, etc.). He who after dividing and uniting these persons, went beyond (the Samāna), that person, taught in the Upanishads, I now ask thee (to teach me). If thou shalt not explain him to me, thy head will fall.'

Śākalya did not know him, and his head fell, nay, thieves took away his bones, mistaking them for something else.

27. Then Yājñavalkya said: 'Reverend Brāhmaṇas, whosoever among you desires to do so, may now question me. Or question me, all of you. Or whosoever among you desires it, I shall question him, or I shall question all of you.'

But those Brāhmaṇas durst not (say anything).

28. Then Yājñavalkya questioned them with these Ślokas:

'As a mighty tree in the forest, so in truth is man, his hairs are the leaves, his outer skin is the bark.

'From his skin flows forth blood, sap from the skin (of the tree); and thus from the wounded man comes forth blood, as from a tree that is struck.

'The lumps of his flesh are (in the tree) the layers of wood, the fibre is strong like the tendons. The bones are the (hard) wood within, the marrow is made like the marrow of the tree.

'But, while the tree, when felled, grows up again more young from the root, from what root, tell me, does a mortal grow up, after he has been felled by death?

'Do not say, "from seed," for seed is produced from the living; but a tree, springing from a grain, clearly rises again after death.

'If a tree is pulled up with the root, it will not grow again; from what root then, tell me, does a mortal grow up, after he has been felled by death?

'Once born, he is not born (again); for who should create him again?

'Brahman, who is knowledge and bliss, he is the principle, both to him who gives gifts, and also to him who stands firm, and knows.'

Fourth Adhyāya

FIRST BRĀHMAṆA

1. When Janaka Vaideha was sitting (to give audience), Yājñavalkya approached, and Janaka Vaideha said: 'Yājñavalkya, for what object did you come, wishing for cattle, or for subtle questions?'

Yājñavalkya replied: 'For both, your Majesty;

2. 'Let us hear what anybody may have told you.'

Janaka Vaideha replied: 'Jitvan Śailini told me that speech (vāch) is Brahman.'

Yājñavalkya said: 'As one who had (the benefit of a good) father, mother, and teacher might tell, so did Śailini tell you, that speech is Brahman; for what is the use of a dumb person? But did he tell you the body (āyatana) and the resting-place (pratishṭhā) of that Brahman?'

Janaka Vaideha said: 'He did not tell me.'

Yājñavalkya said: 'Your Majesty, this (Brahman) stands on one leg only.'

Janaka Vaideha said: 'Then tell me, Yājñavalkya.'

Yājñavalkya said: 'The tongue is its body, ether its place, and one should worship it as knowledge.'

Janaka Vaideha said: 'What is the nature of that knowledge?'

Yājñavalkya replied: 'Your Majesty, speech itself (is knowledge). For through speech, your Majesty, a friend is known (to be a friend), and likewise the Ṛigveda, Yajur-veda, Sāma-veda, the Atharvāṇgirasas, the Itihāsa (tradition), Purāṇa-vidyā (knowledge of the past), the Upanishads, Ślokas (verses), Sūtras (rules), Anuvyākhyānas and Vyākhyānas (commentaries, etc.); what is sacrificed, what is poured out, what is (to be) eaten and drunk, this world and the other world, and all creatures. By speech alone, your Majesty, Brahman is known, speech indeed, O king, is the highest Brahman. Speech does not desert him who worships that (Brahman) with such knowledge, all creatures approach him, and having become a god, he goes to the gods.'

Janaka Vaideha said: 'I shall give you (for this) a thousand cows with a bull as big as an elephant.'

Yājñavalkya said: 'My father was of opinion that one should not accept a reward without having fully instructed a pupil.'

3. Yājñavalkya said: 'Let us hear what anybody may have told you.'

Janaka Vaideha replied: 'Udaṅka Śaulbāyana told me that life (prāṇa) is Brahman.'

Yājñavalkya said: 'As one who had (the benefit of a good) father, mother, and teacher might tell, so did Udaṅka Śaulbāyana tell you that life is Brahman; for what is the use of a person without life? But did he tell you the body and the resting-place of that Brahman?'

Janaka Vaideha said: 'He did not tell me.'

Yājñavalkya said: 'Your Majesty, this (Brahman) stands on one leg only.'

Janaka Vaideha said: 'Then tell me, Yājñavalkya.'

Yājñavalkya said: 'Breath is its body, ether its place, and one should worship it as what is dear.'

Janaka Vaideha said: 'What is the nature of that which is dear?'

Yājñavalkya replied: 'Your Majesty, life itself (is that which is dear); because for the sake of life, your Majesty, a man sacrifices even for him who is unworthy of sacrifice, he accepts presents from him who is not worthy to bestow presents, nay, he goes to a country, even when there is fear of being hurt, for the sake of life. Life, O king, is the highest Brahman. Life does not desert him who worships that (Brahman) with such knowledge, all creatures approach him, and having become a god, he goes to the gods.'

Janaka Vaideha said: 'I shall give you (for this) a thousand cows with a bull as big as an elephant.'

Yājñavalkya said: 'My father was of opinion that one should not accept a reward without having fully instructed a pupil.'

4. Yājñavalkya said: 'Let us hear what anybody may have told you.'

Janaka Vaideha replied: 'Barku Vārshṇa told me that sight (chakshus) is Brahman.'

Yājñavalkya said: 'As one who had (the benefit of a good) father, mother, and teacher might tell, so did Barku Vārshṇa tell you that sight is Brahman; for what is the use of a person who cannot see? But did he tell you the body and the resting-place of that Brahman?'

Janaka Vaideha said: 'He did not tell me.'

Yājñavalkya said: 'Your Majesty, this (Brahman) stands on one leg only.'

Janaka Vaideha said: 'Then tell me, Yājñavalkya.'

Yājñavalkya said: 'The eye is its body, ether its place, and one should worship it as what is true.'

Janaka Vaideha said: 'What is the nature of that which is true?'

Yājñavalkya replied: 'Your Majesty, sight itself (is that which is true); for if they say to a man who sees with his eye, "Didst thou see?" and he says, "I saw," then it is true. Sight, O king, is the highest Brahman. Sight does not desert him who worships that (Brahman) with such knowledge, all creatures approach him, and having become a god, he goes to the gods.'

Janaka Vaideha said: 'I shall give you (for this) a thousand cows with a bull as big as an elephant.'

Yājñavalkya said: 'My father was of opinion that one should not accept a reward without having fully instructed a pupil.'

5. Yājñavalkya said: 'Let us hear what anybody may have told you.'

Janaka Vaideha replied: 'Gardabhīvibhīta Bhāradvāja told me that hearing (śrotra) is Brahman.'

Yājñavalkya said: 'As one who had (the benefit of a good) father, mother, and teacher might tell, so did Gardabhīvibhīta Bhāradvāja tell you that hearing is Brahman; for what is the use of a person who cannot hear? But did he tell you the body and the resting-place of that Brahman?'

Janaka Vaideha said: 'He did not tell me.'

Yājñavalkya said: 'Your Majesty, this (Brahman) stands on one leg only.'

Janaka Vaideha said: 'Then tell me, Yājñavalkya.'

Yājñavalkya said: 'The ear is its body, ether its place, and we should worship it as what is endless."

Janaka Vaideha said: 'What is the nature of that which is endless?'

Yājñavalkya replied: 'Your Majesty, space (diśah) itself (is that which is endless), and therefore to whatever space (quarter) he goes, he never comes to the end of it. For space is endless. Space indeed, O king, is hearing, and hearing indeed, O king, is the highest Brahman. Hearing does not desert him who worships that (Brahman) with such knowledge, all creatures approach him, and having become a god, he goes to the gods.'

Janaka Vaideha said: 'I shall give you (for this) a thousand cows with a bull as big as an elephant.'

Yājñavalkya said: 'My father was of opinion that one should not accept a reward without having fully instructed a pupil.'

6. Yājñavalkya said: 'Let us hear what anybody may have told you.'

Janaka Vaideha replied: 'Satyakāma Jābāla told me that mind (manas) is Brahman.'

Yājñavalkya said: 'As one who had (the benefit of a good) father, mother, and teacher might tell, so did Satyakāma Jābāla tell you that mind is Brahman; for what is the use of a person without mind? But did he tell you the body and the resting-place of that Brahman?'

Janaka Vaideha said: 'He did not tell me.'

Yājñavalkya said: 'Your Majesty, this (Brahman) stands on one leg only.'

Janaka Vaideha said: 'Then tell me, Yājñavalkya.'

Yājñavalkya said: 'Mind itself is its body, ether its place, and we should worship it as bliss.'

Janaka Vaideha said: 'What is the nature of bliss?'

Yājñavalkya replied: 'Your Majesty, mind itself; for with the mind does a man desire a woman, and a like son is born of her, and he is bliss. Mind indeed, O king, is the highest Brahman. Mind does not desert him who worships that (Brahman) with such knowledge, all creatures approach him, and having become a god, he goes to the gods.'

Janaka Vaideha said: 'I shall give you (for this) a thousand cows with a bull as big as an elephant.'

Yājñavalkya said: 'My father was of opinion that one should not accept a reward without having fully instructed a pupil.'

7. Yājñavalkya said: 'Let us hear what anybody may have told you.'

Janaka Vaideha replied: 'Vidagdha Śākalya told me that the heart (hṛidaya) is Brahman.'

Yājñavalkya said: 'As one who had (the benefit of a good) father, mother, and teacher might tell, so did Vidagdha Śākalya tell you that the heart is Brahman; for what is the use of a person without a heart? But did he tell you the body and the resting-place of that Brahman?'

Janaka Vaideha said: 'He did not tell me.'

Yājñavalkya said: 'Your Majesty, this (Brahman) stands on one leg only.'

Janaka Vaideha said: 'Then tell me, Yājñavalkya.'

Yājñavalkya said: 'The heart itself is its body, ether its place, and we should worship it as certainty (sthiti).'

Janaka Vaideha said: 'What is the nature of certainty?'

Yājñavalkya replied: 'Your Majesty, the heart itself; for the heart indeed, O king, is the body of all things, the heart is the resting-place of all things, for in the heart, O king, all things rest. The heart indeed, O king, is the highest Brahman. The heart does not desert him who worships that (Brahman) with such knowledge, all creatures approach him, and having become a god, he goes to the gods.'

Janaka Vaideha said: 'I shall give you (for this) a thousand cows with a bull as big as an elephant.'

Yājñavalkya said: 'My father was of opinion that one should not accept a reward without having fully instructed a pupil.'

SECOND BRĀHMAṆA

1. Janaka Vaideha, descending from his throne, said: 'I bow to you, O Yājñavalkya, teach me.'

Yājñavalkya said: 'Your Majesty, as a man who wishes to make a long journey, would furnish himself with a chariot or a ship, thus is your mind well furnished by these Upanishads. You are honourable, and wealthy, you have learnt the Vedas and been told the Upanishads. Whither then will you go when departing hence?'

Janaka Vaideha said: 'Sir, I do not know whither I shall go.'

Yājñavalkya said: 'Then I shall tell you this, whither you will go.'

Janaka Vaideha said: 'Tell it, Sir.'

2. Yājñavalkya said: 'That person who is in the right eye, he is called Indha, and him who is Indha they call indeed Indra mysteriously, for the gods love what is mysterious, and dislike what is evident.

3. 'Now that which in the shape of a person is in the right eye, is his wife, Virāj. Their meeting-place is the ether within the heart, and their food the red lump within the heart. Again, their covering is that which is like net-work within the heart, and the road on which they move (from sleep to waking) is the artery that rises upwards from the heart. Like a hair divided into a thousand parts, so are the veins of it, which are called Hita, placed firmly within the heart. Through these indeed that (food) flows on flowing, and he (the Taijasa) receives as it were purer food than the corporeal Self (the Vaiśvānara).

4. 'His (the Taijasa's) eastern quarter are the prāṇas (breath) which go to the east;

'His southern quarter are the prāṇas which go to the south;

'His western quarter are the prāṇas which go to the west;

'His northern quarter are the prāṇas which go to the north;

'His upper (zenith) quarter are the prāṇas which go upward;

'His lower (nadir) quarter are the prāṇas which go downward;

'All the quarters are all the prāṇas. And he (the Ātman in that state) can only be described by No, no! He is incomprehensible, for he cannot be comprehended; he is undecaying, for he cannot decay; he is not attached, for he does not attach himself; he is unbound, he does not suffer, he does not perish. O Janaka, you have indeed reached fearlessness'—thus said Yājñavalkya.

Then Janaka said: 'May that fearlessness come to you also who teachest us fearlessness. I bow to you. Here are the Videhas, and here am I (thy slave).'

THIRD BRĀHMAṆA

1. Yājñavalkya came to Janaka Vaideha, and he did not mean to speak with him.[1] But when formerly Janaka Vaideha and Yājñavalkya had a disputation on the Agnihotra, Yājñavalkya had granted him a boon, and he chose (for a boon) that he might be free to ask him any question he liked. Yājñavalkya granted it, and thus the king was the first to ask him a question.

2. 'Yājñavalkya,' he said, 'what is the light of man?'

Yājñavalkya replied: 'The sun, O king; for, having the sun alone for his light, man sits, moves about, does his work, and returns.'

Janaka Vaideha said: 'So indeed it is, O Yājñavalkya.'

3. Janaka Vaideha said: 'When the sun has set, O Yājñavalkya, what is then the light of man?'

Yājñavalkya replied: 'The moon indeed is his light; for, having the moon alone for his light, man sits, moves about, does his work, and returns.'

Janaka Vaideha said: 'So indeed it is, O Yājñavalkya.'

4. Janaka Vaideha said: 'When the sun has set, O Yājñavalkya, and the moon has set, what is the light of man?'

Yājñavalkya replied: 'Fire indeed is his light; for, having fire alone for his light, man sits, moves about, does his work, and returns.'

5. Janaka Vaideha said: 'When the sun has set, O Yājñavalkya, and the moon has set, and the fire is gone out, what is then the light of man?'

Yājñavalkya replied: 'Sound indeed is his light; for, having sound alone for his light, man sits, moves about, does his work, and returns. Therefore, O king, when one cannot see even

1 The introduction to this Brāhmaṇa has a very peculiar interest, as showing the close coherence of the different portions which together form the historical groundwork of the Upanishads. Janaka Vaideha and Yājñavalkya are leading characters in the Bṛihadāraṇyaka Upanishad, and whenever they meet they seem to converse quite freely, though each retains his own character, and Yājñavalkya honours Janaka as king quite as much as Janaka honours Yājñavalkya as a Brāhmaṇa. Now in our chapter we read that Yājñavalkya did not wish to enter on a discussion, but that Janaka was the first to address him (pūrvam papraccha). This was evidently considered not quite correct, and an explanation is given.

one's own hand, yet when a sound is raised, one goes towards it.'

Janaka Vaideha said: 'So indeed it is, O Yājñavalkya.'

6. Janaka Vaideha said: 'When the sun has set, O Yājñavalkya, and the moon has set, and the fire is gone out, and the sound hushed, what is then the light of man?'

Yājñavalkya said: 'The Self indeed is his light; for, having the Self alone as his light, man sits, moves about, does his work, and returns.'

7. Janaka Vaideha said: 'Who is that Self?'

Yājñavalkya replied: 'He who is within the heart, surrounded by the prāṇas (senses), the person of light, consisting of knowledge. He, remaining the same, wanders along the two worlds, as if thinking, as if moving. During sleep (in dream) he transcends this world and all the forms of death (all that falls under the sway of death, all that is perishable).

8. 'On being born that person, assuming his body, becomes united with all evils; when he departs and dies, he leaves all evils behind.

9. 'And there are two states for that person, the one here in this world, the other in the other world, and as a third an intermediate state, the state of sleep. When in that intermediate state, he sees both those states together, the one here in this world, and the other in the other world. Now whatever his admission to the other world may be, having gained that admission, he sees both the evils and the blessings.

'And when he falls asleep, then after having taken away with him the material from the whole world, destroying and building it up again, he sleeps (dreams) by his own light. In that state the person is self-illuminated.

10. 'There are no (real) chariots in that state, no horses, no roads, but he himself sends forth (creates) chariots, horses, and roads. There are no blessings there, no happiness, no joys, but he himself sends forth (creates) blessings, happiness, and joys. There are no tanks there, no lakes, no rivers, but he himself sends forth (creates) tanks, lakes, and rivers. He indeed is the maker.

11. 'On this there are these verses:

'"After having subdued by sleep all that belongs to the body, he, not asleep himself, looks down upon the sleeping (senses). Having assumed light, he goes again to his place, the golden person, the lonely bird.

12. '"Guarding with the breath (prāṇa, life) the lower nest, the immortal moves away from the nest; that immortal one goes wherever he likes, the golden person, the lonely bird.

13. '"Going up and down in his dream, the god makes manifold shapes for himself, either rejoicing together with women, or laughing (with his friends), or seeing terrible sights.

14. '"People may see his playground, but himself no one ever sees."

'Therefore they say, "Let no one wake a man suddenly, for it is not easy to remedy, if he does not get back (rightly to his body)."

'Here some people (object and) say: "No, this (sleep) is the same as the place of waking, for what he sees while awake, that only he sees when asleep." No, here (in sleep) the person is self-illuminated (as we explained before).'

Janaka Vaideha said: 'I give you, Sir, a thousand. Speak on for the sake of (my) emancipation.'

15. Yājñavalkya said: 'That (person) having enjoyed himself in that state of bliss (samprasāda, deep sleep), having moved about and seen both good and evil, hastens back again as he came, to the place from which he started (the place of sleep), to dream. And whatever he may have seen there, he is not followed (affected) by it, for that person is not attached to anything.'

Janaka Vaideha said: 'So it is indeed, Yājñavalkya. I give you, Sir, a thousand. Speak on for the sake of emancipation.'

16. Yājñavalkya said: 'That (person) having enjoyed himself in that sleep (dream), having moved about and seen both good and evil, hastens back again as he came, to the place from which he started, to be awake. And whatever he may have seen there, he is not followed (affected) by it, for that person is not attached to anything.'

Janaka Vaideha said: 'So it is indeed, Yājñavalkya. I give you, Sir, a thousand. Speak on for the sake of emancipation.'

17. Yājñavalkya said: 'That (person) having enjoyed himself in that state of waking, having moved about and seen both good and evil, hastens back again as he same, to the place from which he started, to the state of sleeping (dream).

18. 'In fact, as a large fish moves along the two banks of a river, the right and the left, so does that person move along these two states, the state of sleeping and the state of waking.

19. 'And as a falcon, or any other (swift) bird, after he has roamed about here in the air, becomes tired, and folding his

wings is carried to his nest, so does that person hasten to that state where, when asleep, he desires no more desires, and dreams no more dreams.

20. 'There are in his body the veins called Hitā, which are as small as a hair divided a thousandfold, full of white, blue, yellow, green, and red. Now when, as it were, they kill him, when, as it were, they overcome him, when, as it were, an elephant chases him, when, as it were, he falls into a well, he fancies, through ignorance, that danger which he (commonly) sees in waking. But when he fancies that he is, as it were, a god, or that he is, as it were, a king, or "I am this altogether," that is his highest world.

21. 'This indeed is his (true) form, free from desires, free from evil, free from fear. Now as a man, when embraced by a beloved wife, knows nothing that is without, nothing that is within, thus this person, when embraced by the intelligent (prājña) Self, knows nothing that is without, nothing that is within. This indeed is his (true) form, in which his wishes are fulfilled, in which the Self (only) is his wish, in which no wish is left—free from any sorrow.

22. 'Then a father is not a father, a mother not a mother, the worlds not worlds, the gods not gods, the Vedas not Vedas. Then a thief is not a thief, a murderer not a murderer, a Chāṇḍāla not a Chāṇḍāla, a Paulkasa not a Paulkasa, a Śramaṇa not a Śramaṇa, a Tāpasa not a Tāpasa. He is not followed by good, not followed by evil, for he has then overcome all the sorrows of the heart.

23. 'And when (it is said that) there (in the Sushupti) he does not see, yet he is seeing, though he does not see. For sight is inseparable from the seer, because it cannot perish. But there is then no second, nothing else different from him that he could see.

24. 'And when (it is said that) there (in the Sushupti) he does not smell, yet he is smelling, though he does not smell. For smelling is inseparable from the smeller, because it cannot perish. But there is then no second, nothing else different from him that he could smell.

25. 'And when (it is said that) there (in the Sushupti) he does not taste, yet he is tasting, though he does not taste. For tasting is inseparable from the taster, because it cannot perish. But there is then no second, nothing else different from him that he could taste.

26. 'And when (it is said that) there (in the Sushupti) he does not speak, yet he is speaking, though he does not speak. For speaking is inseparable from the speaker, because it cannot perish. But there is then no second, nothing else different from him that he could speak.

27. 'And when (it is said that) there (in the Sushupti) he does not hear, yet he is hearing, though he does not hear. For hearing is inseparable from the hearer, because it cannot perish. But there is then no second, nothing else different from him that he could hear.

28. 'And when (it is said that) there (in the Sushupti) he does not think, yet he is thinking, though he does not think. For thinking is inseparable from the thinker, because it cannot perish. But there is then no second, nothing else different from him that he could think.

29. 'And when (it is said that) there (in the Sushupti) he does not touch, yet he is touching, though he does not touch. For touching is inseparable from the toucher, because it cannot perish. But there is then no second, nothing else different from him that he could think.

30. 'And when (it is said that) there (in the Sushupti) he does not know, yet he is knowing, though he does not know. For knowing is inseparable from the knower, because it cannot perish. But there is then no second, nothing else different from him that he could know.

31. 'When (in waking and dreaming) there is, as it were, another, then can one see the other, then can one smell the other, then can one speak to the other, then can one hear the other, then can one think the other, then can one touch the other, then can one know the other.

32. 'An ocean is that one seer, without any duality; this is the Brahma-world, O king.' Thus did Yājñavalkya teach him. 'This is his highest goal, this is his highest success, this is his highest world, this is his highest bliss. All other creatures live on a small portion of that bliss.

33. 'If a man is healthy, wealthy, and lord of others, surrounded by all human enjoyments, that is the highest blessing of men. Now a hundred of these human blessings make one blessing of the fathers who have conquered the world (of the fathers). A hundred blessings of the fathers who have conquered this world make one blessing in the Gandharva world. A hundred blessings in the Gandharva world make one blessing

of the Devas by merit (work, sacrifice), who obtain their godhead by merit. A hundred blessings of the Devas by merit make one blessing of the Devas by birth, also (of) a Śrotriya who is without sin, and not overcome by desire. A hundred blessings of the Devas by birth make one blessing in the world of Prajāpati, also (of) a Śrotriya who is without sin, and not overcome by desire. A hundred blessings in the world of Prajāpati make one blessing in the world of Brahman, also (of) a Śrotriya who is without sin, and not overcome by desire. And this is the highest blessing.

'This is the Brahma-world, O king,' thus spake Yājñavalkya.

Janaka Vaideha said: 'I give you, Sir, a thousand. Speak on for the sake of (my) emancipation.'

Then Yājñavalkya was afraid lest the king, having become full of understanding, should drive him from all his positions.

34. And Yājñavalkya said: 'That (person), having enjoyed himself in that state of sleeping (dream), having moved about and seen both good and bad, hastens back again as he came, to the place from which he started, to the state of waking.

35. 'Now as a heavy-laden carriage moves along groaning, thus does this corporeal Self, mounted by the intelligent Self, move along groaning, when a man is thus going to expire.

36. 'And when (the body) grows weak through old age, or ecomes weak through illness, at that time that person, after eparating himself from his members, as an Amra (mango), r Udumbara (fig), or Pippala-fruit is separated from the stalk, astens back again as he came, to the place from which he tarted, to (new) life.

37. 'And as policemen, magistrates, equerries, and governors ait for a king who is coming back, with food and drink, saying, He comes back, he approaches," thus do all the elements wait n him who knows this, saying, "That Brahman comes, that rahman approaches."

38. 'And as policemen, magistrates, equerries, and governors ather round a king who is departing, thus do all the senses rāṇas) gather round the Self at the time of death, when a man thus going to expire.'

FOURTH BRĀHMAṆA

1. Yājñavalkya continued: 'Now when that Self, having sunk to weakness, sinks, as it were, into unconsciousness, then ther those senses (prāṇas) around him, and he, taking with

him those elements of light, descends into the heart. When that person in the eye turns away, then he ceases to know any forms.

2. '"He has become one," they say, "he does not see." "He has become one," they say, "he does not smell." "He has become one," they say, "he does not taste." "He has become one," they say, "he does not speak." "He has become one," they say, "he does not hear." "He has become one," they say, "he does not think." "He has become one," they say, "he does not touch." "He has become one," they say, "he does not know." The point of his heart becomes lighted up, and by that light the Self departs, either through the eye, or through the skull, or through other places of the body. And when he thus departs, life (the chief prāṇa) departs after him, and when life thus departs, all the other vital spirits (prāṇas) depart after it. He is conscious, and being conscious he follows and departs.

'Then both his knowledge and his work take hold of him, and his acquaintance with former things.

3. 'And as a caterpillar, after having reached the end of a blade of grass, and after having made another approach (to another blade), draws itself together towards it, thus does this Self, after having thrown off this body and dispelled all ignorance, and after making another approach (to another body), draw himself together towards it.

4. 'And as a goldsmith, taking a piece of gold, turns it into another, newer and more beautiful shape, so does this Self, after having thrown off this body and dispelled all ignorance, make unto himself another, newer and more beautiful shape, whether it be like the fathers, or like the Gandharvas, or like the Devas, or like Prajāpati, or like Brahman, or like other beings.

5. 'That Self is indeed Brahman, consisting of knowledge, mind, life, sight, hearing, earth, water, wind, ether, light and no light, desire and no desire, anger and no anger, right or wrong, and all things. Now as a man is like this or like that, according as he acts and according as he behaves, so will he be—a man of good acts will become good, a man of bad acts, bad. He becomes pure by pure deeds, bad by bad deeds.

'And here they say that a person consists of desires. And as is his desire, so is his will; and as is his will, so is his deed; and whatever deed he does, that he will reap.

6. 'And here there is this verse: "To whatever object a

man's own mind is attached, to that he goes strenuously together with his deed; and having obtained the end (the last results) of whatever deed he does here on earth, he returns again from that world (which is the temporary reward of his deed) to this world of action."

'So much for the man who desires. But as to the man who does not desire, who, not desiring, freed from desires, is satisfied in his desires, or desires the Self only, his vital spirits do not depart elsewhere—being Brahman, he goes to Brahman.

7. 'On this there is this verse: "When all desires which once entered his heart are undone, then does the mortal become immortal, then he obtains Brahman."

'And as the slough of a snake lies on an ant-hill, dead and cast away, thus lies this body; but that disembodied immortal spirit (prāṇa, life) is Brahman only, is only light.'

Janaka Vaideha said: 'Sir, I give you a thousand.'

8. 'On this there are these verses:

'"The small, old path stretching far away has been found by me. On it sages who know Brahman move on to the Svarga-loka (heaven), and thence higher on, as entirely free.

9. '"On that path they say that there is white, or blue, or yellow, or green, or red; that path was found by Brahman, and on it goes whoever knows Brahman, and who has done good, and obtained splendour.

10. '"All who worship what is not knowledge (avidyā) enter into blind darkness: those who delight in knowledge, enter, as it were, into greater darkness.

11. '"There are indeed those unblessed worlds, covered with blind darkness. Men who are ignorant and not enlightened go after death to those worlds.

12. '"If a man understands the Self, saying, "I am He," what could be wish or desire that he should pine after the body?

13. '"Whoever has found and understood the Self that has entered into this patched-together hiding-place, he indeed is the creator, for he is the maker of everything, his is the world, and he is the world itself.

14. '"While we are here, we may know this; if not, I am ignorant, and there is great destruction. Those who know it become immortal, but others suffer pain indeed.

15. '"If a man clearly beholds this Self as God, and as the lord of all that is and will be, then he is no more afraid.

16. '" He behind whom the year revolves with the days, him the gods worship as the light of lights, as immortal time.

17. '" He in whom the five beings and the ether rest, him alone I believe to be the Self—I who know, believe him to be Brahman; I who am immortal, believe him to be immortal.

18. '" They who know the life of life, the eye of the eye, the ear of the ear, the mind of the mind, they have comprehended the ancient, primeval Brahman.

19. '" By the mind alone it is to be perceived, there is in it no diversity. He who perceives therein any diversity, goes from death to death.

20. '" This eternal being that can never be proved, is to be perceived in one way only; it is spotless, beyond the ether, the unborn Self, great and eternal.

21. '" Let a wise Brāhmaṇa, after he has discovered him, practise wisdom. Let him not seek after many words, for that is mere weariness of the tongue."

22. 'And he is that great unborn Self, who consists of knowledge, is surrounded by the Prāṇas, the ether within the heart. In it there reposes the ruler of all, the lord of all, the king of all. He does not become greater by good works, nor smaller by evil works. He is the lord of all, the king of all things, the protector of all things. He is a bank and a boundary, so that these worlds may not be confounded. Brāhmaṇas seek to know him by the study of the Veda, by sacrifice, by gifts, by penance, by fasting, and he who knows him becomes a Muni. Wishing for that world (for Brahman) only, mendicants leave their homes.

'Knowing this, the people of old did not wish for offspring. What shall we do with offspring, they said, we who have this Self and this world (of Brahman). And they, having risen above the desire for sons, wealth, and new worlds, wander about as mendicants. For desire for sons is desire for wealth, and desire for wealth is desire for worlds. Both these are indeed desires only. He, the Self, is to be described by No, no! He is incomprehensible, for he cannot be comprehended; he is imperishable, for he cannot perish; he is unattached, for he does not attach himself; unfettered, he does not suffer, he does not fail. Him (who knows), these two do not overcome, whether he says that for some reason he has done evil, or for some reason he has done good—he overcomes both, and neither what he has done, nor what he has omitted to do, burns (affects) him.

23. 'This has been told by a verse (Ṛich): "This eternal greatness of the Brāhmaṇa does not grow larger by work, nor does it grow smaller. Let man try to find (know) its trace, for having found (known) it, he is not sullied by any evil deed."

'He therefore that knows it, after having become quiet, subdued, satisfied, patient, and collected, sees self in Self, sees all as Self. Evil does not overcome him, he overcomes all evil. Evil does not burn him, he burns all evil. Free from evil, free from spots, free from doubt, he becomes a (true) Brāhmaṇa; this is the Brahma-world, O king'—thus spoke Yājñavalkya.

Janaka Vaideha said: 'Sir, I give you the Videhas, and also myself, to be together your slaves.'

24. This indeed is the great, the unborn Self, the strong, the giver of wealth. He who knows this obtains wealth.

25. This great, unborn Self, undecaying, undying, immortal, fearless, is indeed Brahman. Fearless is Brahman, and he who knows this becomes verily the fearless Brahman.

FIFTH BRĀHMAṆA

1. Yājñavalkya had two wives, Maitreyī and Kātyāyanī. Of these Maitreyī was conversant with Brahman, but Kātyāyanī possessed such knowledge only as women possess. And Yājñavalkya, when he wished to get ready for another state of life (when he wished to give up the state of a householder, and retire into the forest),

2. Said, 'Maitreyī, verily I am going away from this my house (into the forest). Forsooth, let me make a settlement between thee and that Kātyāyanī.'

3. Maitreyī said: 'My lord, if this whole earth, full of wealth, belonged to me, tell me, should I be immortal by it, or no?'

'No,' replied Yājñavalkya, 'like the life of rich people will be my life. But there is no hope of immortality by wealth.'

4. And Maitreyī said: 'What should I do with that by which I do not become immortal? What my lord knoweth (of immortality), tell that clearly to me.'

5. Yājñavalkya replied: 'Thou who art truly dear to me, thou hast increased what is dear (to me in thee.) Therefore, if you like, Lady, I will explain it to thee, and mark well what I say.'

6. And he said: 'Verily, a husband is not dear, that you may love the husband; but that you may love the Self, therefore a husband is dear.

'Verily, a wife is not dear, that you may love the wife; but that you may love the Self, therefore a wife is dear.

'Verily, sons are not dear, that you may love the sons; but that you may love the Self, therefore sons are dear.

'Verily, wealth is not dear, that you may love wealth; but that you may love the Self, therefore wealth is dear.

'Verily, cattle are not dear, that you may love cattle; but that you may love the Self, therefore cattle are dear.

'Verily, the Brahman-class is not dear, that you may love the Brahman-class; but that you may love the Self, therefore the Brahman-class is dear.

'Verily, the Kshatra-class is not dear, that you may love the Kshatra-class; but that you may love the Self, therefore the Kshatra-class is dear.

'Verily, the worlds are not dear, that you may love the worlds but that you may love the Self, therefore the worlds are dear.

'Verily, the Devas are not dear, that you may love the Devas but that you may love the Self, therefore the Devas are dear.

'Verily, the Vedas are not dear, that you may love the Vedas but that you may love the Self, therefore the Vedas are dear.

'Verily, creatures are not dear, that you may love the creatures; but that you may love the Self, therefore are creature dear.

'Verily, everything is not dear, that you may love everything but that you may love the Self, therefore everything is dear.

'Verily, the Self is to be seen, to be heard, to be perceived, t be marked, O Maitreyī! When the Self has been seen, heard perceived, and known, then all this is known.

7. 'Whosoever looks for the Brahman-class elsewhere tha in the Self, was abandoned by the Brahman-class. Whosoeve looks for the Kshatra-class elsewhere than in the Self, wa abandoned by the Kshatra-class. Whosoever looks for th worlds elsewhere than in the Self, was abandoned by the world Whosoever looks for the Devas elsewhere than in the Self, wa abandoned by the Devas. Whosoever looks for the Veda elsewhere than in the Self, was abandoned by the Vedas. Wh soever looks for the creatures elsewhere than in the Self, wa abandoned by the creatures. Whosoever looks for anythin elsewhere than in the Self, was abandoned by everything.

'This Brahman-class, this Kshatra-class, these worlds, the Devas, these Vedas, all these beings, this everything, all is th Self.

8. 'Now as the sounds of a drum, when beaten, cannot be seized externally (by themselves), but the sound is seized, when the drum is seized, or the beater of the drum;

9. 'And as the sounds of a conch-shell, when blown, cannot be seized externally (by themselves), but the sound is seized, when the shell is seized, or the blower of the shell;

10. 'And as the sounds of a lute, when played, cannot be seized externally (by themselves), but the sound is seized, when the lute is seized, or the player of the lute;

11. 'As clouds of smoke proceed by themselves out of lighted fire kindled with damp fuel, thus verily, O Maitreyī, has been breathed forth from this great Being what we have as Ṛigveda, Yajur-veda, Sāma-veda, Atharvāṅgirasas, Itihāsa, Purāṇa, Vidyā, the Upanishads, Ślokas, Sūtras, Anuvyākhyānas, Vyākhyānas, what is sacrificed, what is poured out, food, drink, this world and the other world, and all creatures. From him alone all these were breathed forth.

12. 'As all waters find their centre in the sea, all touches in the skin, all tastes in the tongue, all smells in the nose, all colours in the eye, all sounds in the ear, all percepts in the mind, all knowledge in the heart, all actions in the hands, all movements in the feet, and all the Vedas in speech—

13. 'As a mass of salt has neither inside nor outside, but is altogether a mass of taste, thus indeed has that Self neither inside nor outside, but is altogether a mass of knowledge; and having risen from out these elements, vanishes again in them. When he has departed, there is no more knowledge (name), I say, O Maitreyī'—thus spoke Yājñavalkya.

14. Then Maitreyī said: 'Here, Sir, thou hast landed me in utter bewilderment. Indeed, I do not understand him.'

But he replied: 'O Maitreyī, I say nothing that is bewildering. Verily, beloved, that Self is imperishable, and of an indestructible nature.

15. 'For when there is as it were duality, then one sees the other, one smells the other, one tastes the other, one salutes the other, one hears the other, one perceives the other, one touches the other, one knows the other; but when the Self only is all this, how should he see another, how should he smell another, how should he taste another, how should he salute another, how should he hear another, how should he touch another, how should he know another? How should he know him by whom he knows all this? That Self is to be described by No, no! He is

incomprehensible, for he cannot be comprehended; he is imperishable, for he cannot perish; he is unattached, for he does not attach himself; unfettered, he does not suffer, he does not fail. How, O beloved, should he know the Knower? Thus, O Maitreyī, thou hast been instructed. Thus far goes immortality.' Having said so, Yājñavalkya went away (into the forest).

[The SIXTH BRĀHMAṆA is omitted.]

FIFTH ADHYĀYA

FIRST BRĀHMAṆA[1]

That (the invisible Brahman) is full, this (the visible Brahman) is full. This full (visible Brahman) proceeds from that full (invisible Brahman). On grasping the fullness of this full (visible Brahman) there is left that full (invisible Brahman).

Om (is) ether, (is) Brahman. 'There is the old ether (the invisible), and the (visible) ether of the atmosphere,' thus said Kauravyāyaṇīputra. This (the Om) is the Veda (the means of knowledge), thus the Brāhmaṇas know. One knows through it all that has to be known.

SECOND BRĀHMAṆA

1. The threefold descendants of Prajāpati, gods, men, and Asuras (evil spirits), dwelt as Brahmachārins (students) with their father Prajāpati. Having finished their studentship the gods said: 'Tell us (something), Sir.' He told them the syllable da. Then he said: 'Did you understand?' They said: 'We did understand. You told us "Dāmyata," Be subdued.' 'Yes,' he said, 'you have understood.'

2. Then the men said to him: 'Tell us something, Sir.' He told them the same syllable da. Then he said: 'Did you understand?' They said: 'We did understand. You told us, "Datta," Give.' 'Yes,' he said, 'you have understood.'

3. Then the Asuras said to him: 'Tell us something, Sir.' He told them the same syllable da. Then he said: 'Did you understand?' They said: 'We did understand. You told us, "Dayadham," Be merciful.' 'Yes,' he said, 'you have understood.'

The divine voice of thunder repeats the same, Da da da, that

[1] This is called a Khila, or supplementary chapter, treating of various auxiliary means of arriving at a knowledge of Brahman.

is, Be subdued, Give, Be merciful. Therefore let that triad be taught, Subduing, Giving, and Mercy.

THIRD BRĀHMAṆA

Prajāpati is the heart, is this Brahman, is all this. The heart, hṛidayam consists of three syllables. One syllable is hṛi, and to him who knows this, his own people and others bring offerings. One syllable is da, and to him who knows this, his own people and others bring gifts. One syllable is yam, and he who knows this, goes to heaven (svarga) as his world.

FOURTH BRĀHMAṆA

This (heart) indeed is even that, it was indeed the true (Brahman). And whosoever knows this great glorious first-born as the true Brahman, he conquers these worlds, and conquered likewise may that (enemy) be! yes, whosoever knows this great glorious first-born as the true Brahman; for Brahman is the true.

FIFTH BRĀHMAṆA

1. In the beginning this (world) was water. Water produced the true, and the true is Brahman. Brahman produced Prajāpati, Prajāpati the Devas (gods). The Devas adore the true (satyam) alone. This satyam consists of three syllables. One syllable is sa, another t(i), the third yam. The first and last syllables are true, in the middle there is the untrue. This untrue is on both sides enclosed by the true, and thus the true preponderates. The untrue does not hurt him who knows this.

2. Now what is the true, that is the Āditya (the sun), the person that dwells in yonder orb, and the person in the right eye. These two rest on each other, the former resting with his rays in the latter, the latter with his prāṇas (senses) in the former. When the latter is on the point of departing this life, he sees that orb as white only, and those rays (of the sun) do not return to him.

3. Now of the person in that (solar) orb Bhūr is the head, for the head is one, and that syllable is one; Bhuvar the two arms, for the arms are two, and these syllables are two; Svar the foot, for the feet are two, and these syllables are two. Its secret name is Ahar (day), and he who knows this, destroys (hanti) evil and leaves (jahāti) it.

4. Of the person in the right eye Bhūr is the head, for the

head is one, and that syllable is one; Bhuvar the two arms, for the arms are two, and these syllables are two; Svar the foot, for the feet are two, and these syllables are two. Its secret name is Aham (ego), and he who knows this, destroys (hanti) evil and leaves (jahāti) it.

SIXTH BRĀHMAṆA

That person, under the form of mind (manas), being light indeed, is within the heart, small like a grain of rice or barley. He is the ruler of all, the lord of all—he rules all this, whatsoever exists.

SEVENTH BRĀHMAṆA

They say that lightning is Brahman, because lightning (vidyut) is called so from cutting off (vidānāt). Whosoever knows this, that lightning is Brahman, him (that Brahman) cuts off from evil, for lightning indeed is Brahman.

EIGHTH BRĀHMAṆA

Let him meditate on speech as a cow. Her four udders are the words Svāhā, Vashaṭ, Hanta, and Svadhā. The gods live on two of her udders, the Svāhā and the Vashaṭ, men on the Hanta, the fathers on the Svadhā. The bull of that cow is breath (prāṇa), the calf the mind.

NINTH BRĀHMAṆA

Agni Vaiśvānara is the fire within man by which the food that is eaten is cooked, i.e. digested. Its noise is that which one hears, if one covers one's ears. When he is on the point of departing this life, he does not hear that noise.

TENTH BRĀHMAṆA

When the person goes away from this world, he comes to the wind. Then the wind makes room for him, like the hole of a carriage wheel, and through it he mounts higher. He comes to the sun. Then the sun makes room for him, like the hole of a Lambara, and through it he mounts higher. He comes to the moon. Then the moon makes room for him, like the hole of a drum, and through it he mounts higher, and arrives at the world where there is no sorrow, no snow. There he dwells eternal years.

ELEVENTH BRĀHMAṆA

This is indeed the highest penance, if a man, laid up with sickness, suffers pain. He who knows this, conquers the highest world.

This is indeed the highest penance, if they carry a dead person into the forest. He who knows this, conquers the highest world.

This is indeed the highest penance, if they place a dead person on the fire. He who knows this, conquers the highest world.

TWELFTH BRĀHMAṆA

1. Some say that food is Brahman, but this is not so, for food decays without life (prāṇa). Others say that life (prāṇa) is Brahman, but this is not so, for life dries up without food. Then these two deities (food and life), when they have become one, reach that highest state (i.e. are Brahman). Thereupon Prātṛida said to his father: 'Shall I be able to do any good to one who knows this, or shall I be able to do him any harm?' The father said to him, beckoning with his hand: 'Not so, O Prātṛida; for who could reach the highest state, if he has only got to the oneness of these two?' He then said to him: 'Vi; verily, food is Vi, for all these beings rest (vishṭāni) on food.' He then said: 'Ram; verily, life is Ram, for all these beings delight (ramante) in life. All beings rest on him, all beings delight in him who knows this.'

THIRTEENTH BRĀHMAṆA

1. Next follows the Uktha. Verily, breath (prāṇa) is Uktha, for breath raises up (utthāpayati) all this. From him who knows this, there is raised a wise son, knowing the Uktha; he obtains union and oneness with the Uktha.

2. Next follows the Yajus. Verily, breath is Yajus, for all these beings are joined in breath. For him who knows this, all beings are joined to procure his excellence; he obtains union and oneness with the Yajus.

3. Next follows the Sāman. Verily, breath is the Sāman, for all these beings meet in breath. For him who knows this, all beings meet to procure his excellence; he obtains union and oneness with the Sāman.

4. Next follows the Kshatra. Verily, breath is the Kshatra,

for breath is Kshatra, i.e. breath protects (trāyate) him from being hurt (kshaṇitoh). He who knows this, obtains Kshatra (power), which requires no protection; he obtains union and oneness with Kshatra.

FOURTEENTH BRĀHMAṆA

1. The words Bhūmi (earth), Antariksha (sky), and Dyu (heaven) form eight syllables. One foot of the Gāyatrī consists of eight syllables. This (one foot) of it is that (i.e. the three worlds). And he who thus knows that foot of it, conquers as far as the three worlds extend.

2. The Ṛichas, the Yajūṃshi, and the Sāmāni form eight syllables. One foot (the second) of the Gāyatrī consists of eight syllables. This (one foot) of it is that (i.e. the three Vedas, the Ṛigveda, Yajur-veda, and Sāma-veda). And he who thus knows that foot of it, conquers as far as that threefold knowledge extends.

3. The Prāṇa (the up-breathing), the Apāna (the down-breathing), and the Vyāna (the back-breathing) form eight syllables. One foot (the third) of the Gāyatrī consists of eight syllables. This (one foot) of it is that (i.e. the three vital breaths). And he who thus knows that foot of it, conquers as far as there is anything that breathes. And of that (Gāyatrī, or speech) this indeed is the fourth (turīya), the bright (darśata) foot, shining high above the skies. What is here called turīya (the fourth) is meant for chaturtha (the fourth); what is called darśatam padam (the bright foot) is meant for him who is as it were seen (the person in the sun); and what is called parorajas (he who shines high above the skies) is meant for him who shines higher and higher above every sky. And he who thus knows that foot of the Gāyatrī, shines thus himself also with happiness and glory.

4. That Gāyatrī (as described before with its three feet) rests on that fourth foot, the bright one, high above the sky. And that again rests on the True (satyam), and the True is the eye, for the eye is (known to be) true. And therefore even now, if two persons come disputing, the one saying, I saw, the other, I heard, then we should trust the one who says, I saw. And the True again rests on force (balam), and force is life (prāṇa), and that (the True) rests on life. Therefore they say, force is stronger than the True. Thus does that Gāyatrī rest with

respect to the self (as life). That Gāyatrī protects (tatre) the vital breaths (gayas); the gayas are the prāṇas (vital breaths), and it protects them. And because it protects (tatre) the vital breaths (gayas), therefore it is called Gāyatrī. And that Sāvitrī verse which the teacher teaches,[1] that is it (the life, the prāṇa, and indirectly the Gāyatrī); and whomsoever he teaches, he protects his vital breaths.

5. Some teach that Sāvitrī as an Anushṭubh verse, saying that speech is Anushṭubh, and that we teach that speech. Let no one do this, but let him teach the Gāyatrī as Sāvitrī. And even if one who knows this receives what seems to be much as his reward (as a teacher), yet this is not equal to one foot of the Gāyatrī.

6. If a man (a teacher) were to receive as his fee these three worlds full of all things, he would obtain that first foot of the Gāyatrī. And if a man were to receive as his fee everything as far as this threefold knowledge extends, he would obtain that second foot of the Gāyatrī. And if a man were to receive as his fee everything whatsoever breathes, he would obtain that third foot of the Gāyatrī. But 'that fourth bright foot, shining high above the skies,' cannot be obtained by anybody—whence then could one receive such a fee?

7. The adoration of that (Gāyatrī):

'O Gāyatrī, thou hast one foot, two feet, three feet, four feet. Thou art footless, for thou art not known. Worship to thy fourth bright foot above the skies.' If one (who knows this) hates someone and says, 'May he not obtain this,' or 'May this wish not be accomplished to him,' then that wish is not accomplished to him against whom he thus prays, or if he says, 'May I obtain this.'

8. And thus Janaka Vaideha spoke on this point to Buḍila Āśvatarāśvi: 'How is it that thou who spokest thus as knowing the Gāyatrī, hast become an elephant and carriest me?' He answered: 'Your Majesty, I did not know its mouth. Agni, fire, is indeed its mouth; and if people pile even what seems much (wood) on the fire, it consumes it all. And thus a man who knows this, even if he commits what seems much evil, consumes it all and becomes pure, clean, and free from decay and death.'

[1] The teacher teaches his pupil, who is brought to him when eight years old, the Sāvitrī verse, making him repeat each word, and each half verse, till he knows the whole, and by teaching him that Sāvitrī, he is supposed to teach him really the prāṇa, the life, as the Self of the world. See p. 17.

FIFTEENTH BRĀHMAṆA

1. The face of the True (the Brahman) is covered with a golden disk. Open that, O Pūshan, that we may see the nature of the True.

2. O Pūshan, only seer, Yama (judge), Sūrya (sun), son of Prajāpati, spread thy rays and gather them! The light which is thy fairest form, I see it. I am what he is (viz. the person in the sun).

3. Breath to air and to the immortal! Then this my body ends in ashes. Om! Mind, remember! Remember thy deeds! Mind, remember! Remember thy deeds!

4. Agni, lead us on to wealth (beatitude) by a good path, thou, O God, who knowest all things! Keep far from us crooked evil, and we shall offer thee the fullest praise! (Ṛigveda I, 189, 1.)

SIXTH ADHYĀYA

FIRST BRĀHMAṆA

1. Hari, Om. He who knows the first and the best, becomes himself the first and the best among his people. Breath is indeed the first and the best. He who knows this, becomes the first and the best among his people, and among whomsoever he wishes to be so.

2. He who knows the richest, becomes himself the richest among his people. Speech is the richest. He who knows this, becomes the richest among his people, and among whomsoever he wishes to be so.

3. He who knows the firm rest, becomes himself firm on even and uneven ground. The eye indeed is the firm rest, for by means of the eye a man stands firm on even and uneven ground. He who knows this, stands firm on even and uneven ground.

4. He who knows success, whatever desire he desires, it succeeds to him. The ear indeed is success. For in the ear are all these Vedas successful. He who knows this, whatever desire he desires, it succeeds to him.

5. He who knows the home, becomes a home of his own people, a home of all men. The mind indeed is the home. He who knows this, becomes a home of his own people and a home of all men.

6. He who knows generation, becomes rich in offspring and cattle. Seed indeed is generation. He who knows this, becomes rich in offspring and cattle.

7. These prāṇas (senses), when quarrelling together as to who was the best, went to Brahman and said: 'Who is the richest of us?' He replied: 'He by whose departure this body seems worst, he is the richest.'

8. The tongue (speech) departed, and having been absent for a year, it came back and said: 'How have you been able to live without me?' They replied: 'Like unto people, not speaking with the tongue, but breathing with breath, seeing with the eye, hearing with the ear, knowing with the mind, generating with seed. Thus we have lived.' Then speech entered in.

9. The eye (sight) departed, and having been absent for a year, it came back and said: 'How have you been able to live without me?' They replied: 'Like blind people, not seeing with the eye, but breathing with the breath, speaking with the tongue, hearing with the ear, knowing with the mind, generating with seed. Thus we have lived.' Then the eye entered in.

10. The ear (hearing) departed, and having been absent for a year, it came back and said: 'How have you been able to live without me?' They replied: 'Like deaf people, not hearing with the ear, but breathing with the breath, speaking with the tongue, seeing with the eye, knowing with the mind, generating with seed. Thus we have lived.' Then the ear entered in.

11. The mind departed, and having been absent for a year, it came back and said: 'How have you been able to live without me?' They replied: 'Like fools, not knowing with the mind, but breathing with the breath, seeing with the eye, hearing with the ear, generating with seed. Thus we have lived.' Then the mind entered in.

12. The seed departed, and having been absent for a year, it came back and said: 'How have you been able to live without me?' They replied: 'Like impotent people, not generating with seed, but breathing with the breath, seeing with the eye, hearing with the ear, knowing with the mind. Thus we have lived.' Then the seed entered in.

13. The (vital) breath, when on the point of departing, tore up these senses, as a great, excellent horse of the Sindhu country might tear up the pegs to which he is tethered. They said to him: 'Sir, do not depart. We shall not be able to live without thee.' He said: 'Then make me an offering.' They said: 'Let it be so.'

14. Then the tongue said: 'If I am the richest, then thou art the richest by it.' The eye said: 'If I am the firm rest, then

thou art possessed of firm rest by it.' The ear said: 'If I am success, then thou art possessed of success by it.' The mind said: 'If I am the home, thou art the home by it.' The seed said: 'If I am generation, thou art possessed of generation by it.' He said: 'What shall be food, what shall be dress for me?'

They replied: 'Whatever there is, even unto dogs, worms, insects, and birds, that is thy food, and water thy dress. He who thus knows the food of Ana (the breath), by him nothing is eaten that is not (proper) food, nothing is received that is not (proper) food. Śrotriyas (Vedic theologians) who know this, rinse the mouth with water when they are going to eat, and rinse the mouth with water after they have eaten, thinking that thereby they make the breath dressed (with water).'

SECOND BRĀHMAṆA

1. Śvetaketu Āruṇeya went to the settlement of the Pañchālas. He came near to Pravāhaṇa Jaivali who was walking about (surrounded by his men). As soon as he (the king) saw him, he said: 'My boy!' Śvetaketu replied: 'Sir!'

Then the king said: 'Have you been taught by your father?' 'Yes,' he replied.

2. The king said: 'Do you know how men, when they depart from here, separate from each other?' 'No,' he replied.

'Do you know how they come back to this world?' 'No,' he replied.

'Do you know how that world does never become full with the many who again and again depart thither?' 'No,' he replied.

'Do you know at the offering of which libation the waters become endowed with a human voice and rise and speak?' 'No,' he replied.

'Do you know the access to the path leading to the Devas and to the path leading to the Fathers, i.e. by what deeds men gain access to the path leading to the Devas or to that leading to the Fathers? For we have heard even the saying of a Ṛishi: "I heard of two paths for men, one leading to the Fathers, the other leading to the Devas. On those paths all that lives moves on, whatever there is between father (sky) and mother (earth)."'

Śvetaketu said: 'I do not know even one of all these questions.'

3. Then the king invited him to stay and accept his hospitality. But the boy, not caring for hospitality, ran away, went back to his father, and said: 'Thus then you called me formerly well-instructed!' The father said: 'What then, you sage?'

The son replied: 'That fellow of a Rājanya asked me five questions, and I did not know one of them.'

'What were they?' said the father.

'These were they,' the son replied, mentioning the different heads.

4. The father said: 'You know me, child, that whatever I know, I told you. But come, we shall go thither, and dwell there as students.'

'You may go, Sir,' the son replied.

Then Gautama went where (the place of) Pravāhaṇa Jaivali was, and the king offered him a seat, ordered water for him, and gave him the proper offerings. Then he said to him: 'Sir, we offer a boon to Gautama.'

5. Gautama said: 'That boon is promised to me; tell me the same speech which you made in the presence of my boy.'

6. He said: 'That belongs to divine boons, name one of the human boons.'

7. He said: 'You know well that I have plenty of gold, plenty of cows, horses, slaves, attendants, and apparel; do not heap on me what I have already in plenty, in abundance, and superabundance.'

The king said: 'Gautama, do you wish (for instruction from me) in the proper way?'

Gautama replied: 'I come to you as a pupil.'

In word only have former sages (though Brahmans) come as pupils (to people of lower rank), but Gautama actually dwelt as a pupil (of Pravāhaṇa, who was a Rājanya) in order to obtain the fame of having respectfully served his master.

8. The king said: 'Do not be offended with us, neither you nor your forefathers, because this knowledge has before now never dwelt with any Brāhmaṇa. But I shall tell it to you, for who could refuse you when you speak thus?

9. 'The altar (fire), O Gautama, is that world (heaven); the fuel is the sun itself, the smoke his rays, the light the day, the coals the quarters, the sparks the intermediate quarters. On that altar the Devas offer the śraddhā libation (consisting of water). From that oblation rises Soma, the king (the moon).

10. 'The altar, O Gautama, is Parjanya (the god of rain); the fuel is the year itself, the smoke the clouds, the light the lightning, the coals the thunderbolt, the sparks the thunderings. On that altar the Devas offer Soma, the king (the moon). From that oblation rises rain.

11. 'The altar, O Gautama, is this world; the fuel is the earth itself, the smoke the fire, the light the night, the coals the moon, the sparks the stars. On that altar the Devas offer rain. From that oblation rises food.

12. 'The altar, O Gautama, is man; the fuel the opened mouth, the smoke the breath, the light the tongue, the coals the eye, the sparks the ear. On that altar the Devas offer food. From that oblation rises seed.

13. 'The altar, O Gautama, is woman. On that altar the Devas offer seed. From that oblation rises man. He lives so long as he lives, and then when he dies,

14. 'They take him to the fire (the funeral pile), and then the altar-fire is indeed fire, the fuel fuel, the smoke smoke, the light light, the coals coals, the sparks sparks. In that very altar-fire the Devas offer man, and from that oblation man rises, brilliant in colour.

15. 'Those who thus know this (even Gṛihasthas), and those who in the forest worship faith and the True (Brahman Hiraṇyagarbha), go to light (archis), from light to day, from day to the increasing half, from the increasing half to the six months when the sun goes to the north, from those six months to the world of the Devas (Devaloka), from the world of the Devas to the sun, from the sun to the place of lightning. When they have thus reached the place of lightning a spirit comes near them, and leads them to the worlds of the (conditioned) Brahman. In these worlds of Brahman they dwell exalted for ages. There is no returning for them.

16. 'But they who conquer the worlds (future states) by means of sacrifice, charity, and austerity, go to smoke, from smoke to night, from night to the decreasing half of the moon, from the decreasing half of the moon to the six months when the sun goes to the south, from these months to the world of the fathers, from the world of the fathers to the moon. Having reached the moon they become food, and then the Devas feed on them there, as sacrificers feed on soma, as it increases and decreases. But when this (the result of their good works on earth) ceases, they return again to that ether, from ether to the air, from the air to rain, from rain to the earth. And when they have reached the earth, they become food, they are offered again in the altar-fire, which is man (see § 11), and thence are born in the fire of woman. Thus they rise up towards the worlds, and go the same round as before.

'Those, however, who know neither of these two paths, become worms, birds, and creeping things.'

THIRD BRĀHMAṆA

1. If a man wishes to reach greatness (wealth for performing sacrifices), he performs the upasad rule during twelve days (i.e. he lives on small quantities of milk), beginning on an auspicious day of the light half of the moon during the northern progress of the sun, collecting at the same time in a cup or a dish made of udumbara wood all sorts of herbs, including fruits. He sweeps the floor (near the house-altar, āvasathya), sprinkles it, lays the fire, spreads grass round it according to rule, prepares the clarified butter (ājya), and on a day, presided over by a male star (nakshatra), after having properly mixed the mantha (the herbs, fruits, milk, honey, etc.), he sacrifices (he pours ajya into the fire), saying: 'O Jātavedas, whatever adverse gods there are in thee, who defeat the desires of men, to them I offer this portion; may they, being pleased, please me with all desires.' Svāhā!

'That cross deity who lies down, thinking that all things are kept asunder by her, I worship thee as propitious with this stream of ghee.' Svāhā!

2. He then says, Svāhā to the first, Svāhā to the best, pours ghee into the fire, and throws what remains into the mantha (mortar).

He then says, Svāhā to breath, Svāhā to her who is the richest, pours ghee into the fire, and throws what remains into the mantha (mortar).

He then says, Svāhā to speech, Svāhā to the support, pours ghee into the fire, and throws what remains into the mantha (mortar).

He then says, Svāhā to the eye, Svāhā to success, pours ghee into the fire, and throws what remains into the mantha (mortar).

He then says, Svāhā to the ear, Svāhā to the home, pours ghee into the fire, and throws what remains into the mantha (mortar).

He then says, Svāhā to the mind, Svāhā to offspring, pours ghee into the fire, and throws what remains into the mantha (mortar).

He then says, Svāhā to seed, pours ghee into the fire, and throws what remains into the mantha (mortar).

3. He then says, Svāhā to Agni (fire), pours ghee into the fire, and throws what remains into the mantha (mortar).

He then says, Svāhā to Soma, pours ghee into the fire, and throws what remains into the mantha (mortar).

He then says, Bhūr (earth), Svāhā, pours ghee into the fire, and throws what remains into the mantha (mortar).

He then says, Bhuvas (sky), Svāhā, pours ghee into the fire, and throws what remains into the mantha (mortar).

He then says, Svar (heaven), Svāhā, pours ghee into the fire, and throws what remains into the mantha (mortar).

He then says, Bhūr, Bhuvas, Svar, Svāhā, pours ghee into the fire, and throws what remains into the mantha (mortar).

He then says, Svāhā to Brahman (the priesthood), pours ghee into the fire, and throws what remains into the mantha (mortar).

He then says, Svāhā to Kshatra (the knighthood), pours ghee into the fire, and throws what remains into the mantha (mortar).

He then says, Svāhā to the past, pours ghee into the fire, and throws what remains into the mantha (mortar).

He then says, Svāhā to the future, pours ghee into the fire, and throws what remains into the mantha (mortar).

He then says, Svāhā to the universe, pours ghee into the fire, and throws what remains into the mantha (mortar).

He then says, Svāhā to all things, pours ghee into the fire, and throws what remains into the mantha (mortar).

He then says, Svāhā to Prajāpati, pours ghee into the fire, and throws what remains into the mantha (mortar).

4. Then he touches it (the mantha, which is dedicated to Prāṇa, breath), saying: 'Thou art fleet (as breath). Thou art burning (as fire). Thou art full (as Brahman). Thou art firm (as the sky). Thou art the abode of all (as the earth). Thou hast been saluted with Hiṅ (at the beginning of the sacrifice by the prastotṛi). Thou art saluted with Hiṅ (in the middle of the sacrifice by the prastotṛi). Thou hast been sung (by the udgātṛi at the beginning of the sacrifice). Thou art sung (by the udgātṛi in the middle of the sacrifice). Thou hast been celebrated (by the adhvaryu at the beginning of the sacrifice). Thou art celebrated again (by the āgnīdhra in the middle of the sacrifice). Thou art bright in the wet (cloud). Thou art great. Thou art powerful. Thou art food (as Soma). Thou art light (as Agni, fire, the eater). Thou art the end. Thou art the absorption (of all things).'

5. Then he holds it (the mantha) forth, saying: 'Thou knowest all, we know thy greatness. He is indeed a king, a ruler, the

highest lord. May that king, that ruler make me the highest lord.'

6. Then he eats it, saying: 'Tat savitur vareṇyam[1] (We meditate on that adorable light)—The winds drop honey for the righteous, the rivers drop honey, may our plants be sweet as honey! Bhūr (earth), Svāhā!

'Bhargo devasya dhīmahi (of the divine Savitṛi)—May the night be honey in the morning, may the air above the earth, may heaven, our father, be honey! Bhuvas (sky), Svāhā!

'Dhiyo you nar prochodayāt (who should rouse our thoughts)—May the tree be full of honey, may the sun be full of honey, may our cows be sweet like honey! Svar (heaven), Svāhā!'

He repeats the whole Sāvitrī verse, and all the verses about the honey, thinking, May I be all this! Bhūr, Bhuvas, Svar, Svāhā! Having thus swallowed all, he washes his hands, and sits down behind the altar, turning his head to the east. In the morning he worships Āditya (the sun), with the hymn, 'Thou art the best lotus of the four quarters, may I become the best lotus among men.' Then returning as he came, he sits down behind the altar and recites the genealogical list.

7. Uddālaka Āruṇi told this (mantha-doctrine) to his pupil Vājasaneya Vājñavalkya, and said: 'If a man were to pour it on a dry stick, branches would grow, and leaves spring forth.'

8. Vājasaneya Yājñavalkya told the same to his pupil Madhuka Paiṅgya, and said: 'If a man were to pour it on a dry stick, branches would grow, and leaves spring forth.'

9. Madhuka Paiṅgya told the same to his pupil Chhūla Bhāgavitti, and said: 'If a man were to pour it on a dry stick, branches would grow, and leaves spring forth.'

10. Chhūla Bhāgavitti told the same to his pupil Janaki Āyasthūṇa, and said: 'If a man were to pour it on a dry stick, branches would grow, and leaves spring forth.'

11. Jānaki Āyasthūṇa told the same to his pupil Satyakāma Jābāla, and said: 'If a man were to pour it on a dry stick, branches would grow, and leaves spring forth.'

12. Satyakāma Jābāla told the same to his pupils, and said: 'If a man were to pour it on a dry stick, branches would grow, and leaves spring forth.'

Let no one tell this to anyone, except to a son or to a pupil.

13. Four things are made of the wood of the udumbara tree,

[1] Ṛigveda III, 62, 10; see p. 17.

the sacrificial ladle (sruva), the cup (chamasa), the fuel, and the two churning sticks.

There are ten kinds of village (cultivated) seeds, viz. rice and barley (brīhiyavās), sesamum and kidney-beans (tilamāshās), millet and panic seed (aṇupriyaṅgavas), wheat (godhūmās), lentils (masūrās), pulse (khalvās), and vetches (khalakulās). After having ground these, he sprinkles them with curds (dadhi), honey, and ghee, and then offers (the proper portions) of clarified butter (ājya).

[The FOURTH and FIFTH BRĀHMAṆAS are omitted.]

CHHĀNDOGYA UPANISHAD

First Prapāṭhaka

FIRST KHAṆḌA [1]

1. Let a man meditate on the syllable Om, called the udgītha; for the udgītha (a portion of the Sāma-veda) is sung, beginning with Om.

The full account, however, of Om is this:

2. The essence of all beings is the earth, the essence of the earth is water, the essence of water the plants, the essence of plants man, the essence of man speech, the essence of speech the Ṛigveda, the essence of the Ṛigveda the Sāma-veda, the essence of the Sāma-veda the udgītha (which is Om).

3. That udgītha (Om) is the best of all essences, the highest, deserving the highest place, the eighth.

4. What then is the Ṛig? What is the Sāman? What is the udgītha? This is the question.

5. The Ṛig indeed is speech, Sāman is breath, the udgītha is the syllable Om. Now speech and breath, or Ṛig and Sāman, form one couple.

6. And that couple is joined together in the syllable Om. When two people come together, they fulfil each other's desire.

7. Thus, he who knowing this, meditates on the syllable (Om), the udgītha, becomes indeed a fulfiller of desires.

8. That syllable is a syllable of permission, for whenever we permit anything, we say Om, yes. Now permission is gratification. He who knowing this meditates on the syllable (Om), the udgītha, becomes indeed a gratifier of desires.

9. By that syllable does the threefold knowledge (the sacrifice, more particularly the soma-sacrifice, as founded on the three vedas) proceed. When the Adhvaryu priest gives an order, he

[1] The Chhāndogya Upanishad begins with recommending meditation on the syllable Om, a sacred syllable that had to be pronounced at the beginning of each veda and of every recitation of Vedic hymns. As connected with the Sāma-veda, that syllable Om is called udgītha. Its more usual name is praṇava. The object of the upanishad is to explain the various meanings which the syllable Om may assume in the mind of a devotee, some of them being extremely artificial and senseless, till at last the highest meaning of Om is reached, viz. Brahman, the intelligent cause of the universe.

says Om. When the Hotṛi priest recites, he says Om. When the Udgātṛi priest sings, he says Om—all for the glory of that syllable. The threefold knowledge (the sacrifice) proceeds by the greatness of that syllable (the vital breaths), and by its essence (the oblations).

10. Now therefore it would seem to follow, that both he who knows this (the true meaning of the syllable Om), and he who does not, perform the same sacrifice. But this is not so, for knowledge and ignorance are different. The sacrifice which a man performs with knowledge, faith, and the upanishad is more powerful. This is the full account of the syllable Om.

SECOND KHAṆḌA [1]

1. When the Devas and Asuras struggled together, both of the race of Prajāpati, the Devas took the udgītha (Om), thinking they would vanquish the Asuras with it.

2. They meditated on the udgītha (Om) as the breath (scent) in the nose, but the Asuras pierced it (the breath) with evil. Therefore we smell by the breath in the nose both what is good-smelling and what is bad-smelling. For the breath was pierced by evil.

3. Then they meditated on the udgītha (Om) as speech, but the Asuras pierced it with evil. Therefore we speak both truth and falsehood. For speech is pierced by evil.

4. Then they meditated on the udgītha (Om) as the eye, but the Asuras pierced it with evil. Therefore we see both what is sightly and unsightly. For the eye is pierced by evil.

5. Then they meditated on the udgītha (Om) as the ear, but the Asuras pierced it with evil. Therefore we hear both what should be heard and what should not be heard. For the ear is pierced by evil.

6. Then they meditated on the udgītha (Om) as the mind, but the Asuras pierced it with evil. Therefore we conceive both what should be conceived and what should not be conceived. For the mind is pierced by evil.

7. Then comes this breath (of life) in the mouth. They meditated on the udgītha (Om) as that breath. When the Asuras came to it, they were scattered, as (a ball of earth) would be scattered when hitting a solid stone.

[1] A very similar story is told in the Bṛihadāraṇyaka I, iii, 1. But though the coincidences between the two are considerable amounting sometimes to verbal identity, the purport of the two seems to be different.

8. Thus, as a ball of earth is scattered when hitting on a solid stone, will he be scattered who wishes evil to one who knows this, or who persecutes him; for he is a solid stone.

9. By it (the breath in the mouth) he distinguishes neither what is good- nor what is bad-smelling, for that breath is free from evil. What we eat and drink with it supports the other vital breaths (i.e. the senses, such as smell, etc.). When at the time of death he does not find that breath (in the mouth, through which he eats and drinks and lives), then he departs. He opens the mouth at the time of death (as if wishing to eat).

10. Aṅgiras meditated on the udgītha (Om) as that breath, and people hold it to be Aṅgiras, i.e. the essence of the members (angānām rasah);

11. Therefore Bṛihaspati meditated on udgītha (Om) as that breath, and people hold it to be Bṛihaspati, for speech is bṛihatī, and he (that breath) is the lord (pati) of speech;

12. Therefore Ayāsya meditated on the udgītha (Om) as that breath, and people hold it to be Ayāsya, because it comes (ayati) from the mouth (āsya);

13. Therefore Vaka Dālbhya knew it. He was the Udgātṛi (singer) of the Naimishīya-sacrificers, and by singing he obtained for them their wishes.

14. He who knows this, and meditates on the syllable Om (the imperishable udgītha) as the breath of life in the mouth, he obtains all wishes by singing. So much for the udgītha (Om) as meditated on with reference to the body.

THIRD KHAṆḌA

1. Now follows the meditation on the udgītha with reference o the gods. Let a man meditate on the udgītha (Om) as he vho sends warmth (the sun in the sky). When the sun rises it ings as Udgātṛi for the sake of all creatures. When it rises it estroys the fear of darkness. He who knows this, is able to estroy the fear of darkness (ignorance).

2. This (the breath in the mouth) and that (the sun) are the ame. This is hot and that is hot. This they call svara (sound), nd that they call pratyāsavara (reflected sound). Therefore t a man meditate on the udgītha (Om) as this and that (as reath and as sun).

3. Then let a man meditate on the udgītha (Om) as vyāna

indeed. If we breathe up, that is prāṇa, the up-breathing. If we breathe down, that is apāna, the down-breathing. The combination of prāṇa and apāna is vyāna, back-breathing or holding in of the breath. This vyāna is speech. Therefore when we utter speech, we neither breathe up nor down.

4. Speech is Ṛich, and therefore when a man utters a Ṛich verse he neither breathes up nor down.

Ṛich is Sāman, and therefore when a man utters a Sāman verse he neither breathes up nor down.

Sāman is udgītha, and therefore when a man sings (the udgītha, Om) he neither breathes up nor down.

5. And other works also which require strength, such as the production of fire by rubbing, running a race, stringing a strong bow, are performed without breathing up or down. Therefore let a man meditate on the udgītha (Om) as vyāna.

6. Let a man meditate on the syllables of the udgītha, i.e. of the word udgītha. Ut is breath (prāṇa), for by means of breath a man rises (uttishṭhati). Gī is speech, for speeches are called girah. Tha is food, for by means of food all subsists (sthita).

7. Ut is heaven, gī the sky, tha the earth. Ut is the sun, gī the air, tha the fire. Ut is the Sāma-veda, gī the Yajur-veda, tha the Ṛigveda. Speech yields the milk, which is the milk of speech itself, to him who thus knowing meditates on those syllables of the name of udgītha, he becomes rich in food and able to eat food.

8. Next follows the fulfilment of prayers. Let a man thus meditate on the Upasaraṇas, i.e. the objects which have to be approached by meditation: Let him (the Udgātṛi) quickly reflect on the Sāman with which he is going to praise;

9. Let him quickly reflect on the Ṛich in which that Sāman occurs; on the Ṛishi (poet) by whom it was seen or composed; on the Devatā (object) which he is going to praise;

10. On the metre in which he is going to praise; on the tune with which he is going to sing for himself;

11. On the quarter of the world which he is going to praise. Lastly, having approached himself (his name, family, etc.) by meditation, let him sing the hymn of praise, reflecting on his desire, and avoiding all mistakes in pronunciation, etc. Quickly will the desire be then fulfilled to him, for the sake of which he may have offered his hymn of praise, yea, for which he may have offered his hymn of praise.

FOURTH KHAṆḌA

1. Let a man meditate on the syllable Om, for the udgītha is sung beginning with Om. And this is the full account of the syllable Om:

2. The Devas, being afraid of death, entered upon (the performance of the sacrifice prescribed in) the threefold knowledge (the three vedas). They covered themselves with the metrical hymns. Because they covered (chhad) themselves with the hymns, therefore the hymns are called chhāndas.

3. Then, as a fisherman might observe a fish in the water, death observed the Devas in the Ṛich, Yajus, and Sāman-(sacrifices). And the Devas seeing this, rose from the Ṛich, Yajus, and Sāman-sacrifices, and entered the Svara, i.e. the Om (they meditated on the Om).

4. When a man has mastered the Ṛigveda, he says quite loud Om; the same, when he has mastered the Sāman and the Yajus. This Svara is the imperishable (syllable), the immortal, free from fear. Because the Devas entered it, therefore they became immortal, and free from fear.

5. He who knowing this loudly pronounces (praṇauti) that syllable, enters the same (imperishable) syllable, the Svara, the immortal, free from fear, and having entered it, becomes immortal, as the Devas are immortal.

FIFTH KHAṆḌA

1. The udgītha is the praṇava, the praṇava is the udgītha. And as the udgītha is the sun, so is the praṇava, for he (the sun) goes sounding Om.

2. 'Him I sang praises to, therefore art thou my only one,' thus said Kaushītaki to his son. 'Do thou revolve his rays, then thou wilt have many sons.' So much in reference to the Devas.

3. Now with reference to the body. Let a man meditate on the udgītha as the breath (in the mouth), for he goes sounding Om.

4. 'Him I sang praises to, therefore art thou my only son,' thus said Kaushītaki to his son. 'Do thou therefore sing praises to the breath as manifold, if thou wishest to have many son's.

5. He who knows that the udgītha is the praṇava, and the praṇava the udgītha, rectifies from the seat of the Hotṛi priest

any mistake committed by the Udgātṛi priest in performing the udgītha, yea, in performing the udgītha.

SIXTH KHAṆḌA

1. The Ṛich (veda) is this earth, the Sāman (veda) is fire. This Sāman (fire) rests on that Ṛich (earth). Therefore the Sāman is sung as resting on the Ṛich. Sā is this earth, ama is fire, and that makes Sāma.

2. The Ṛich is the sky, the Sāman air. This Sāman (air) rests on that Ṛich (sky). Therefore the Sāman is sung as resting on the Ṛich. Sā is the sky, ama the air, and that makes Sāma.

3. Ṛich is heaven, Sāman the sun. This Sāman (sun) rests on that Ṛich (heaven). Therefore the Sāman is sung as resting on the Ṛich, Sā is heaven, ama the sun, and that makes Sāma.

4. Ṛich is the stars, Sāman the moon. This Sāman (moon) rests on that Ṛich (stars). Therefore the Sāman is sung as resting on the Ṛich. Sā is the stars, ama the moon, and that makes Sāma.

5. Ṛich is the white light of the sun, Sāman the blue exceeding darkness (in the sun). This Sāman (darkness) rests on that Ṛich (brightness). Therefore the Sāman is sung as resting on the Ṛich.

6. Sā is the white light of the sun, ama the blue exceeding darkness, and that makes Sāma.

Now that golden person, who is seen within the sun, with golden beard and golden hair, golden altogether to the very tips of his nails,

7. Whose eyes are like blue lotus's, his name is ut, for he has risen (udita) above all evil. He also who knows this, rises above all evil.

8. Ṛich and Sāman are his joints, and therefore he is udgītha. And therefore he who praises him (the ut) is called the Udgātṛi (the out-singer). He (the golden person, called ut) is lord of the worlds beyond that (sun), and of all the wishes of the Devas (inhabiting those worlds). So much with reference to the Devas.

SEVENTH KHAṆḌA

1. Now with reference to the body. Ṛich is speech, Sāman breath. This Sāman (breath) rests on that Ṛich (speech).

Therefore the Sāman is sung as resting on the Ṛich. Sā is speech, ama is breath, and that makes Sāma.

2. Ṛich is the eye, Sāman the self. This Sāman (shadow) rests on that Ṛich (eye). Therefore the Sāman is sung as resting on the Ṛich. Sā is the eye, ama the self, and that makes Sāma.

3. Ṛich is the ear, Sāman the mind. This Sāman (mind) rests on that Ṛich (ear). Therefore the Sāman is sung as resting on the Ṛich. Sā is the ear, ama the mind, and that makes Sāma.

4. Ṛich is the white light of the eye, Sāman the blue exceeding darkness. This Sāman (darkness) rests on the Ṛich (brightness). Therefore the Sāman is sung as resting on the Ṛich. Sā is the white light of the eye, ama the blue exceeding darkness, and that makes Sāma.

5. Now the person who is seen in the eye, he is Ṛich, he is Sāman, Uktha, Yajus, Brahman. The form of that person (in the eye) is the same as the form of the other person (in the sun), the joints of the one (Ṛich and Sāman) are the joints of the other, the name of the one (ut) is the name of the other.

6. He is lord of the worlds beneath that (the self in the eye), and of all the wishes of men. Therefore all who sing to the vīṇā (lyre), sing him, and from him also they obtain wealth.

7. He who knowing this sings a Sāman, sings to both (the adhidaivata and adhyātma self, the person in the sun and the person in the eye, as one and the same person). He obtains through the one, yea, he obtains the worlds beyond that, and the wishes of the Devas;

8. And he obtains through the other the worlds beneath that, and the wishes of men.

Therefore an Udgātṛi priest who knows this, may say (to the sacrificer for whom he officiates):

9. 'What wish shall I obtain for you by my songs?' For he who knowing this sings a Sāman is able to obtain wishes through his song, yea, through his song.

EIGHTH KHAṆḌA

1. There were once three men, well-versed in udgītha, Śilaka Śālāvatya, Chaikitāyana Dālbhya, and Pravāhaṇa Jaivali. They said: 'We are well-versed in udgītha. Let us have a discussion on udgītha.'

2. They all agreed and sat down. Then Pravāhaṇa Jaivali

said: 'Sirs, do you both speak first, for I wish to hear what two Brāhmaṇas have to say.'

3. Then Śilaka Śālāvatya said to Chaikitāyana Dālbhya: 'Let me ask you.'

'Ask,' he replied.

4. 'What is the origin of the Sāman?' 'Tone (svara),' he replied.

'What is the origin of tone?' 'Breath,' he replied.

'What is the origin of breath?' 'Food,' he replied.

'What is the origin of food?' 'Water,' he replied.

5. 'What is the origin of water?' 'That world (heaven),' he replied.

'And what is the origin of that world?'

He replied: 'Let no man carry the Sāman beyond the world of svarga (heaven). We place (recognize) the Sāman in the world of svarga, for the Sāman is extolled as svarga (heaven).'

6. Then said Śilaka Śālāvatya to Chaikitāyana Dālbhya: 'O Dālbhya, thy Sāman is not firmly established. And if anyone were to say, Your head shall fall off (if you be wrong), surely your head would now fall.'

7. 'Well then, let me know this from you, Sir,' said Dālbhya.

'Know it,' replied Śilaka Śālāvatya.

'What is the origin of that world (heaven)?' 'This world,' he replied.

'And what is the origin of this world?'

He replied: 'Let no man carry the Sāman beyond this world as its rest. We place the Sāman in this world as its rest, for the Sāman is extolled as rest.'

8. Then said Pravāhaṇa Jaivali to Śilaka Śālāvatya: 'Your Sāman (the earth), O Śālāvatya, has an end. And if anyone were to say, Your head shall fall off (if you be wrong), surely your head would now fall.'

'Well then, let me know this from you, Sir,' said Śālāvatya.

'Know it,' replied Jaivali.

NINTH KHAṆḌA

1. 'What is the origin of this world?' 'Ether,' he replied. For all these beings take their rise from the ether, and return into the ether. Ether is older than these, ether is their rest.

2. He is indeed the udgītha (Om = Brahman), greater than great (parovarīyas), he is without end.

He who knowing this meditates on the udgītha, the greater than great, obtains what is greater than great, he conquers the worlds which are greater than great.

3. Atidhanvan Śaunaka, having taught this udgītha to Udara-śāṇḍilya, said: 'As long as they will know in your family this udgītha, their life in this world will be greater than great.

4. 'And thus also will be their state in the other world.' He who thus knows the udgītha, and meditates on it thus, his life in this world will be greater than great, and also his state in the other world, yea, in the other world.

TENTH KHAṆḌA

1. When the Kurus had been destroyed by (hail) stones Ushasti Chākrāyaṇa lived as a beggar with his virgin wife at Ibhyagrāma.

2. Seeing a chief eating beans, he begged of him. The chief said: 'I have no more, except those which are put away for me here.'

3. Ushasti said: 'Give me to eat of them.' He gave him the beans, and said: 'There is something to drink also.' Then said Ushasti: 'If I drank of it, I should have drunk what was left by another, and is therefore unclean.'

4. The chief said: 'Were not those beans also left over and therefore unclean?'

'No,' he replied; 'for I should not have lived, if I had not eaten them, but the drinking of water would be mere pleasure.'

5. Having eaten himself, Ushasti gave the remaining beans to his wife. But she, having eaten before, took them and put them away.

6. Rising the next morning, Ushasti said to her: 'Alas, if we could only get some food, we might gain a little wealth. The king here is going to offer a sacrifice, he should choose me for all the priestly offices.'

7. His wife said to him: 'Look, here are those beans of yours.' Having eaten them, he went to the sacrifice which was being performed.

8. He went and sat down on the orchestra near the Udgātṛis, who were going to sing their hymns of praise. And he said to the Prastotṛi (the leader):

9. 'Prastotṛi, if you, without knowing the deity which belongs to the prastâva (the hymns, etc., of the Prastotṛi), are going to sing it, your head will fall off.'

10. In the same manner he addressed the Udgātṛi: 'Udgātṛi, if you, without knowing the deity which belongs to the udgītha (the hymns of the Udgātṛi), are going to sing it, your head will fall off.'

11. In the same manner he addressed the Pratihartṛi: 'Pratihartṛi, if you, without knowing the deity which belongs to the pratihāra (the hymns of the Pratihartṛi), are going to sing it, your head will fall off.'

They stopped, and sat down in silence.

ELEVENTH KHAṆḌA

1. Then the sacrificer said to him: 'I should like to know who you are, Sir.' He replied: 'I am Ushasti Chākrāyaṇa.'

2. He said: 'I looked for you, Sir, for all these sacrificial offices, but not finding you, I chose others.

3. 'But now, Sir, take all the sacrificial offices.'

Ushasti said: 'Very well; but let those, with my permission, perform the hymns of praise. Only as much wealth as you give to them, so much give to me also.'

The sacrificer assented.

4. Then the Prastotṛi approached him, saying: 'Sir, you said to me, "Prastotṛi, if you, without knowing the deity which belongs to the prastâva, are going to sing it, your head will fall off"—which then is that deity?'

5. He said: 'Breath (prāṇa). For all these beings merge into breath alone, and from breath they arise. This is the deity belonging to the prastâva. If, without knowing that deity, you had sung forth your hymns, your head would have fallen off, after you had been warned by me.'

6. Then the Udgātṛi approached him, saying: 'Sir, you said to me, "Udgātṛi, if you, without knowing the deity which belongs to the udgītha, are going to sing it, your head will fall off"—which then is that deity?'

7. He said: 'The sun (âditya). For all these beings praise the sun when it stands on high. This is the deity belonging to the udgītha. If, without knowing that deity, you had sung out your hymns, your head would have fallen off, after you had been warned by me.'

8. Then the Pratihartṛi approached him, saying: 'Sir, you said to me, "Pratihartṛi, if you, without knowing the deity belonging to the pratihāra, are going to sing it, your head will fall off"—which then is that deity?'

9. He said: 'Food (anna). For all these beings live when they partake of food. This is the deity belonging to the pratihāra. If, without knowing that deity, you had sung your hymns, your head would have fallen off, after you had been warned by me.'

TWELFTH KHAṆḌA

1. Now follows the udgītha of the dogs. Vaka Dālbhya, or, as he was also called, Glāva Maitreya, went out to repeat the Veda (in a quiet place).

2. A white (dog) appeared before him, and other dogs gathering round him, said to him: 'Sir, sing and get us food, we are hungry.'

3. The white dog said to them: 'Come to me to-morrow morning.' Vaka Dālbhya, or, as he was also called, Glāva Maitreya, watched.

4. The dogs came on, holding together, each dog keeping the tail of the preceding dog in his mouth, as the priests do when they are going to sing praises with the Vahishpavamāna hymn. After they had settled down, they began to say Hiṅ.

5. 'Om, let us eat! Om, let us drink! Om, may the ivine Varuṇa, Prajāpati, Savitṛi bring us food! Lord of food, ring hither food, bring it, Om!'

THIRTEENTH KHAṆḌA

1. The syllable Hāu is this world (the earth), the syllable Iai the air, the syllable Atha the moon, the syllable Iha the elf, the syllable I is Agni, fire.

2. The syllable U is the sun, the syllable E is the Nihava or vocation, the syllable Auhoi is the Viśve Devas, the syllable Iiṅ is Prajāpati, Svara (tone) is breath (prāṇa), the syllable Yā food, the syllable Vāg is Virāj.

3. The thirteenth stobha syllable, viz. the indistinct syllable uv, is the undefinable (the highest Brahman).

4. Speech yields the milk, which is the milk of speech itself him who knows this upanishad (secret doctrine) of the āmans in this wise. He becomes rich in food, and able to eat od—yea, able to eat food.

Second Prapāṭhaka

FIRST KHAṆḌA

1. Meditation on the whole of the Sāman is good, and people, when anything is good, say it is Sāman; when it is not good, it is not Sāman.

2. Thus they also say, he approached him with Sāman, i.e. becomingly; and he approached him without Sāman, i.e. unbecomingly.

3. And they also say, truly this is Sāman for us, i.e. it is good for us, when it is good; and truly that is not Sāman for us, i.e. it is not good for us, when it is not good.

4. If anyone knowing this meditates on the Sāman as good, depend upon it all good qualities will approach quickly, aye, they will become his own.

SECOND KHAṆḌA

1. Let a man meditate on the fivefold Sāman as the five worlds. The hiṅkāra is the earth, the prastāva the fire, the udgītha the sky, the pratihāra the sun, the nidhana heaven; so in an ascending line.

2. In a descending line, the hiṅkāra is heaven, the prastāva the sun, the udgītha the sky, the pratihāra the fire, the nidhana the earth.

3. The worlds in an ascending and in a descending line belong to him who knowing this meditates on the fivefold Sāman as the worlds.

THIRD KHAṆḌA

1. Let a man meditate on the fivefold Sāman as rain. The hiṅkāra is wind (that brings the rain); the prastāva is, 'the cloud is come'; the udgītha is, 'it rains'; the pratihāra, 'it flashes, it thunders';

2. The nidhana is 'it stops.' There is rain for him, and he brings rain for others, who thus knowing meditates on the fivefold Sāman as rain.

FOURTH KHAṆḌA

1. Let a man meditate on the fivefold Sāman in all waters. When the clouds gather, that is the hiṅkāra; when it rains, that is the prastāva; that which flows in the east, that is the udgītha

that which flows in the west, that is the pratihāra; the sea is the nidhana.

2. He does not die in water, nay, he is rich in water who knowing this meditates on the fivefold Sāman as all waters.

FIFTH KHAṆḌA

1. Let a man meditate on the fivefold Sāman as the seasons. The hiṅkāra is spring, the prastāva summer (harvest of yava, etc.), the udgītha the rainy season, the pratihāra autumn, the nidhana winter.

2. The seasons belong to him, nay, he is always in season (successful) who knowing this meditates on the fivefold Sāman as the seasons.

SIXTH KHAṆḌA

1. Let a man meditate on the fivefold Sāman in animals. The hiṅkāra is goats, the prastāva sheep, the udgītha cows, the pratihāra horses, the nidhana man.

2. Animals belong to him, nay, he is rich in animals who knowing this meditates on the fivefold Sāman as animals.

SEVENTH KHAṆḌA

1. Let a man meditate on the fivefold Sāman, which is greater than great, as the prāṇas (senses). The hiṅkāra is smell (nose), the prastāva speech (tongue), the udgītha sight (eye), the pratihāra hearing (ear), the nidhana mind. These are one greater than the other.

2. What is greater than great belongs to him, nay, he conquers the worlds which are greater than great, who knowing this meditates on the fivefold Sāman, which is greater than great, as the prāṇas (senses).

EIGHTH KHAṆḌA

1. Next for the sevenfold Sāman. Let a man meditate on the sevenfold Sāman in speech. Whenever there is in speech the syllable huṅ, that is hiṅkāra, pra is the prastāva, ā is the ādi, the first, i.e. Om.

2. Ud is the udgītha, pra the pratihāra, upa the upadrava, ni the nidhana.

3. Speech yields the milk, which is the milk of speech itself,

to him who knowing this meditates on the sevenfold Sāman in speech. He becomes rich in food, and able to eat food.

NINTH KHAṆḌA

1. Let a man meditate on the sevenfold Sāman as the sun. The sun is Sāman, because he is always the same (sama); he is Sāman, because he is the same, everybody thinking he looks towards me, he looks towards me.

2. Let him know that all beings are dependent on him (the sun). What he is before his rising, that is the hiṅkāra. On it animals are dependent. Therefore animals say hiṅ (before sunrise), for they share the hiṅkāra of that Sāman (the sun).

3. What he is when first risen, that is the prastāva. On it men are dependent. Therefore men love praise (prastuti) and celebrity, for they share the prastāva of that Sāman.

4. What he is at the time of the saṅgava, that is the ādi, the first, the Om. On it birds are dependent. Therefore birds fly about in the sky without support, holding themselves, for they share the ādi (the Om) of that Sāman.

5. What he is just at noon, that is the udgītha. On it the Devas are dependent (because they are brilliant). Therefore they are the best of all the descendants of Prajāpati, for they share the udgītha of that Sāman.

6. What he is after midday and before afternoon, that is the pratihāra. On it all germs are dependent. Therefore these, having been conceived (pratihṛita), do not fall, for they share the pratihāra of that Sāman.

7. What he is after the afternoon and before sunset, that is the upadrava. On it the animals of the forest are dependent. Therefore, when they see a man, they run (upadravanti) to the forest as a safe hiding-place, for they share the upadrava of that Sāman.

8. What he is when he first sets, that is the nidhana. On it the fathers are dependent. Therefore they put them down (nidadhati), for they share the nidhana of that Sāman. Thus a man meditates on the sevenfold Sāman as the sun.

TENTH KHAṆḌA

1. Next let a man meditate on the sevenfold Sāman which is uniform in itself and leads beyond death. The word hiṅkāra has three syllables, the word prastāva has three syllables: that is equal (sama).

2. The word ādi (first, Om) has two syllables, the word pratihāra has four syllables. Taking one syllable from that over, that is equal (sama).

3. The word udgītha has three syllables, the word upadrava has four syllables. With three and three syllables it should be equal. One syllable being left over, it becomes trisyllabic. Hence it is equal.

4. The word nidhana has three syllables, therefore it is equal. These make twenty-two syllables.

5. With twenty-one syllables a man reaches the sun (and death), for the sun is the twenty-first from here; with the twenty-second he conquers what is beyond the sun: that is blessedness, that is freedom from grief.

6. He obtains here the victory over the sun (death), and there is a higher victory than the victory over the sun for him, who knowing this meditates on the sevenfold Sāman as uniform in itself, which leads beyond death, yea, which leads beyond death.

ELEVENTH KHAṆḌA

1. The hiṅkāra is mind, the prastāva speech, the udgītha sight, the pratihāra hearing, the nidhana breath. That is the Gāyatra Sāman, as interwoven in the (five) prāṇas.

2. He who thus knows this Gāyatra interwoven in the prāṇas, keeps his senses, reaches the full life, he lives long; becomes great with children and cattle, great by fame. The rule of him who thus meditates on the Gāyatra is, 'Be not high-minded.'

TWELFTH KHAṆḌA

1. The hiṅkāra is, he rubs (the fire-stick); the prastāva, smoke rises; the udgītha, it burns; the pratihāra, there are glowing coals; the nidhana, it goes down; the nidhana, it is gone out. This is the Rathantara Sāman as interwoven in fire.

2. He who thus knows this Rathantara interwoven in fire, becomes radiant and strong. He reaches the full life, he lives long, becomes great with children and cattle, great by fame. The rule is, 'Do not rinse the mouth or spit before the fire.'

THE THIRTEENTH KHAṆḌA IS OMITTED

FOURTEENTH KHAṆḌA

1. Rising, the sun is the hiṅkāra, risen, he is the prastâva, at noon he is the udgītha, in the afternoon he is the pratihâra, setting, he is the nidhana. That is the Bṛihat Sāman as interwoven in the sun.

2. He who thus knows the Bṛihat as interwoven in the sun, becomes refulgent and strong, he reaches the full life, he lives long, becomes great with children and cattle, great by fame. His rule is, 'Never complain of the heat of the sun.'

FIFTEENTH KHAṆḌA

1. The mists gather, that is the hiṅkāra; the cloud has risen, that is the prastāva; it rains, that is the udgītha; it flashes and thunders, that is the pratihāra; it stops, that is the nidhana. That is the Vairūpa Sāman, as interwoven in Parjanya, the god of rain.

2. He who thus knows the Vairūpa as interwoven in Parjanya, obtains all kinds of cattle (virūpa), he reaches the full life, he lives long, becomes great with children and cattle, great by fame. His rule is, 'Never complain of the rain.'

SIXTEENTH KHAṆḌA

1. The hiṅkāra is spring, the prastâva summer, the udgītha the rainy season, the pratihāra autumn, the nidhana winter. That is the Vairāja Sāman, as interwoven in the seasons.

2. He who thus knows the Vairāja, as interwoven in the seasons, shines (virājati) through children, cattle, and glory of countenance. He reaches the full life, he lives long, becomes great with children and cattle, great by fame. His rule is, 'Never complain of the seasons.'

SEVENTEENTH KHAṆḌA

1. The hiṅkāra is the earth, the prastāva the sky, the udgītha heaven, the pratihāra the regions, the nidhana the sea. These are the Śakvarī Sāmans, as interwoven in the worlds.

2. He who thus knows the Śakvarīs, as interwoven in the worlds, becomes possessed of the worlds, he reaches the full life, he lives long, becomes great with children and cattle, great by fame. His rule is, 'Never complain of the worlds.'

EIGHTEENTH KHAṆḌA

1. The hiṅkāra is goats, the prastāva sheep, the udgītha cows, the pratihāra horses, the nidhana man. These are the Revatī Sāmans, as interwoven in animals.

2. He who thus knows these Revatīs, as interwoven in animals, becomes rich in animals, he reaches the full life, he lives long, becomes great with children and cattle, great by fame. His rule is, 'Never complain of animals.'

NINETEENTH KHAṆḌA

1. The hiṅkāra is hair, the prastāva skin, the udgītha flesh, the pratihāra bone, the nidhana marrow. That is the Yajñāyajñīya Sāman, as interwoven in the members of the body.

2. He who thus knows the Yajñāyajñīya, as interwoven in the members of the body, becomes possessed of strong limbs, he is not crippled in any limb, he reaches the full life, he lives long, becomes great with children and cattle, great by fame. His rule is, 'Do not eat marrow for a year,' or 'Do not eat marrow at all.'

TWENTIETH KHAṆḌA

1. The hiṅkāra is fire, the prastāva air, the udgītha the sun, the pratihāra the stars, the nidhana the moon. That is the Rājana Sāman, as interwoven in the deities.

2. He who thus knows the Rājana, as interwoven in the deities, obtains the same world, the same happiness, the same company as the gods, he reaches the full life, he lives long, becomes great with children and cattle, great by fame. His rule is, 'Do not speak evil of the Brāhmaṇas.'

TWENTY-FIRST KHAṆḌA

1. The hiṅkāra is the threefold knowledge, the prastāva these three worlds, the udgītha Agni (fire), Vāyu (air), and Āditya (sun), the pratihāra the stars, the birds, and the rays, the nidhana the serpents, Gandharvas, and fathers. That is the Sāman, as interwoven in everything.

2. He who thus knows this Sāman, as interwoven in everything, he becomes everything.

3. And thus it is said in the following verse: 'There are the fivefold three (the three kinds of sacrificial knowledge, the three worlds, etc., in their fivefold form, i.e. as identified with the

hiṅkāra, the prastāva, etc.), and the other forms of the Sāman. Greater than these there is nothing else besides.'

4. He who knows this, knows everything. All regions offer him gifts. His rule is, 'Let him meditate (on the Sāman), knowing that he is everything, yea, that he is everything.'

TWENTY-SECOND KHAṆḌA

1. The udgītha, of which a poet said, I choose the deep sounding note of the Sāman as good for cattle, belongs to Agni; the indefinite note belongs to Prajāpati, the definite note to Soma, the soft and smooth note to Vāyu, the smooth and strong note to Indra, the heron-like note to Bṛihaspati, the dull note to Varuṇa. Let a man cultivate all of these, avoiding, however, that of Varuṇa.

2. Let a man sing, wishing to obtain by his song immortality for the Devas. 'May I obtain by my song oblations (svadhā) for the fathers, hope for men, fodder and water for animals, heaven for the sacrificer, food for myself,' thus reflecting on these in his mind, let a man (Udgātṛi priest) sing praises, without making mistakes in pronunciation, etc.

3. All vowels (svara) belong to Indra, all sibilants (ūshman) to Prajāpati, all consonants (sparśa) to Mṛityu (death). If somebody should reprove him for his vowels, let him say, 'I went to Indra as my refuge (when pronouncing my vowels): he will answer thee.'

4. And if somebody should reprove him for his sibilants, let him say, 'I went to Prajāpati as my refuge: he will smash thee.' And if somebody should reprove him for his consonants, let him say, 'I went to Mṛityu as my refuge: he will reduce thee to ashes.'

5. All vowels are to be pronounced with voice (ghosha) and strength (bala), so that the Udgātṛi may give strength to Indra. All sibilants are to be pronounced, neither as if swallowed (agrasta), nor as if thrown out (nirasta), but well opened (vivṛia), so that the Udgātṛi may give himself to Prajāpati. All consonants are to be pronounced slowly, and without crowding them together, so that the Udgātṛi may withdraw himself from Mṛityu.

TWENTY-THIRD KHAṆḌA

1. There are three branches of the law. Sacrifice, study, and charity are the first,

2. Austerity the second, and to dwell as a Brahmachārin in the house of a tutor, always mortifying the body in the house of a tutor, is the third. All these obtain the worlds of the blessed; but the Brahmasaṃstha alone (he who is firmly grounded in Brahman) obtains immortality.

3. Prajāpati brooded on the worlds. From them, thus brooded on, the threefold knowledge (sacrifice) issued forth. He brooded on it, and from it, thus brooded on, issued the three syllables, Bhūr, Bhuvas, Svar.

4. He brooded on them, and from them, thus brooded on, issued the Om. As all leaves are attached to a stalk, so is all speech (all words) attached to the Om (Brahman). Om is all this, yea, Om is all this.

TWENTY-FOURTH KHAṆḌA

1. The teachers of Brahman (Veda) declare, as the Prātar-savana (morning-oblation) belongs to the Vasus, the Mādhyan-dina-savana (noon-libation) to the Rudras, the third Savana (evening-libation) to the Ādityas and the Viśvedevas.

2. Where then is the world of the sacrificer? He who does not know this, how can he perform the sacrifice? He only who knows, should perform it.

3. Before the beginning of the Prātaranuvāka (matin-chant), the sacrificer, sitting down behind the household altar (gārha-patya), and looking towards the north, sings the Sāman, addressed to the Vasus:

4. 'Open the door of the world (the earth), let us see thee, that we may rule (on earth).'

5. Then he sacrifices, saying: 'Adoration to Agni, who dwells on the earth, who dwells in the world! Obtain that world for me, the sacrificer! That is the world for the sacrificer!'

6. 'I (the sacrificer) shall go thither, when this life is over. Take this! (he says, in offering the libation). Cast back the bolt!' Having said this, he rises. For him the Vasus fulfil the morning-oblation.

7. Before the beginning of the Mādhyandina-savana, the noon-oblation, the sacrificer, sitting down behind the Āgnidhrīya altar, and looking towards the north, sings the Sāman, addressed to the Rudras:

8. 'Open the door of the world (the sky), let us see thee, that we may rule wide (in the sky).'

9. Then he sacrifices, saying: 'Adoration to Vāyu (air), who

dwells in the sky, who dwells in the world. Obtain that world for me, the sacrificer! That is the world for the sacrificer!'

10. 'I (the sacrificer) shall go thither, when this life is over. Take this! Cast back the bolt!' Having said this, he rises. For him the Rudras fulfil the noon-oblation.

11. Before the beginning of the third oblation, the sacrificer, sitting down behind the Āhavanīya altar, and looking towards the north, sings the Sāman, addressed to the Ādityas and Viśve Devas:

12. 'Open the door of the world (the heaven), let us see thee, that we may rule supreme (in heaven).' This is addressed to the Ādityas.

13. Next the Sāman addressed to the Viśvedevas: 'Open the door of the world (heaven), let us see thee, that we may rule supreme (in heaven).'

14. Then he sacrifices, saying: 'Adoration to the Ādityas and to the Viśve Devas, who dwell in heaven, who dwell in the world. Obtain that world for me, the sacrificer!'

15. 'That is the world for the sacrificer! I (the sacrificer) shall go thither, when this life is over. Take this! Cast back the bolt!' Having said this, he rises.

16. For him the Ādityas and the Viśvedevas fulfil the third oblation. He who knows this, knows the full measure of the sacrifice, yea, he knows it.

Third Prapāṭhaka

FIRST KHAṆḌA

1. The sun is indeed the honey of the Devas. The heaven is the cross-beam (from which) the sky (hangs as) a hive, and the bright vapours are the eggs of the bees.

2. The eastern rays of the sun are the honey-cells in front. The Ṛich verses are the bees, the Ṛigveda (sacrifice) is the flower, the water (of the sacrificial libations) is the nectar (of the flower).

3. Those very Ṛich verses then (as bees) brooded over the Ṛigveda sacrifice (the flower); and from it, thus brooded on, sprang as its (nectar) essence, fame, glory of countenance, vigour, strength, and health.

4. That (essence) flowed forth and went towards the sun. And that forms what we call the red (rohita) light of the rising sun.

SECOND KHAṆḌA

1. The southern rays of the sun are the honey-cells on the right. The Yajus verses are the bees, the Yajur-veda sacrifice is the flower, the water (of the sacrificial libations) is the nectar (of the flower).

2. Those very Yajus verses (as bees) brooded over the Yajur-veda sacrifice (the flower); and from it, thus brooded on, sprang as its (nectar) essence, fame, glory of countenance, vigour, strength, and health.

3. That flowed forth and went towards the sun. And that forms what we call the white (śukla) light of the sun.

THIRD KHAṆḌA

1. The western rays of the sun are the honey-cells behind. The Sāman verses are the bees, the Sāma-veda sacrifice is the flower, the water is the nectar.

2. Those very Sāman verses (as bees) brooded over the Sāma-veda sacrifice; and from it, thus brooded on, sprang as its (nectar) essence, fame, glory of countenance, vigour, strength, and health.

3. That flowed forth and went towards the sun. And that forms what we call the dark (kṛishṇa) light of the sun.

FOURTH KHAṆḌA

1. The northern rays of the sun are the honey-cells on the left. The (hymns of the) Atharvāṅgiras are the bees, the Itihāsa-purāṇa (the reading of the old stories) is the flower, the water is the nectar.

2. Those very hymns of the Atharvāṅgiras (as bees) brooded over the Itihāsa-purāṇa; and from it, thus brooded on, sprang as its (nectar) essence, fame, glory of countenance, vigour, strength, and health.

3. That flowed forth, and went towards the sun. And that forms what we call the extreme dark (paraḥ kṛishṇam) light of the sun.

FIFTH KHAṆḌA

1. The upward rays of the sun are the honey-cells above. The secret doctrines are the bees, Brahman (the Om) is the flower, the water is the nectar.

2. Those secret doctrines (as bees) brooded over Brahman (the Om); and from it, thus brooded on, sprang as its (nectar) essence, fame, glory of countenance, brightness, vigour, strength, and health.

3. That flowed forth, and went towards the sun. And that forms what seems to stir in the centre of the sun.

4. These (the different colours in the sun) are the essences of the essences. For the Vedas are essences (the best things in the world); and of them (after they have assumed the form of sacrifice) these (the colours rising to the sun) are again the essences. They are the nectar of the nectar. For the Vedas are nectar (immortal), and of them these are the nectar.

SIXTH KHAṆḌA

1. On the first of these nectars (the red light, which represents fame, glory of countenance, vigour, strength, health) the Vasus live, with Agni at their head. True, the Devas do not eat or drink, but they enjoy by seeing the nectar.

2. They enter into that (red) colour, and they rise from that colour.

3. He who thus knows this nectar, becomes one of the Vasus, with Agni at their head, he sees the nectar and rejoices. And he, too, having entered that colour, rises again from that colour.

4. So long as the sun rises in the east and sets in the west, so long does he follow the sovereign supremacy of the Vasus.

SEVENTH KHAṆḌA

1. On the second of these nectars the Rudras live, with Indra at their head. True, the Devas do not eat or drink, but they enjoy by seeing the nectar.

2. They enter into that white colour, and they rise from that colour.

3. He who thus knows this nectar, becomes one of the Rudras, with Indra at their head, he sees the nectar and rejoices. And he, having entered that colour, rises again from that colour.

4. So long as the sun rises in the east and sets in the west, twice as long does it rise in the south and set in the north; and so long does he follow the sovereign supremacy of the Rudras.

EIGHTH KHAṆḌA

1. On the third of these nectars the Ādityas live, with Varuṇa at their head. True, the Devas do not eat or drink, but they enjoy by seeing the nectar.

2. They enter into that (dark) colour, and they rise from that colour.

3. He who thus knows this nectar, becomes one of the Ādityas, with Varuṇa at their head, he sees the nectar and rejoices. And he, having entered that colour, rises again from that colour.

4. So long as the sun rises in the south and sets in the north, twice as long does it rise in the west and set in the east; and so long does he follow the sovereign supremacy of the Ādityas.

NINTH KHAṆḌA

1. On the fourth of these nectars the Maruts live, with Soma at their head. True, the Devas do not eat or drink, but they enjoy by seeing the nectar.

2. They enter in that (very dark) colour, and they rise from that colour.

3. He who thus knows this nectar, becomes one of the Maruts, with Soma at their head, he sees the nectar and rejoices. And he, having entered that colour, rises again from that colour.

4. So long as the sun rises in the west and sets in the east, twice as long does it rise in the north and set in the south; and so long does he follow the sovereign supremacy of the Maruts.

TENTH KHAṆḌA

1. On the fifth of these nectars the Sādhyas live, with Brahman at their head. True, the Devas do not eat or drink, but they enjoy by seeing the nectar.

2. They enter into that colour, and they rise from that colour.

3. He who thus knows this nectar, becomes one of the Sādhyas, with Brahman at their head; he sees the nectar and rejoices. And he, having entered that colour, rises again from that colour.

4. So long as the sun rises in the north and sets in the south,

twice as long does it rise above, and set below; and so long does he follow the sovereign power of the Sādhyas.[1]

ELEVENTH KHAṆḌA

1. When from thence he has risen upwards, he neither rises nor sets. He is alone, standing in the centre. And on this there is this verse:

2. 'Yonder he neither rises nor sets at any time. If this is not true, ye gods, may I lose Brahman.'

3. And indeed to him who thus knows this Brahma-upanishad (the secret doctrine of the Veda) the sun does not rise and does not set. For him there is day, once and for all.

4. This doctrine (beginning with III, 1, 1) Brahman (m. Hiraṇyagarbha) told to Prajāpati (Virāj), Prajāpati to Manu, Manu to his offspring (Ikshvāku, etc.). And the father told that (doctrine of) Brahman (n.) to Uddālaka Āruṇi.

5. A father may therefore tell that doctrine of Brahman to his eldest son, or to a worthy pupil.

But no one should tell it to anybody else, even if he gave him the whole sea-girt earth, full of treasure, for this doctrine is worth more than that, yea, it is worth more.

TWELFTH KHAṆḌA

1. The Gāyatrī (verse) is everything whatsoever here exists. Gāyatrī indeed is speech, for speech sings forth (gāya-ti) and protects (trāya-te) everything that here exists.

2. That Gāyatrī is also the earth, for everything that here exists rests on the earth, and does not go beyond.

3. That earth again is the body in man, for in it the vital airs (prāṇas, which are everything) rest, and do not go beyond.

4. That body again in man is the heart within man, for in it the prāṇas (which are everything) rest, and do not go beyond.

5. That Gāyatrī has four feet and is sixfold. And this is also declared by a Ṛich verse (Ṛigveda X, 90, 3):

6. 'Such is the greatness of it (of Brahman, under the disguise of Gāyatrī); greater than it is the Person (purusha). His feet

[1] The meaning of the five Khaṇḍas from 6 to 10 is clear, in so far as they are intended to show that he who knows or meditates on the sacrifices as described before, enjoys his reward in different worlds with the Vasus, Rudras, etc., for certain periods of time, till at last he reaches the true Brahman. Of these periods each succeeding one is supposed to be double the length of the preceding one.

are all things. The immortal with three feet is in heaven (i.e. in himself).'

7. The Brahman which has been thus described (as immortal with three feet in heaven, and as Gāyatrī) is the same as the ether which is around us;

8. And the ether which is around us, is the same as the ether which is within us. And the ether which is within us,

9. That is the ether within the heart. That ether in the heart (as Brahman) is omnipresent and unchanging. He who knows this obtains omnipresent and unchangeable happiness.

THIRTEENTH KHAṆḌA[1]

1. For that heart there are five gates belonging to the Devas (the senses). The eastern gate is the Prāṇa (up-breathing), that is the eye, that is Āditya (the sun). Let a man meditate on that as brightness (glory of countenance) and health. He who knows this, becomes bright and healthy.

2. The southern gate is the Vyāna (back-breathing), that is the ear, that is the moon. Let a man meditate on that as happiness and fame. He who knows this, becomes happy and famous.

3. The western gate is the Apāna (down-breathing), that is speech, that is Agni (fire). Let a man meditate on that as glory of countenance and health. He who knows this, becomes glorious and healthy.

4. The northern gate is the Samāna (on-breathing), that is mind, that is Parjanya (rain). Let a man meditate on that as celebrity and beauty. He who knows this, becomes celebrated and beautiful.

5. The upper gate is the Udāna (out-breathing), that is air, that is ether. Let a man meditate on that as strength and greatness. He who knows this, becomes strong and great.

6. These are the five men of Brahman, the door-keepers of the Svarga (heaven) world. He who knows these five men of Brahman, the door-keepers of the Svarga world, in his family a strong son is born. He who thus knows these five men of Brahman, as the door-keepers of the Svarga world, enters himself the Svarga world.

7. Now that light which shines above this heaven, higher

[1] The meditation on the five gates and the five gate-keepers of the heart is meant to be subservient to the meditation on Brahman, as the ether in the heart, which, as it is said at the end, is actually seen and heard by the senses as being within the heart.

than all, higher than everything, in the highest world, beyond which there are no other worlds, that is the same light which is within man. And of this we have this visible proof:

8. Namely, when we thus perceive by touch the warmth here in the body. And of it we have this audible proof: Namely, when we thus, after stopping our ears, listen to what is like the rolling of a carriage, or the bellowing of an ox, or the sound of a burning fire (within the ears). Let a man meditate on this as the (Brahman) which is seen and heard. He who knows this, becomes conspicuous and celebrated, yea, he becomes celebrated.

FOURTEENTH KHAṆḌA

1. All this is Brahman (n.). Let a man meditate on that (visible world) as beginning, ending, and breathing in it (the Brahman).

Now man is a creature of will. According to what his will is in this world, so will he be when he has departed this life. Let him therefore have this will and belief:

2. The intelligent, whose body is spirit, whose form is light, whose thoughts are true, whose nature is like ether (omnipresent and invisible), from whom all works, all desires, all sweet odours and tastes proceed; he who embraces all this, who never speaks, and is never surprised,

3. He is my self within the heart, smaller than a corn of rice, smaller than a corn of barley, smaller than a mustard seed, smaller than a canary seed or the kernel of a canary seed. He also is my self within the heart, greater than the earth, greater than the sky, greater than heaven, greater than all these worlds.

4. He from whom all works, all desires, all sweet odours and tastes proceed, who embraces all this, who never speaks and who is never surprised, he, my self within the heart, is that Brahman (n.). When I shall have departed from hence, I shall obtain him (that Self). He who has this faith has no doubt; thus said Sāṇḍilya,[1] yea, thus he said.

FIFTEENTH KHAṆḌA [2]

1. The chest which has the sky for its circumference and the earth for its bottom, does not decay, for the quarters are its

[1] This chapter is frequently quoted as the Sāṇḍilya-vidyā.

[2] The object of this section is to show how the promise made in III, xiii, 6, 'that a strong son should be born in a man's family,' is to be fulfilled.

sides, and heaven its lid above. That chest is a treasury, and all things are within it.

2. Its eastern quarter is called Juhū, its southern Sahamānā, its western Rājñī, its northern Subhūtā. The child of those quarters is Vāyu, the air, and he who knows that the air is indeed the child of the quarters, never weeps for his sons. 'I know the wind to be the child of the quarters, may I never weep for my sons.'

3. 'I turn to the imperishable chest with such and such and such.' 'I turn to the Prāṇa (life) with such and such and such.' 'I turn to Bhūr with such and such and such.' 'I turn to Bhuvas with such and such and such.' 'I turn to Svar with such and such and such.'

4. 'When I said, I turn to Prāṇa, then Prāṇa means all whatever exists here—to that I turn.'

5. 'When I said, I turn to Bhūr, what I said is, I turn to the earth, the sky, and heaven.'

6. 'When I said, I turn to Bhuvas, what I said is, I turn to Agni (fire), Vāyu (air), Āditya (sun).'

7. 'When I said, I turn to Svar, what I said is, I turn to the Ṛigveda, Yajur-veda, and Sāma-veda. That is what I said, yea, that is what I said.'

SIXTEENTH KHAṆḌA [1]

1. Man is sacrifice. His (first) twenty-four years are the morning-libation. The Gāyatrī has twenty-four syllables, the morning-libation is offered with Gāyatrī hymns. The Vasus are connected with that part of the sacrifice. The Prāṇas (the five senses) are the Vasus, for they make all this to abide (vāsayanti).

2. If anything ails him in that (early) age, let him say: 'Ye Prāṇas, ye Vasus, extend this my morning-libation unto the midday-libation, that I, the sacrificer, may not perish in the midst of the Prāṇas or Vasus.' Thus he recovers from his illness, and becomes whole.

3. The next forty-four years are the midday-libation. The Trishṭubh has forty-four syllables, the midday-libation is offered with Trishṭubh hymns. The Rudras are connected with that part of it. The Prāṇas are the Rudras, for they make all this to cry (rodayanti).

[1] The object of this Khaṇḍa is to show how to obtain long life, as promised before.

4. If anything ails him in that (second) age, let him say: 'Ye Prāṇas, ye Rudras, extend this my midday-libation unto the third libation, that I, the sacrificer, may not perish in the midst of the Prāṇas or Rudras.' Thus he recovers from his illness, and becomes whole.

5. The next forty-eight years are the third libation. The Jagatī has forty-eight syllables, the third libation is offered with Jagatī hymns. The Ādityas are connected with that part of it. The Prāṇas are the Ādityas, for they take up all this (ādadate).

6. If anything ails him in that (third) age, let him say: 'Ye Prāṇas, ye Ādityas, extend this my third libation unto the full age, that I, the sacrificer, may not perish in the midst of the Prāṇas or Ādityas.' Thus he recovers from his illness, and becomes whole.

7. Mahidāsa Aitareya (the son of Itarā), who knew this, said (addressing a disease): 'Why dost thou afflict me, as I shall not die by it?' He lived a hundred and sixteen years (i.e. 24 + 44 + 48). He, too, who knows this lives on to a hundred and sixteen years.

SEVENTEENTH KHAṆḌA[1]

1. When a man (who is the sacrificer) hungers, thirsts, and abstains from pleasures, that is the Dīkshā (initiatory rite).

2. When a man eats, drinks, and enjoys pleasures, he does it with the Upasadas (the sacrificial days on which the sacrificer is allowed to partake of food).

3. When a man laughs, eats, and delights himself, he does it with the Stuta-śastras (hymns sung and recited at the sacrifices).

4. Penance, liberality, righteousness, kindness, truthfulness, these form his Dakshiṇās (gifts bestowed on priests, etc.).

5. Therefore when they say, 'There will be a birth,' and 'there has been a birth' (words used at the soma-sacrifice, and really meaning, 'He will pour out the soma-juice,' and 'he has poured out the soma-juice'), that is his new birth. His death is the Avabhṛitha ceremony (when the sacrificial vessels are carried away to be cleansed).

6. Ghora Āṅgirasa, after having communicated this (view of the sacrifice) to Kṛishṇa, the son of Devakī—and he never thirsted again (after other knowledge)—said: 'Let a man,

[1] Here we have a representation of the sacrifice as performed without any ceremonial, and as it is often represented when performed in thought only by a man living in the forest.

when his end approaches, take refuge with this Triad: "Thou art the imperishable," "Thou art the unchangeable," "Thou art the edge of Prāṇa."' On this subject there are two Ṛich verses. (Ṛigveda VIII, 6, 30):—

7. 'Then they see (within themselves) the ever-present light of the old seed (of the world, the Sat), the highest, which is lighted in the brilliant (Brahman).' (Ṛigveda I, 50, 10):—

'Perceiving above the darkness (of ignorance) the higher light (in the sun), as the higher light within the heart, the bright source (of light and life) among the gods, we have reached the highest light, yea, the highest light.'

EIGHTEENTH KHAṆḌA

1. Let a man meditate on mind as Brahman (n.), this is said with reference to the body. Let a man meditate on the ether as Brahman (n.), this is said with reference to the Devas. Thus both the meditation which has reference to the body, and the meditation which has reference to the Devas, has been taught.

2. That Brahman (mind) has four feet (quarters). Speech is one foot, breath is one foot, the eye is one foot, the ear is one foot—so much with reference to the body. Then with reference to the gods, Agni (fire) is one foot, Vāyu (air) is one foot, Āditya (sun) is one foot, the quarters are one foot. Thus both the worship which has reference to the body, and the worship which has reference to the Devas, has been taught.

3. Speech is indeed the fourth foot of Brahman. That foot shines with Agni (fire) as its light, and warms. He who knows this, shines and warms through his celebrity, fame, and glory of countenance.

4. Breath is indeed the fourth foot of Brahman. That foot shines with Vāyu (air) as its light, and warms. He who knows this, shines and warms through his celebrity, fame, and glory of countenance.

5. The eye is indeed the fourth foot of Brahman. That foot shines with Āditya (sun) as its light, and warms. He who knows this, shines and warms through his celebrity, fame, and glory of countenance.

6. The ear is indeed the fourth foot of Brahman. That foot shines with the quarters as its light, and warms. He who knows this, shines and warms through his celebrity, fame, and glory of countenance.

NINETEENTH KHAṆḌA

1. Āditya (the sun) is Brahman, this is the doctrine, and this is the fuller account of it:

In the beginning this was non-existent. It became existent, it grew. It turned into an egg. The egg lay for the time of a year. The egg broke open. The two halves were one of silver, the other of gold.

2. The silver one became this earth, the golden one the sky, the thick membrane (of the white) the mountains, the thin membrane (of the yoke) the mist with the clouds, the small veins the rivers, the fluid the sea.

3. And what was born from it that was Āditya, the sun. When he was born shouts of hurrah arose, and all beings arose, and all things which they desired. Therefore whenever the sun rises and sets, shouts of hurrah arise, and all beings arise, and all things which they desire.

4. If anyone knowing this meditates on the sun as Brahman, pleasant shouts will approach him and will continue, yea, they will continue.

FOURTH PRAPĀṬHAKA

FIRST KHAṆḌA

1. There lived once upon a time Jānaśruti Pautrāyaṇa (the great-grandson of Jānaśruta), who was a pious giver, bestowing much wealth upon the people, and always keeping open house. He built places of refuge everywhere, wishing that people should everywhere eat of his food.

2. Once in the night some Haṁsas (flamingoes) flew over his house, and one flamingo said to another: 'Hey, Bhallāksha, Bhallāksha (short-sighted friend). The light (glory) of Jānaśruti Pautrāyaṇa has spread like the sky. Do not go near, that it may not burn thee.'

3. The other answered him: 'How can you speak of him, being what he is (a rājanya, noble), as if he were like Raikva with the car?'

4. The first replied: 'How is it with this Raikva with the car of whom thou speakest?'

The other answered: 'As (in a game of dice) all the lower casts belong to him who has conquered with the Kṛita cast, so whatever good deeds other people perform, belong to that Raikva. He who knows what he knows, he is thus spoken of by me.'

5. Jānaśruti Pautrāyaṇa overheard this conversation, and as soon as he had risen in the morning, he said to his door-keeper (kshattṛi): 'Friend, dost thou speak of (me, as if I were) Raikva with the car?'

He replied: 'How is it with this Raikva with the car?'

6. The king said: 'As (in a game of dice), all the lower casts belong to him who has conquered with the Kṛita cast, so whatever good deeds other people perform, belong to that Raikva. He who knows what he knows, he is thus spoken of by me.'

7. The door-keeper went to look for Raikva, but returned saying, 'I found him not.' Then the king said: 'Alas! where a Brāhmaṇa should be searched for (in the solitude of the forest), there go for him.'

8. The door-keeper came to a man who was lying beneath a car and scratching his sores. He addressed him, and said: 'Sir, are you Raikva with the car?'

He answered: 'Here I am.'

Then the door-keeper returned, and said: 'I have found him.'

SECOND KHAṆḌA

1. Then Jānaśruti Pautrāyaṇa took six hundred cows, a necklace, and a carriage with mules, went to Raikva and said:

2. 'Raikva, here are six hundred cows, a necklace, and a carriage with mules; teach me the deity which you worship.'

3. The other replied: 'Fie, necklace and carriage be thine, O Śūdra, together with the cows.'

Then Jānaśruti Pautrāyaṇa took again a thousand cows, a necklace, a carriage with mules, and his own daughter, and went to him.

4. He said to him: 'Raikva, there are a thousand cows, a necklace, a carriage with mules, this wife, and this village in which thou dwellest. Sir, teach me!'

5. He, opening her mouth, said: 'You have brought these (cows and other presents), O Śūdra, but only by that mouth did you make me speak.'

These are the Raikva-parṇa villages in the country of the Mahāvṛishas (mahāpuṇyas) where Raikva dwelt under him. And he said to him:

THIRD KHAṆḌA

1. 'Air (vāyu) is indeed the end of all. For when fire goes out, it goes into air. When the sun goes down, it goes into air. When the moon goes down, it goes into air.

2. 'When water dries up, it goes into air. Air indeed consumes them all. So much with reference to the Devas.

3. 'Now with reference to the body. Breath (prāṇa) is indeed the end of all. When a man sleeps, speech goes into breath, so do sight, hearing, and mind. Breath indeed consumes them all.

4. 'These are the two ends, air among the Devas, breath among the senses (prāṇa).'

5. Once while Śaunaka Kāpeya and Abhipratārin Kākshaseni were being waited on at their meal, a religious student begged of them. They gave him nothing.

6. He said: 'One god—who is he?—swallowed the four great ones, he, the guardian of the world. O Kāpeya, mortals see him not, O Abhipratārin, though he dwells in many places. He to whom this food belongs, to him it has not been given.'

7. Śaunaka Kāpeya, pondering on that speech, went to the student and said: 'He is the self of the Devas, the creator of all beings, with golden tusks, the eater, not without intelligence. His greatness is said to be great indeed, because, without being eaten, he eats even what is not food. Thus do we, O Brahmachārin, meditate on that Being.' Then he said: 'Give him food.'

8. They gave him food. Now these five (the eater Vāyu (air), and his food, Agni (fire), Āditya (sun), Chandramas (moon), Ap (water)) and the other five (the eater Prāṇa (breath), and his food, speech, sight, hearing, mind) make ten, and that is the Kṛita (the highest) cast (representing the ten, the eaters and the food). Therefore in all quarters those ten are food (and) Kṛita (the highest cast). These are again the Virāj (of ten syllables) which eats the food. Through this all this becomes seen. He who knows this sees all this and becomes an eater of food, yea he becomes an eater of food.

FOURTH KHAṆḌA

1. Satyakāma, the son of Jabālā, addressed his mother and said: 'I wish to become a Brahmachārin (religious student), mother. Of what family am I?'

2. She said to him: 'I do not know, my child, of what family thou art. In my youth when I had to move about much as a servant (waiting on the guests in my father's house), I conceived thee. I do not know of what family thou art. I am Jabālā b

name, thou art Satyakāma (Philalethes). Say that thou art Satyakāma Jābāla.'

3. He going to Gautama Hāridrumata said to him, 'I wish to become a Brahmachārin with you, Sir. May I come to you, Sir?'

4. He said to him: 'Of what family are you, my friend?' He replied: 'I do not know, Sir, of what family I am. I asked my mother, and she answered: "In my youth when I had to move about much as a servant, I conceived thee. I do not know of what family thou art. I am Jabālā by name, thou art Satyakāma," I am therefore Satyakāma Jābāla, Sir.'

5. He said to him: 'No one but a true Brāhmaṇa would thus speak out. Go and fetch fuel, friend, I shall initiate you. You have not swerved from the truth.'

Having initiated him, he chose four hundred lean and weak cows, and said: 'Tend these, friend.' He drove them out and said to himself, 'I shall not return unless I bring back a thousand.' He dwelt a number of years (in the forest), and when the cows had become a thousand,

FIFTH KHAṆḌA

1. The bull of the herd (meant for Vāyu) said to him: 'Satyakāma!' He replied: 'Sir!' The bull said: 'We have become a thousand, lead us to the house of the teacher;

2. 'And I will declare to you one foot of Brahman.'

'Declare it, Sir,' he replied.

He said to him: 'The eastern region is one quarter, the western region is one quarter, the southern region is one quarter, the northern region is one quarter. This is a foot of Brahman, consisting of the four quarters, and called Prakāśavat (endowed with splendour).

3. 'He who knows this and meditates on the foot of Brahman, consisting of four quarters, by the name of Prakāśavat, becomes endowed with splendour in this world. He conquers the resplendent worlds, whoever knows this and meditates on the foot of Brahman, consisting of the four quarters, by the name of Prakāśavat.

SIXTH KHAṆḌA

1. 'Agni will declare to you another foot of Brahman.'

(After these words of the bull), Satyakāma, on the morrow, drove the cows (toward the house of the teacher). And when they came towards the evening, he lighted a fire, penned the cows, laid wood on the fire, and sat down behind the fire, looking to the east.

2. Then Agni (the fire) said to him: 'Satyakāma!' He replied: 'Sir.'

3. Agni said: 'Friend, I will declare unto you one foot of Brahman.'

'Declare it, Sir,' he replied.

He said to him: 'The earth is one quarter, the sky is one quarter, the heaven is one quarter, the ocean is one quarter. This is a foot of Brahman, consisting of four quarters, and called Anantavat (endless).

4. 'He who knows this and meditates on the foot of Brahman, consisting of four quarters, by the name of Anantavat, becomes endless in this world. He conquers the endless worlds, whoever knows this and meditates on the foot of Brahman, consisting of four quarters, by the name of Anantavat.

SEVENTH KHAṆḌA

1. 'A Haṁsa (flamingo, meant for the sun) will declare to you another foot of Brahman.'

(After these words of Agni), Satyakāma, on the morrow, drove the cows onward. And when they came towards the evening, he lighted a fire, penned the cows, laid wood on the fire, and sat down behind the fire, looking toward the east.

2. Then a Haṁsa flew near and said to him: 'Satyakāma.' He replied: 'Sir.'

3. The Haṁsa said: 'Friend, I will declare unto you one foot of Brahman.'

'Declare it, Sir,' he replied.

He said to him: 'Fire is one quarter, the sun is one quarter, the moon is one quarter, lightning is one quarter. This is a foot of Brahman, consisting of four quarters, and called Jyotishmat (full of light).

4. 'He who knows this and meditates on the foot of Brahman consisting of four quarters, by the name of Jyotishmat, becomes full of light in this world. He conquers the worlds which are full of light, whoever knows this and meditates on the foot o Brahman, consisting of four quarters, by the name of Jyotishmat

EIGHTH KHAṆḌA

1. 'A diver-bird (Madgu, meant for Prāṇa) will declare t you another foot of Brahman.'

(After these words of the Haṁsa), Satyakāma, on the morrow, drove the cows onward. And when they came towards the evening, he lighted a fire, penned the cows, laid wood on the fire, and sat down behind the fire, looking toward the east.

2. Then a diver flew near and said to him: 'Satyakāma.' He replied: 'Sir.'

3. The diver said: 'Friend, I will declare unto you one foot of Brahman.'

'Declare it, Sir,' he replied.

He said to him: 'Breath is one quarter, the eye is one quarter, he ear is one quarter, the mind is one quarter. This is a foot of Brahman, consisting of four quarters, and called Āyatanavat having a home).

'He who knows this and meditates on the foot of Brahman, onsisting of four quarters, by the name of Āyatanavat, becomes ossessed of a home in this world. He conquers the worlds which offer a home, whoever knows this and meditates on the oot of Brahman, consisting of four quarters, by the name of yatanavat.'

NINTH KHAṆḌA

1. Thus he reached the house of his teacher. The teacher aid to him: 'Satyakāma.' He replied: 'Sir.'

2. The teacher said: 'Friend, you shine like one who knows rahman. Who then has taught you?' He replied: 'Not ien. But you only, Sir, I wish, should teach me;

3. 'For I have heard from men like you, Sir, that only knowdge which is learnt from a teacher (Āchārya) leads to real ood.' Then he taught him the same knowledge. Nothing was ft out, yea, nothing was left out.

TENTH KHAṆḌA

1. Upakośala Kāmalāyana dwelt as a Brahmachārin (religious udent) in the house of Satyakāma Jābāla. He tended his es for twelve years. But the teacher, though he allowed her pupils (after they had learnt the sacred books) to depart their own homes, did not allow Upakośala to depart.

2. Then his wife said to him: 'This student, who is quite hausted (with austerities), has carefully tended your fires. t not the fires themselves blame you, but teach him.' The icher, however, went away on a journey without having ight him.

3. The student from sorrow was not able to eat. Then the wife of the teacher said to him: ‘Student, eat! Why do you not eat?’ He said: ‘There are many desires in this man here, which lose themselves in different directions. I am full of sorrows, and shall take no food.’

4. Thereupon the fires said among themselves: ‘This student, who is quite exhausted, has carefully tended us. Well, let us teach him.’ They said to him:

5. ‘Breath is Brahman, Ka (pleasure) is Brahman, Kha (ether) is Brahman.’

He said: ‘I understand that breath is Brahman, but I do not understand Ka or Kha.’

They said: ‘What is Ka is Kha, what is Kha is Ka.’ They therefore taught him Brahman as breath, and as the ether (in the heart).

ELEVENTH KHAṆḌA

1. After that the Gārhapatya fire taught him: ‘Earth, fire, food, and the sun (these are my forms, or forms of Brahman). The person that is seen in the sun, I am he, I am he indeed.

2. ‘He who knowing this meditates on him, destroys sin, obtains the world (of Agni Gārhapatya), reaches his full age, and lives long; his descendants do not perish. We guard him in this world and in the other, whosoever knowing this meditates on him.’

TWELFTH KHAṆḌA

1. Then the Anvāhārya fire taught him: ‘Water, the quarters, the stars, the moon (these are my forms). The person that is seen in the moon, I am he, I am he indeed.

2. ‘He who knowing this meditates on him, destroys sin, obtains the world (of Agni Anvāhārya), reaches his full age, and lives long; his descendants do not perish. We guard him in this world and in the other, whosoever knowing this meditates on him.’

THIRTEENTH KHAṆḌA

1. Then the Āhavanīya fire taught him: ‘Breath, ether, heaven, and lightning (these are my forms). The person that is seen in the lightning, I am he, I am he indeed.

2. ‘He who knowing this meditates on him, destroys sin, obtains the world (of Agni Āhavanīya), reaches his full age, and lives long; his descendants do not perish. We guard him in th

vorld and in the other, whosoever knowing this meditates on im.'

FOURTEENTH KHAṆḌA

1. Then they all said: 'Upakośala, this is our knowledge, our friend, and the knowledge of the Self, but the teacher will ell you the way (to another life).'

2. In time his teacher came back, and said to him: 'Upakośala.' He answered: 'Sir.' The teacher said: 'Friend, your ace shines like that of one who knows Brahman. Who has aught you?'

'Who should teach me, Sir?' he said. He denies, as it were. And he said (pointing) to the fires: 'Are these fires other than ires?'

The teacher said: 'What, my friend, have these fires told you?'

3. He answered: 'This' (repeating some of what they had old him).

The teacher said: 'My friend, they have taught you about the vorlds, but I shall tell you this; and as water does not cling to a otus leaf, so no evil deed clings to one who knows it.' He said: Sir, tell it me.'

FIFTEENTH KHAṆḌA

1. He said: 'The person that is seen in the eye, that is the Self. This is the immortal, the fearless, this is Brahman. Even hough they drop melted butter or water on him, it runs away on both sides.

2. 'They call him Saṁyadvāma, for all blessings (vāma) go towards him (saṁyanti). All blessings go towards him who knows this.

3. 'He is also Vāmanī, for he leads (nayati) all blessings vāma). He leads all blessings who knows this.

4. 'He is also Bhāmanī, for he shines (bhāti) in all worlds. He who knows this, shines in all worlds.

5. 'Now (if one who knows this, dies), whether people perorm obsequies for him or no, he goes to light (archis), from light o day, from day to the light half of the moon, from the light half of the moon to the six months during which the sun goes o the north, from the months to the year, from the year to the un, from the sun to the moon, from the moon to the lightning. There is a person not human,

6. 'He leads them to Brahman. This is the path of the

Devas, the path that leads to Brahman. Those who proceed on that path, do not return to the life of man, yea, they do not return.'

SIXTEENTH KHAṆḌA

1. Verily, he who purifies (Vāyu) is the sacrifice, for he (the air) moving along, purifies everything. Because moving along he purifies everything, therefore he is the sacrifice. Of that sacrifice there are two ways, by mind and by speech.

2. The Brahman priest performs one of them in his mind, the Hotṛi, Adhvaryu, and Udgātṛi priests perform the other by words. When the Brahman priest, after the Prātaranuvāka ceremony has begun, but before the recitation of the Paridhānīyā hymn, has (to break his silence and) to speak,

3. He performs perfectly the one way only (that by words), but the other is injured. As a man walking on one foot, or a carriage going on one wheel, is injured, his sacrifice is injured, and with the injured sacrifice the sacrificer is injured; yes, having sacrificed, he becomes worse.

4. But when after the Prātaranuvāka ceremony has begun, and before the recitation of the Paridhānīyā hymn, the Brahman priest has not (to break his silence and) to speak, they perform both ways perfectly, and neither of them is injured.

5. As a man walking on two legs and a carriage going on two wheels gets on, so his sacrifice gets on, and with the successful sacrifice the sacrificer gets on; yes, having sacrificed, he becomes better.

SEVENTEENTH KHAṆḌA

1. Prajāpati brooded over the worlds, and from them thus brooded on he squeezed out the essences, Agni (fire) from the earth, Vāyu (air) from the sky, Āditya (the sun) from heaven.

2. He brooded over these three deities, and from them thus brooded on he squeezed out the essences, the Ṛich verses from Agni, the Yajus verses from Vāyu, the Sāman verses from Āditya.

3. He brooded over the threefold knowledge (the three Vedas), and from it thus brooded on he squeezed out the essences, the sacred interjection Bhūs from the Ṛich verses, the sacred interjection Bhuvas from the Yajus verses, the sacred interjection Svar from the Sāman verses.

4. If the sacrifice is injured from the Ṛigveda side, let him offer a libation in the Gārhapatya fire, saying, Bhūr, Svāha

Thus does he bind together and heal, by means of the essence and the power of the Ṛich verses themselves, whatever break the Ṛich sacrifice may have suffered.

5. If the sacrifice is injured from the Yajur-veda side, let him offer a libation in the Dakshiṇa fire, saying, Bhuvas, Svāhā! Thus does he bind together and heal, by means of the essence and the power of the Yajus verses themselves, whatever break the Yajus sacrifice may have suffered.

6. If the sacrifice is injured by the Sāma-veda side, let him offer a libation in the Āhavanīya fire, saying, Svar, Svāhā! Thus does he bind together and heal, by means of the essence and the power of the Sāman verses themselves, whatever break the Sāman sacrifice may have suffered.

7. As one binds (softens) gold by means of lavaṇa (borax), and silver by means of gold, and tin by means of silver, and lead by means of tin, and iron (loha) by means of lead, and wood by means of iron, or also by means of leather,

8. Thus does one bind together and heal any break in the sacrifice by means of (the Vyāhṛitis or sacrificial interjections which are) the essence and strength of the three worlds, of the deities, and of the threefold knowledge. That sacrifice is healed in which there is a Brahman priest who knows this.

9. That sacrifice is inclined towards the north (in the right way) in which there is a Brahman priest who knows this. And with regard to such a Brahman priest there is the following Gāthā: 'Wherever it falls back, thither the man goes'—viz. the Brahman only, as one of the Ṛitvij priests. 'He saves the Kurus as a mare' (viz. a Brahman priest who knows this, saves the sacrifice, the sacrificer, and all the other priests). Therefore let a man make him who knows this his Brahman priest, not one who does not know it, who does not know it.

FIFTH PRAPĀṬHAKA [1]

FIRST KHAṆḌA

1. He who knows the oldest and the best becomes himself the oldest and the best. Breath indeed is the oldest and the best.

[1] The chief object is to show the different ways on which people proceed after death. One of these ways, the Devapatha that leads to Brahman and from which there is no return, has been described, IV, xv. The other ways for those who on earth know the conditioned Brahman only, have to be discussed now.

2. He who knows the richest, becomes himself the richest Speech indeed is the richest.

3. He who knows the firm rest, becomes himself firm in this world and in the next. The eye indeed is the firm rest.

4. He who knows success, his wishes succeed, both his divine and human wishes. The ear indeed is success.

5. He who knows the home, becomes a home of his people. The mind indeed is the home.

6. The five senses quarrelled together, who was the best saying, I am better, I am better.

7. They went to their father Prajāpati and said: 'Sir, who is the best of us?' He replied: 'He by whose departure the body seems worse than worst, he is the best of you.'

8. The tongue (speech) departed, and having been absent for a year, it came round and said: 'How have you been able to live without me?' They replied: 'Like mute people, not speaking, but breathing with the breath, seeing with the eye hearing with the ear, thinking with the mind. Thus we lived.' Then speech went back.

9. The eye (sight) departed, and having been absent for a year it came round and said: 'How have you been able to live without me?' They replied: 'Like blind people, not seeing, but breathing with the breath, speaking with the tongue, hearing with the ear, thinking with the mind. Thus we lived.' Then the eye went back.

10. The ear (hearing) departed, and having been absent for a year, it came round and said: 'How have you been able to live without me?' They replied: 'Like deaf people, not hearing but breathing with the breath, speaking with the tongue, thinking with the mind. Thus we lived.' Then the ear went back

11. The mind departed, and having been absent for a year it came round and said: 'How have you been able to live without me?' They replied: 'Like children whose mind is not yet formed, but breathing with the breath, speaking with the tongue, seeing with the eye, hearing with the ear. Thus we lived.' Then the mind went back.

12. The breath, when on the point of departing, tore up the other senses, as a horse, going to start, might tear up the pegs to which he is tethered. They came to him and said: 'Sir, be thou (our lord); thou art the best among us. Do not depart from us!'

13. Then the tongue said to him: 'If I am the richest, thou

rt the richest.' The eye said to him: 'If I am the firm rest, ɪou art the firm rest.'

14. The ear said to him: 'If I am success, thou art success.' he mind said to him: 'If I am the home, thou art the home.'

15. And people do not call them, the tongues, the eyes, the ırs, the minds, but the breaths (prâṇa, the senses). For reath are all these.

SECOND KHAṆḌA

1. Breath said: 'What shall be my food?' They answered: Whatever there is, even unto dogs and birds.' Therefore this food for Ana (the breather). His name is clearly Ana. To im who knows this there is nothing that is not (proper) food.

2. He said: 'What shall be my dress?' They answered: Water.' Therefore wise people, when they are going to eat od, surround their food before and after with water. He râṇa) thus gains a dress, and is no longer naked.

3. Satyakâma Jâbâla, after he had communicated this to ośruti Vaiyâghrapadya, said to him: 'If you were to tell this a dry stick, branches would grow, and leaves spring from it.'

4. If a man wishes to reach greatness, let him perform the îkshâ (preparatory rite) on the day of the new moon, and then, ı the night of the full moon, let him stir a mash of all kinds of ːrbs with curds and honey, and let him pour ghee on the fire vasthya laukika), saying, 'Svâhâ to the oldest and the best.' fter that let him throw all that remains (of the ghee) into the ash.

5. In the same manner let him pour ghee on the fire, saying, Svâhâ to the richest.' After that let him throw all that mains together into the mash.

In the same manner let him pour ghee on the fire, saying, Svâhâ to the firm rest.' After that let him throw all that mains together into the mash.

In the same manner let him pour ghee on the fire, saying, Svâhâ to success.' After that let him throw all that remains gether into the mash.

6. Then going forward and placing the mash in his hands, he ːites: 'Thou (Prâṇa) art Ama by name, for all this together ists in thee. He is the oldest and best, the king, the sovereign. ıy he make me the oldest, the best, the king, the sovereign. ıy I be all this.'

7. Then he eats with the following Ṛich verse at every foot: 'We choose that food'—here he swallows—'Of the divine Savitṛi (prāṇa)'—here he swallows—'The best and all-supporting food'—here he swallows—'We meditate on the speed of Bhaga (Savitṛi, prāṇa)'—here he drinks all.

8. Having cleansed the vessel, whether it be a kaṁsa or a chamasa, he sits down behind the fire on a skin or on the bare ground, without speaking or making any other effort. If in his dream he sees a woman, let him know this to be a sign that his sacrifice has succeeded.

9. On this there is a Śloka: 'If during sacrifices which are to fulfil certain wishes he sees in his dreams a woman, let him know success from this vision in a dream, yea, from this vision in a dream.'

THIRD KHAṆḌA

1. Śvetaketu Āruṇeya went to an assembly of the Pañchālas. Pravāhaṇa Jaivali said to him: 'Boy, has your father instructed you?' 'Yes, Sir,' he replied.

2. 'Do you know to what place men go from here?' 'No, Sir,' he replied.

'Do you know how they return again?' 'No, Sir,' he replied.

'Do you know where the path of Devas and the path of the fathers diverge?' 'No, Sir,' he replied.

3. 'Do you know why that world never becomes full?' 'No, Sir,' he replied.

'Do you know why in the fifth libation water is called man?' 'No, Sir,' he replied.

4. 'Then why did you say (you had been) instructed? How could anybody who did not know these things say that he had been instructed?' Then the boy went back sorrowful to the place of his father, and said: 'Though you had not instructed me, Sir, you said you had instructed me.

5. 'That fellow of a Rājanya asked me five questions, and I could not answer one of them.' The father said: 'As you have told me these questions of his, I do not know any one of them. If I knew these questions, how should I not have told you?'

6. Then Gautama went to the king's place, and when he had come to him, the king offered him proper respect. In the morning the king went out on his way to the assembly. The king said to him: 'Sir, Gautama, ask a boon of such things as

nen possess.' He replied: 'Such things as men possess may emain with you. Tell me the speech which you addressed to he boy.'

7. The king was perplexed, and commanded him, saying: Stay with me some time.' Then he said: 'As (to what) you ave said to me, Gautama, this knowledge did not go to any Brāhmaṇa before you, and therefore this teaching belonged in all he worlds to the Kshatra class alone.' Then he began:

FOURTH KHAṆḌA[1]

1. 'The altar (on which the sacrifice is supposed to be ffered) is that world (heaven), O Gautama; its fuel is the sun tself, the smoke his rays, the light the day, the coals the moon, he sparks the stars.

2. 'On that altar the Devas (or prāṇas, represented by Agni, tc.) offer the śraddhā libation (consisting of water). From that blation rises Soma, the king (the moon).

FIFTH KHAṆḌA

1. 'The altar is Parjanya (the god of rain), O Gautama; its uel is the air itself, the smoke the cloud, the light the lightning, he coals the thunderbolt, the sparks the thunderings.

2. 'On that altar the Devas offer Soma, the king (the moon). rom that oblation rises rain.

SIXTH KHAṆḌA

1. 'The altar is the earth, O Gautama; its fuel is the year self, the smoke the ether, the light the night, the coals the uarters, the sparks the intermediate quarters.

2. 'On that altar the Devas (prāṇas) offer rain. From that blation rises food (corn, etc.).

SEVENTH KHAṆḌA

1. 'The altar is man, O Gautama; its fuel speech itself, the noke the breath, the light the tongue, the coals the eye, the parks the ear.

2. 'On that altar the Devas (prāṇas) offer food. From that blation rises seed.

[1] He answers the last question, why water in the fifth libation is called an, first.

EIGHTH KHAṆḌA

1. 'The altar is woman, O Gautama.

2. 'On that altar the Devas (prāṇas) offer seed. From tha oblation rises the germ.

NINTH KHAṆḌA

1. 'For this reason is water in the fifth oblation called man This germ, covered in the womb, having dwelt there ten months or more or less, is born.

2. 'When born, he lives whatever the length of his life may be When he has departed, his friends carry him, as appointed, t the fire (of the funeral pile) from whence he came, from whenc he sprang.

TENTH KHAṆḌA

1. 'Those who know this (even though they still be gṛihasthas householders) and those who in the forest follow faith an austerities (the vānaprasthas, and of the parivrājakas those wh do not yet know the highest Brahman) go to light (archis), fron light to day, from day to the light half of the moon, from th light half of the moon to the six months when the sun goes t the north, from the six months when the sun goes to the nort to the year, from the year to the sun, from the sun to the moon from the moon to the lightning. There is a person not human–

2. 'He leads them to Brahman (the conditioned Brahman) This is the path of the Devas.

3. 'But they who living in a village practise (a life o sacrifices, works of public utility, and alms, they go to th smoke, from smoke to night, from night to the dark half of th moon, from the dark half of the moon to the six months when th sun goes to the south. But they do not reach the year.

4. 'From the months they go to the world of the father from the world of the fathers to the ether, from the ether to th moon. That is Soma, the king. Here they are loved (eate by the Devas, yes, the Devas love (eat) them.

5. 'Having dwelt there, till their (good) works are consume they return again that way as they came, to the ether, fro the ether to the air. Then the sacrificer, having become ai becomes smoke, having become smoke, he becomes mist,

6. 'Having become mist, he becomes a cloud, having becon a cloud, he rains down. Then he is born as rice and corn, her and trees, sesamum and beans. From thence the escape is bes

with most difficulties. For whoever the persons may be that eat the food, and beget offspring, he henceforth becomes like unto them.

7. 'Those whose conduct has been good, will quickly attain some good birth, the birth of a Brâhmaṇa, or a Kshatriya, or a Vaiśya. But those whose conduct has been evil, will quickly attain an evil birth, the birth of a dog, or a hog, or a Chaṇḍâla.

8. 'On neither of these two ways those small creatures (flies, worms, etc.) are continually returning of whom it may be said, Live and die. Theirs is a third place.

'Therefore that world never becomes full[1] (cf. V, iii, 3).

'Hence let a man take care to himself! And thus it is said in the following Śloka:

9. '"A man who steals gold, who drinks spirits, who dishonours his Guru's bed, who kills a Brahman, these four fall, and as a fifth he who associates with them."

10. 'But he who thus knows the five fires is not defiled by sin even though he associates with them. He who knows this, is pure, clean, and obtains the world of the blessed, yea, he obtains the world of the blessed.'

ELEVENTH KHAṆḌA

1. Prâchînaśâla Aupamanyava, Satyayajña Paulushi, Indradyumna Bhâllaveya, Jana Śârkarâkshya, and Buḍila Âśvatarâśvi, these five great householders and great theologians came once together and held a discussion as to what is our Self, and what is Brahman.

2. They reflected and said: 'Sirs, there is that Uddâlaka Âruṇi, who knows at present that Self, called Vaiśvânara. Well, let us go to him.' They went to him.

3. But he reflected: 'Those great householders and great theologians will examine me, and I shall not be able to tell them all; therefore I shall recommend another teacher to them.'

4. He said to them: 'Sirs, Aśvapati Kaikeya knows at present

[1] In this manner all the five questions have been answered. First, why in the fifth oblation water is called man; secondly, to what place men go after death, some by the path of the Devas, others by the path of the fathers, others again by neither of these paths; thirdly, how they return, some returning to Brahman, others returning to the earth; fourthly, where the paths of the Devas and the fathers diverge, viz. when from the half-year the path of the Devas goes on to the year, while that of the fathers branches off to the world of the fathers; fifthly, why that world, the other world, does never become full, viz. because men either go on to Brahman or return again to this world.

that Self, called Vaiśvānara. Well, let us go to him.' They went to him.

5. When they arrived (the king) ordered proper presents to be made separately to each of them. And rising the next morning he said: 'In my kingdom there is no thief, no miser, no drunkard, no man without an altar in his house, no ignorant person, no adulterer, much less an adulteress. I am going to perform a sacrifice, Sirs, and as much wealth as I give to each Ṛitvij priest, I shall give to you, Sirs. Please to stay here.'

6. They replied: 'Every man ought to say for what purpose he comes. You know at present that Vaiśvānara Self, tell us that.'

7. He said: 'To-morrow I shall give you an answer.' Therefore on the next morning they approached him, carrying fuel in their hands (like students), and he, without first demanding any preparatory rites, said to them:

TWELFTH KHAṆḌA

1. 'Aupamanyava, whom do you meditate on as the Self?' He replied: 'Heaven only, venerable king.' He said: 'The Self which you meditate on is the Vaiśvānara Self, called Sutejas (having good light). Therefore every kind of soma libation is seen in your house.

2. 'You eat food, and see your desire (a son, etc.), and whoever thus meditates on that Vaiśvānara Self, eats food, sees his desire, and has Vedic glory (arising from study and sacrifice) in his house. That, however, is but the head of the Self, and thus your head would have fallen (in a discussion), if you had not come to me.'

THIRTEENTH KHAṆḌA

1. Then he said to Satyayajña Paulushi: 'O Prāchīnayogya, whom do you meditate on as the Self?' He replied: 'The sun only, venerable king.' He said: 'The Self which you meditate on is the Vaiśvānara Self, called Viśvarūpa (multiform). Therefore much and manifold wealth is seen in your house.

2. 'There is a car with mules, full of slaves and jewels. You eat food and see your desire, and whoever thus meditates on that Vaiśvānara Self, eats food and sees his desire, and has Vedic glory in his house.

'That, however, is but the eye of the Self, and you would have become blind, if you had not come to me.'

FOURTEENTH KHAṆḌA

1. Then he said to Indradyumna Bhâllaveya: 'O Vaiyâghrapadya, whom do you meditate on as the Self?' He replied: 'Air only, venerable king.' He said: 'The Self which you meditate on is the Vaiśvānara Self, called Pṛithagvartman (having various courses). Therefore offerings come to you in various ways, and rows of cars follow you in various ways.

2. 'You eat food and see your desire, and whoever thus meditates on that Vaiśvānara Self, eats food and sees his desire, and has Vedic glory in his house.

'That, however, is but the breath of the Self, and your breath would have left you, if you had not come to me.'

FIFTEENTH KHAṆḌA

1. Then he said to Jana Śârkarâkshya: 'Whom do you meditate on as the Self?' He replied: 'Ether only, venerable king.' He said: 'The Self which you meditate on is the Vaiśvānara Self, called Bahula (full). Therefore you are full of offspring and wealth.

2. 'You eat food and see your desire, and whoever thus meditates on that Vaiśvānara Self, eats food and sees his desire, and has Vedic glory in his house.

'That, however, is but the trunk of the Self, and your trunk would have perished, if you had not come to me.'

SIXTEENTH KHAṆḌA

1. Then he said to Buḍila Âśvatarâśvi, 'O Vaiyâghrapadya, whom do you meditate on as the Self?' He replied: 'Water only, venerable king.' He said: 'The Self which you meditate on is the Vaiśvānara Self, called Rayi (wealth). Therefore are you wealthy and flourishing.

2. 'You eat food and see your desire, and whoever thus meditates on that Vaiśvānara Self, eats food and sees his desire, and has Vedic glory in his house.

'That, however, is but the bladder of the Self, and your bladder would have burst, if you had not come to me.'

SEVENTEENTH KHAṆḌA

1. Then he said to Uddâlaka Āruṇi: 'O Gautama, whom do you meditate on as the Self?' He replied: 'The earth only, venerable king.' He said: 'The Self which you meditate on is

the Vaiśvānara Self, called Pratishṭhā (firm rest). Therefore you stand firm with offspring and cattle.

2. 'You eat food and see your desire, and whoever thus meditates on that Vaiśvānara Self, eats food and sees his desire, and has Vedic glory in his house.

'That, however, is but the feet of the Self, and your feet would have given way, if you had not come to me.'

EIGHTEENTH KHAṆḌA

1. Then he said to them all: 'You eat your food, knowing that Vaiśvānara Self as if it were many. But he who worships the Vaiśvānara Self as a span long, and as identical with himself, he eats food in all worlds, in all beings, in all Selfs.

2. 'Of that Vaiśvānara Self the head is Sutejas (having good light), the eye Viśvarūpa (multiform), the breath Pṛithagvartman (having various courses), the trunk Bahula (full), the bladder Rayi (wealth), the feet the earth, the chest the altar, the hairs the grass on the altar, the heart the Gārhapatya fire, the mind the Anvāhārya fire, the mouth the Āhavanīya fire.

NINETEENTH KHAṆḌA

1. 'Therefore the first food which a man may take, is in the place of Homa. And he who offers that first oblation, should offer it to Prāṇa (up-breathing), saying Svāhā. Then Prāṇa (up-breathing) is satisfied.

2. 'If Prāṇa is satisfied, the eye is satisfied, if the eye is satisfied, the sun is satisfied, if the sun is satisfied, heaven is satisfied, if heaven is satisfied, whatever is under heaven and under the sun is satisfied. And through their satisfaction he (the sacrificer or eater) himself is satisfied with offspring, cattle, health, brightness, and Vedic splendour.

TWENTIETH KHAṆḌA

1. 'And he who offers the second oblation, should offer it to Vyāna (back-breathing), saying Svāhā. Then Vyāna is satisfied.

2. 'If Vyāna is satisfied, the ear is satisfied, if the ear is satisfied, the moon is satisfied, if the moon is satisfied, the quarters are satisfied, if the quarters are satisfied, whatever is under the quarters and under the moon is satisfied. And through their satisfaction he (the sacrificer or eater) himself is satisfied with offspring, cattle, health, brightness, and Vedic splendour.

TWENTY-FIRST KHAṆḌA

1. 'And he who offers the third oblation, should offer it to Apāna (down-breathing), saying Svāhā. Then Apāna is satisfied. If Apāna is satisfied, the tongue is satisfied, if the tongue is satisfied, Agni (fire) is satisfied, if Agni is satisfied, the earth is satisfied, if the earth is satisfied, whatever is under the earth and under fire is satisfied.

2. 'And through their satisfaction he (the sacrificer or eater) himself is satisfied with offspring, cattle, health, brightness, and Vedic splendour.

TWENTY-SECOND KHAṆḌA

1. 'And he who offers the fourth oblation, should offer it to Samāna (on-breathing), saying Svāhā. Then Samāna is satisfied.

2. 'If Samāna is satisfied, the mind is satisfied, if the mind is satisfied, Parjanya (god of rain) is satisfied, if Parjanya is satisfied, lightning is satisfied, if lightning is satisfied, whatever is under Parjanya and under lightning is satisfied. And through their satisfaction he (the sacrificer or eater) himself is satisfied with offspring, cattle, health, brightness, and Vedic splendour.

TWENTY-THIRD KHAṆḌA

1. 'And he who offers the fifth oblation, should offer it to Udāna (out-breathing), saying Svāhā. Then Udāna is satisfied.

2. 'If Udāna is satisfied, Vāyu (air) is satisfied, if Vāyu is satisfied, ether is satisfied, if ether is satisfied, whatever is under Vāyu and under the ether is satisfied. And through their satisfaction he (the sacrificer or eater) himself is satisfied with offspring, cattle, health, brightness, and Vedic splendour.

TWENTY-FOURTH KHAṆḌA

1. 'If, without knowing this, one offers an Agnihotra, it would be as if a man were to remove the live coals and pour his libation on dead ashes.

2. 'But he who offers this Agnihotra with a full knowledge of its true purport, he offers it (i.e. he eats food) in all worlds, in all beings, in all Selfs.

3. 'As the soft fibres of the Ishīkā reed, when thrown into the fire, are burnt, thus all his sins are burnt whoever offers this Agnihotra with a full knowledge of its true purport.

4. 'Even if he gives what is left of his food to a Chaṇḍāla,

it would be offered in his (the Chaṇḍāla's) Vaiśvānara Self. And so it is said in this Śloka:

'"As hungry children here on earth sit (expectantly) round their mother, so do all beings sit round the Agnihotra, yea, round the Agnihotra."'

Sixth Prapāṭhaka

First Khaṇḍa

1. Hari, Om. There lived once Śvetaketu Āruṇeya (the grandson of Aruṇa). To him his father (Uddālaka, the son of Aruṇa) said: 'Śvetaketu, go to school; for there is none belonging to our race, darling, who, not having studied (the Veda), is, as it were, a Brāhmaṇa by birth only.'

2. Having begun his apprenticeship (with a teacher) when he was twelve years of age, Śvetaketu returned to his father, when he was twenty-four, having then studied all the Vedas—conceited, considering himself well-read, and stern.

3. His father said to him: 'Śvetaketu, as you are so conceited, considering yourself so well-read, and so stern, my dear, have you ever asked for that instruction by which we hear what cannot be heard, by which we perceive what cannot be perceived, by which we know what cannot be known?'

4. 'What is that instruction, Sir?' he asked.

The father replied: 'My dear, as by one clod of clay all that is made of clay is known, the difference being only a name, arising from speech, but the truth being that all is clay;

5. 'And as, my dear, by one nugget of gold all that is made of gold is known, the difference being only a name, arising from speech, but the truth being that all is gold;

6. 'And as, my dear, by one pair of nail-scissors all that is made of iron (kārshṇāyasam) is known, the difference being only a name, arising from speech, but the truth being that all is iron—thus, my dear, is that instruction.'

7. The son said: 'Surely those venerable men (my teachers) did not know that. For if they had known it, why should they not have told it me? Do you, Sir, therefore tell me that.' 'Be it so,' said the father.

Second Khaṇḍa

1. 'In the beginning, my dear, there was that only which is (τὸ ὄν), one only, without a second. Others say, in the

beginning there was that only which is not (τὸ μὴ ὄν), one only, without a second; and from that which is not, that which is was born.

2. 'But how could it be thus, my dear?' the father continued. 'How could that which is, be born of that which is not? No, my dear, only that which is, was in the beginning, one only, without a second.

3. 'It thought, may I be many, may I grow forth. It sent forth fire.

'That fire thought, may I be many, may I grow forth. It sent forth water.

'And therefore whenever anybody anywhere is hot and perspires, water is produced on him from fire alone.

4. 'Water thought, may I be many, may I grow forth. It sent forth earth (food).

'Therefore whenever it rains anywhere, most food is then produced. From water alone is eatable food produced.

THIRD KHAṆḌA

1. 'Of all living things there are indeed three origins only, that which springs from an egg (oviparous), that which springs from a living being (viviparous), and that which springs from a germ.

2. 'That Being (i.e. that which had produced fire, water, and earth) thought, let me now enter those three beings (fire, water, earth) with this living Self (jīva ātmā), and let me then reveal (develop) names and forms.

3. 'Then that Being having said, Let me make each of these three tripartite (so that fire, water, and earth should each have itself for its principal ingredient, besides an admixture of the other two) entered into those three beings (devatā) with this living Self only, and revealed names and forms.

4. 'He made each of these tripartite; and how these three beings become each of them tripartite, that learn from me now, my friend!

FOURTH KHAṆḌA

1. 'The red colour of burning fire (agni) is the colour of fire, the white colour of fire is the colour of water, the black colour of fire the colour of earth. Thus vanishes what we call fire, as a mere variety, being a name, arising from speech. What is true (satya) are the three colours (or forms).

2. 'The red colour of the sun (āditya) is the colour of fire, the white of water, the black of earth. Thus vanishes what we call the sun, as a mere variety, being a name, arising from speech. What is true are the three colours.

3. 'The red colour of the moon is the colour of fire, the white of water, the black of earth. Thus vanishes what we call the moon, as a mere variety, being a name, arising from speech. What is true are the three colours.

4. 'The red colour of the lightning is the colour of fire, the white of water, the black of earth. Thus vanishes what we call the lightning, as a mere variety, being a name, arising from speech. What is true are the three colours.

5. 'Great householders and great theologians of olden times who knew this, have declared the same, saying, "No one can henceforth mention to us anything which we have not heard, perceived, or known." Out of these (three colours or forms) they knew all.

6. 'Whatever they thought looked red, they knew was the colour of fire. Whatever they thought looked white, they knew was the colour of water. Whatever they thought looked black, they knew was the colour of earth.

7. 'Whatever they thought was altogether unknown, they knew was some combination of those three beings (devatā).

'Now learn from me, my friend, how those three beings, when they reach man, become each of them tripartite.

FIFTH KHAṆḌA

1. 'The earth (food) when eaten becomes threefold; its grossest portion becomes faeces, its middle portion flesh, its subtilest portion mind.

2. 'Water when drunk becomes threefold; its grossest portion becomes water, its middle portion blood, its subtilest portion breath.

3. 'Fire (i.e. in oil, butter, etc.) when eaten becomes threefold; its grossest portion becomes bone, its middle portion marrow, its subtilest portion speech.

4. 'For truly, my child, mind comes of earth, breath of water, speech of fire.'

'Please, Sir, inform me still more,' said the son.

'Be it so, my child,' the father replied.

SIXTH KHAṆḌA

1. 'That which is the subtile portion of curds, when churned, rises upwards, and becomes butter.

2. 'In the same manner, my child, the subtile portion of earth (food), when eaten, rises upwards, and becomes mind.

3. 'That which is the subtile portion of water, when drunk, rises upwards, and becomes breath.

4. 'That which is the subtile portion of fire, when consumed, rises upwards, and becomes speech.

5. 'For mind, my child, comes of earth, breath of water, speech of fire.'

'Please, Sir, inform me still more,' said the son.

'Be it so, my child,' the father replied.

SEVENTH KHAṆḌA

1. 'Man (purusha), my son, consists of sixteen parts. Abstain from food for fifteen days, but drink as much water as you like, for breath comes from water, and will not be cut off, if you drink water.'

2. Śvetaketu abstained from food for fifteen days. Then he came to his father and said: 'What shall I say?' The father said: 'Repeat the Ṛich, Yajus, and Sāman verses.' He replied: 'They do not occur to me, Sir.'

3. The father said to him: 'As of a great lighted fire one coal only of the size of a firefly may be left, which would not burn much more than this (i.e. very little), thus, my dear son, one part only of the sixteen parts (of you) is left, and therefore with that one part you do not remember the Vedas. Go and eat!

4. 'Then wilt thou understand me.' Then Śvetaketu ate, and afterwards approached his father. And whatever his father asked him, he knew it all by heart. Then his father said to him:

5. 'As of a great lighted fire one coal of the size of a firefly, if left, may be made to blaze up again by putting grass upon it, and will thus burn more than this,

6. 'Thus, my dear son, there was one part of the sixteen parts left to you, and that, lighted up with food, burnt up, and by it you remember now the Vedas.' After that, he understood what his father meant when he said: 'Mind, my son, comes from food, breath from water, speech from fire.' He understood what he said, yea, he understood it.

EIGHTH KHAṆḌA

1. Uddālaka Āruṇi said to his son Śvetaketu: 'Learn from me the true nature of sleep (svapna). When a man sleeps here, then, my dear son, he becomes united with the True, he is gone to his own (Self). Therefore they say, svapiti, he sleeps, because he is gone (apīta) to his own (sva).

2. 'As a bird when tied by a string flies first in every direction, and finding no rest anywhere, settles down at last on the very place where it is fastened, exactly in the same manner, my son, that mind (the jīva, or living Self in the mind, see VI, iii, 2), after flying in every direction, and finding no rest anywhere, settles down on breath; for indeed, my son, mind is fastened to breath.

3. 'Learn from me, my son, what are hunger and thirst. When a man is thus said to be hungry, water is carrying away (digests) what has been eaten by him. Therefore as they speak of a cow-leader (go-nāya), a horse-leader (aśva-nāya), a man-leader (purusha-nāya), so they call water (which digests food and causes hunger) food-leader (aśanāya). Thus (by food digested, etc.), my son, know this offshoot (the body) to be brought forth, for this (body) could not be without a root (cause).

4. 'And where could its root be except in food (earth)? And in the same manner, my son, as food (earth) too is an offshoot, seek after its root, viz. water. And as water too is an offshoot, seek after its root, viz. fire. And as fire too is an offshoot, seek after its root, viz. the True. Yes, all these creatures, my son, have their root in the True, they dwell in the True, they rest in the True.

5. 'When a man is thus said to be thirsty, fire carries away what has been drunk by him. Therefore as they speak of a cow-leader (go-nāya), of a horse-leader (aśva-nāya), of a man-leader (purusha-nāya), so they call fire udanyā, thirst, i.e. water-leader. Thus (by water digested, etc.), my son, know this offshoot (the body) to be brought forth: this (body) could not be without a root (cause).

6. 'And where could its root be except in water? As water is an offshoot, seek after its root, viz. fire. As fire is an offshoot, seek after its root, viz. the True. Yes, all these creatures, O son, have their root in the True, they dwell in the True, they rest in the True.

'And how these three beings (devatā), fire, water, earth, O

son, when they reach man, become each of them tripartite, has been said before (VI, iv, 7). When a man departs from hence, his speech is merged in his mind, his mind in his breath, his breath in heat (fire), heat in the highest Being.

7. 'Now that which is that subtile essence (the root of all), in it all that exists has its self. It is the True. It is the Self, and thou, O Śvetaketu, art it.'

'Please, Sir, inform me still more,' said the son.

'Be it so, my child,' the father replied.

NINTH KHAṆḌA

1. 'As the bees, my son, make honey by collecting the juices of distant trees, and reduce the juice into one form.

2. 'And as these juices have no discrimination, so that they might say, I am the juice of this tree or that, in the same manner, my son, all these creatures, when they have become merged in the True (either in deep sleep or in death), know not that they are merged in the True.

3. 'Whatever these creatures are here, whether a lion, or a wolf, or a boar, or a worm, or a midge, or a gnat, or a mosquito, that they become again and again.

4. 'Now that which is that subtile essence, in it all that exists has its self. It is the True. It is the Self, and thou, O Śvetaketu, art it.'

'Please, Sir, inform me still more,' said the son.

'Be it so, my child,' the father replied.

TENTH KHAṆḌA

1. 'These rivers, my son, run, the eastern (like the Gaṅgā) toward the east, the western (like the Sindhu) toward the west. They go from sea to sea (i.e. the clouds lift up the water from the sea to the sky, and send it back as rain to the sea). They become indeed sea. And as those rivers, when they are in the sea, do not know, I am this or that river.

2. 'In the same manner, my son, all these creatures, when they have come back from the True, know not that they have come back from the True. Whatever these creatures are here, whether a lion, or a wolf, or a boar, or a worm, or a midge, or a gnat, or a mosquito, that they become again and again.

3. 'That which is that subtile essence, in it all that exists has its self. It is the True. It is the Self, and thou, O Śvetaketu, art it.'

'Please, Sir, inform me still more,' said the son.

'Be it so, my child,' the father replied.

ELEVENTH KHAṆḌA

1. 'If someone were to strike at the root of this large tree here, it would bleed, but live. If he were to strike at its stem, it would bleed, but live. If he were to strike at its top, it would bleed, but live. Pervaded by the living Self that tree stands firm, drinking in its nourishment and rejoicing;

2. 'But if the life (the living Self) leaves one of its branches, that branch withers; if it leaves a second, that branch withers; if it leaves a third, that branch withers. If it leaves the whole tree, the whole tree withers. In exactly the same manner, my son, know this.' Thus he spoke:

3. 'This (body) indeed withers and dies when the living Self has left it; the living Self dies not.

'That which is that subtile essence, in it all that exists has its self. It is the True. It is the Self, and thou, Śvetaketu, art it.'

'Please, Sir, inform me still more,' said the son.

'Be it so, my child,' the father replied.

TWELFTH KHAṆḌA

1. 'Fetch me from thence a fruit of the nyagrodha tree.'

'Here is one, Sir.'

'Break it.'

'It is broken, Sir.'

'What do you see there?'

'These seeds, almost infinitesimal.'

'Break one of them.'

'It is broken, Sir.'

'What do you see there?'

'Not anything, Sir.'

2. The father said: 'My son, that subtile essence which you do not perceive there, of that very essence this great nyagrodha tree exists.

3. 'Believe it, my son. That which is the subtile essence, in it all that exists has its self. It is the True. It is the Self, and thou, O Śvetaketu, art it.'

'Please, Sir, inform me still more,' said the son.

'Be it so, my child,' the father replied.

THIRTEENTH KHAṆḌA

1. 'Place this salt in water, and then wait on me in the morning.'

The son did as he was commanded.

The father said to him: 'Bring me the salt, which you placed in the water last night.'

The son having looked for it, found it not, for, of course, it was melted.

2. The father said: 'Taste it from the surface of the water. How is it?'

The son replied: 'It is salt.'

'Taste it from the middle. How is it?'

The son replied: 'It is salt.'

'Taste it from the bottom. How is it?'

The son replied: 'It is salt.'

The father said: 'Throw it away and then wait on me.'

He did so; but salt exists for ever.

Then the father said: 'Here also, in this body, forsooth, you do not perceive the True (Sat), my son; but there indeed it is.

3. 'That which is the subtile essence, in it all that exists has its self. It is the True. It is the Self, and thou, O Śvetaketu, art it.'

'Please, Sir, inform me still more,' said the son.

'Be it so, my child,' the father replied.

FOURTEENTH KHAṆḌA

1. 'As one might lead a person with his eyes covered away from the Gandhāras, and leave him then in a place where there are no human beings; and as that person would turn towards the east, or the north, or the west, and shout, "I have been brought here with my eyes covered, I have been left here with my eyes covered,"

2. 'And as thereupon someone might loose his bandage and say to him, "Go in that direction, it is Gandhāra, go in that direction"; and as thereupon, having been informed and being able to judge for himself, he would by asking his way from village to village arrive at last at Gandhāra—in exactly the same manner does a man, who meets with a teacher to inform him, obtain the true knowledge. For him there is only delay so long as he is not delivered (from the body); then he will be perfect.

3. 'That which is the subtile essence, in it all that exists has its self. It is the True. It is the Self, and thou, O Śvetaketu, art it.'

'Please, Sir, inform me still more,' said the son.

'Be it so, my child,' the father replied.

FIFTEENTH KHAṆḌA

1. 'If a man is ill, his relatives assemble round him and ask: "Dost thou know me? Dost thou know me?" Now as long as his speech is not merged in his mind, his mind in breath, breath in heat (fire), heat in the Highest Being (devatā), he knows them.

2. 'But when his speech is merged in his mind, his mind in breath, breath in heat (fire), heat in the Highest Being, then he knows them not.

'That which is the subtile essence, in it all that exists has its self. It is the True. It is the Self, and thou, O Śvetaketu, art it.'

'Please, Sir, inform me still more,' said the son.

'Be it so, my child,' the father replied.

SIXTEENTH KHAṆḌA

1. 'My child, they bring a man hither whom they have taken by the hand, and they say: "He has taken something, he has committed a theft." (When he denies, they say), "Heat the hatchet for him." If he committed the theft, then he makes himself to be what he is not. Then the false-minded, having covered his true Self by a falsehood, grasps the heated hatchet—he is burnt, and he is killed.

2. 'But if he did not commit the theft, then he makes himself to be what he is. Then the true-minded, having covered his true Self by truth, grasps the heated hatchet—he is not burnt, and he is delivered.

'As that (truthful) man is not burnt, thus has all that exists its self in That. It is the True. It is the Self, and thou, O Śvetaketu, art it.' He understood what he said, yea, he understood it.

Seventh Prapāṭhaka

FIRST KHAṆḌA

1. Nārada approached Sanatkumāra and said, 'Teach me, Sir!' Sanatkumāra said to him: 'Please to tell me what you know; afterward I shall tell you what is beyond.'

2. Nārada said: 'I know the Ṛigveda, Sir, the Yajur-veda, the Sāma-veda, as the fourth the Ātharvaṇa, as the fifth the Itihāsa-purāṇa (the Bhārata); the Veda of the Vedas (grammar); the Pitrya (the rules for the sacrifices for the ancestors); the Rāśi (the science of numbers); the Daiva (the science of portents); the Nidhi (the science of time); the Vākovākya (logic); the Ekāyana (ethics); the Deva-vidyā (etymology); the Brahma-vidyā (pronunciation, śikshā, ceremonial, kalpa, prosody, chhandas); the Bhūta-vidyā (the science of demons); the Kshatra-vidyā (the science of weapons); the Nakshatra-vidyā (astronomy); the Sarpa and Devajana-vidyā (the science of serpents or poisons, and the sciences of the genii, such as the making of perfumes, dancing, singing, playing, and other fine arts). All this I know, Sir.

3. 'But, Sir, with all this I know the Mantras only, the sacred books, I do not know the Self. I have heard from men like you, that he who knows the Self overcomes grief. I am in grief. Do, Sir, help me over this grief of mine.'

Sanatkumāra said to him: 'Whatever you have read, is only a name.

4. 'A name is the Ṛigveda, Yajur-veda, Sāma-veda, and as the fourth the Ātharvaṇa, as the fifth the Itihāsa-purāṇa, the Veda of the Vedas, the Pitrya, the Rāśi, the Daiva, the Nidhi, the Vākovākya, the Ekāyana, the Deva-vidyā, the Brahma-vidyā, the Bhūta-vidyā, the Kshatra-vidyā, the Nakshatra-vidyā, the Sarpa and Devajana-vidyā. All these are a name only. Meditate on the name.

5. 'He who meditates on the name as Brahman, is, as it were, lord and master as far as the name reaches—he who meditates on the name as Brahman.'

'Sir, is there something better than a name?'

'Yes, there is something better than a name.'

'Sir, tell it me.'

SECOND KHAṆḌA

1. 'Speech is better than a name. Speech makes us understand the Ṛigveda, Yajur-veda, Sāma-veda, and as the fourth the Ātharvaṇa, as the fifth the Itihāsa-purāṇa, the Veda of the Vedas, the Pitrya, the Rāśi, the Daiva, the Nidhi, the Vākovākya, the Ekāyana, the Deva-vidyā, the Brahma-vidyā, the Kshatra-vidyā, the Nakshatra-vidyā, the Sarpa and Devajana-vidyā; heaven, earth, air, ether, water, fire, gods, men, cattle, birds, herbs, trees, all beasts down to worms, midges, and ants; what is right and what is wrong; what is true and what is false; what is good and what is bad; what is pleasing and what is not pleasing. For if there were no speech, neither right nor wrong would be known, neither the true nor the false, neither the good nor the bad, neither the pleasant nor the unpleasant. Speech makes us understand all this. Meditate on speech.

2. 'He who meditates on speech as Brahman, is, as it were, lord and master as far as speech reaches—he who meditates on speech as Brahman.'

'Sir, is there something better than speech?'

'Yes, there is something better than speech.'

'Sir, tell it me.'

THIRD KHAṆḌA

1. 'Mind (manas) is better than speech. For as the closed fist holds two amalaka or two kola or two aksha fruits, thus does mind hold speech and name. For if a man is minded in his mind to read the sacred hymns, he reads them; if he is minded in his mind to perform any actions, he performs them; if he is minded to wish for sons and cattle, he wishes for them; if he is minded to wish for this world and the other, he wishes for them. For mind is indeed the Self, mind is the world, mind is Brahman. Meditate on the mind.

2. 'He who meditates on the mind as Brahman, is, as it were, lord and master as far as the mind reaches—he who meditates on the mind as Brahman.'

'Sir, is there something better than mind?'

'Yes, there is something better than mind.'

'Sir, tell it me.'

FOURTH KHAṆḌA

1. 'Will (saṁkalpa) is better than mind. For when a man wills, then he thinks in his mind, then he sends forth speech

and he sends it forth in a name. In a name the sacred hymns are contained, in the sacred hymns all sacrifices.

2. 'All these therefore (beginning with mind and ending in sacrifice) centre in will, consist of will, abide in will. Heaven and earth willed, air and ether willed, water and fire willed. Through the will of heaven and earth, etc., rain wills; through the will of rain food wills; through the will of food the vital airs will; through the will of the vital airs the sacred hymns will; through the will of the sacred hymns the sacrifices will; through the will of the sacrifices the world (as their reward) wills; through the will of the world everything wills. This is will. Meditate on will.

3. 'He who meditates on will as Brahman, he, being himself safe, firm, and undistressed, obtains the safe, firm, and undistressed worlds which he has willed; he is, as it were, lord and master as far as will reaches—he who meditates on will as Brahman.'

'Sir, is there something better than will?'

'Yes, there is something better than will.'

'Sir, tell it me.'

FIFTH KHAṆḌA

1. 'Consideration (chitta) is better than will. For when a man considers, then he wills, then he thinks in his mind, then he sends forth speech, and he sends it forth in a name. In a name the sacred hymns are contained, in the sacred hymns all sacrifices.

2. 'All these (beginning with mind and ending in sacrifice) centre in consideration, consist of consideration, abide in consideration. Therefore if a man is inconsiderate, even if he possesses much learning, people say of him, he is nothing, whatever he may know; for, if he were learned, he would not be so inconsiderate. But if a man is considerate, even though he knows but little, to him indeed do people listen gladly. Consideration is the centre, consideration is the Self, consideration is the support of all these. Meditate on consideration.

3. 'He who meditates on consideration as Brahman, he, being himself safe, firm, and undistressed, obtains the safe, firm, and undistressed worlds which he has considered; he is, as it were, lord and master as far as consideration reaches—he who meditates on consideration as Brahman.'

'Sir, is there something better than consideration?'

'Yes, there is something better than consideration.'

'Sir, tell it me.'

SIXTH KHAṆḌA

1. 'Reflection (dhyāna) is better than consideration. The earth reflects, as it were, and thus does the sky, the heaven, the water, the mountains, gods and men. Therefore those who among men obtain greatness here on earth, seem to have obtained a part of the object of reflection (because they show a certain repose of manner). Thus while small and vulgar people are always quarrelling, abusive, and slandering, great men seem to have obtained a part of the reward of reflection. Meditate on reflection.

2. 'He who meditates on reflection as Brahman, is lord and master, as it were, as far as reflection reaches—he who meditates on reflection as Brahman.'

'Sir, is there something better than reflection?'

'Yes, there is something better than reflection.'

'Sir, tell it me.'

SEVENTH KHAṆḌA

1. 'Understanding (vijñāna) is better than reflection. Through understanding we understand the Ṛigveda, the Yajur-veda, the Sāma-veda, and as the fourth the Ātharvaṇa, as the fifth the Itihāsa-purāṇa, the Veda of the Vedas, the Pitrya, the Rāśi, the Daiva, the Nidhi, the Vākovākya, the Ekāyana, the Deva-vidyā, the Brahma-vidyā, the Bhūta-vidyā, the Kshatra-vidyā, the Nakshatra-vidyā, the Sarpa and Devajana-vidyā, heaven, earth, air, ether, water, fire, gods, men, cattle, birds, herbs, trees, all beasts down to worms, midges, and ants; what is right and what is wrong; what is true and what is false; what is good and what is bad; what is pleasing and what is not pleasing; food and savour, this world and that, all this we understand through understanding. Meditate on understanding.

2. 'He who meditates on understanding as Brahman, reaches the worlds where there is understanding and knowledge; he is, as it were, lord and master as far as understanding reaches—he who meditates on understanding as Brahman.'

'Sir, is there something better than understanding?'

'Yes, there is something better than understanding.'

'Sir, tell it me.'

EIGHTH KHAṆḌA

1. 'Power (bala) is better than understanding. One powerful man shakes a hundred men of understanding. If a man is powerful, he becomes a rising man. If he rises, he becomes a man who visits wise people. If he visits, he becomes a follower of wise people. If he follows them, he becomes a seeing, a hearing, a perceiving, a knowing, a doing, an understanding man. By power the earth stands firm, and the sky, and the heaven, and the mountains, gods and men, cattle, birds, herbs, trees, all beasts down to worms, midges, and ants; by power the world stands firm. Meditate on power.

2. 'He who meditates on power as Brahman, is, as it were, lord and master as far as power reaches—he who meditates on power as Brahman.'

'Sir, is there something better than power?'

'Yes, there is something better than power.'

'Sir, tell it me.'

NINTH KHAṆḌA

1. 'Food (anna) is better than power. Therefore if a man abstain from food for ten days, though he live, he would be unable to see, hear, perceive, think, act, and understand. But when he obtains food, he is able to see, hear, perceive, think, act, and understand. Meditate on food.

2. 'He who meditates on food as Brahman, obtains the worlds rich in food and drink; he is, as it were, lord and master as far as food reaches—he who meditates on food as Brahman.'

'Sir, is there something better than food?'

'Yes, there is something better than food.'

'Sir, tell it me.'

TENTH KHAṆḌA

1. 'Water (ap) is better than food. Therefore if there is not sufficient rain, the vital spirits fail from fear that there will be less food. But if there is sufficient rain, the vital spirits rejoice, because there will be much food. This water, on assuming different forms, becomes this earth, this sky, this heaven, the mountains, gods and men, cattle, birds, herbs and trees, all beasts down to worms, midges, and ants. Water indeed assumes all these forms. Meditate on water.

2. 'He who meditates on water as Brahman, obtains all wishes, he becomes satisfied; he is, as it were, lord and master as far as water reaches—he who meditates on water as Brahman.'

'Sir, is there something better than water?'

'Yes, there is something better than water.'

'Sir, tell it me.'

ELEVENTH KHAṆḌA

1. 'Fire (tejas) is better than water. For fire united with air, warms the ether. Then people say, It is hot, it burns, it will rain. Thus does fire, after showing this sign (itself) first, create water. And thus again thunderclaps come with lightnings, flashing upwards and across the sky. Then people say, There is lightning and thunder, it will rain. Then also does fire, after showing this sign first, create water. Meditate on fire.

2. 'He who meditates on fire as Brahman, obtains, resplendent himself, resplendent worlds, full of light and free of darkness; he is, as it were, lord and master as far as fire reaches—he who meditates on fire as Brahman.'

'Sir, is there something better than fire?'

'Yes, there is something better than fire.'

'Sir, tell it me.'

TWELFTH KHAṆḌA

1. 'Ether (or space) is better than fire. For in the ether exist both sun and moon, the lightning, stars, and fire (agni). Through the ether we call, through the ether we hear, through the ether we answer. In the ether or space we rejoice (when we are together), and rejoice not (when we are separated). In the ether everything is born, and towards the ether everything tends when it is born. Meditate on ether.

2. 'He who meditates on ether as Brahman, obtains the worlds of ether and of light, which are free from pressure and pain, wide and spacious; he is, as it were, lord and master as far as ether reaches—he who meditates on ether as Brahman.'

'Sir, is there something better than ether?'

'Yes, there is something better than ether.'

'Sir, tell it me.'

THIRTEENTH KHAṆḌA

1. 'Memory (smara) is better than ether. Therefore where many are assembled together, if they have no memory, they

would hear no one, they would not perceive, they would not understand. Through memory we know our sons, through memory our cattle. Meditate on memory.

2. 'He who meditates on memory as Brahman, is, as it were, lord and master as far as memory reaches—he who meditates on memory as Brahman.'

'Sir, is there something better than memory?'

'Yes, there is something better than memory.'

'Sir, tell it me.'

FOURTEENTH KHAṆḌA

1. 'Hope (āśā) is better than memory. Fired by hope does memory read the sacred hymns, perform sacrifices, desire sons and cattle, desire this world and the other. Meditate on hope.

2. 'He who meditates on hope as Brahman, all his desires are fulfilled by hope, his prayers are not in vain; he is, as it were, lord and master as far as hope reaches—he who meditates on hope as Brahman.'

'Sir, is there something better than hope?'

'Yes, there is something better than hope.'

'Sir, tell it me.'

FIFTEENTH KHAṆḌA

1. 'Spirit (prāṇa) is better than hope. As the spokes of a wheel hold to the nave, so does all this (beginning with names and ending in hope) hold to spirit. That spirit moves by the spirit, it gives spirit to the spirit. Father means spirit, mother is spirit, brother is spirit, sister is spirit, tutor is spirit, Brāhmaṇa is spirit.

2. 'For if one says anything unbecoming to a father, mother, brother, sister, tutor, or Brāhmaṇa, then people say, Shame on thee! thou hast offended thy father, mother, brother, sister, tutor, or a Brāhmaṇa.

3. 'But, if after the spirit has departed from them, one shoves them together with a poker, and burns them to pieces, no one would say, Thou offendest thy father, mother, brother, sister, tutor, or a Brāhmaṇa.

4. 'Spirit then is all this. He who sees this, perceives this, and understands this, becomes an ativādin. If people say to such a man, Thou art an ativādin, he may say, I am an ativādin; he need not deny it.'

SIXTEENTH KHAṆḌA

'But in reality he is an ativādin who declares the Highest Being to be the True (Satya, τὸ ὄντως ὄν).'

'Sir, may I become an ativādin by the True?'

'But we must desire to know the True.'

'Sir, I desire to know the True.'

SEVENTEENTH KHAṆḌA

'When one understands the True, then one declares the True. One who does not understand it, does not declare the True. Only he who understands it, declares the True. This understanding, however, we must desire to understand.'

'Sir, I desire to understand it.'

EIGHTEENTH KHAṆḌA

'When one perceives, then one understands. One who does not perceive, does not understand. Only he who perceives, understands. This perception, however, we must desire to understand.'

'Sir, I desire to understand it.'

NINETEENTH KHAṆḌA

'When one believes, then one perceives. One who does not believe, does not perceive. Only he who believes, perceives. This belief, however, we must desire to understand.'

'Sir, I desire to understand it.'

TWENTIETH KHAṆḌA

'When one attends on a tutor (spiritual guide), then one believes. One who does not attend on a tutor, does not believe. Only he who attends, believes. This attention on a tutor, however, we must desire to understand.'

'Sir, I desire to understand it.'

TWENTY-FIRST KHAṆḌA

'When one performs all sacred duties, then one attends really on a tutor. One who does not perform his duties, does not really attend on a tutor. Only he who performs his duties attends on his tutor. This performance of duties, however, we must desire to understand.'

'Sir, I desire to understand it.'

TWENTY-SECOND KHAṆḌA

'When one obtains bliss (in oneself), then one performs duties. One who does not obtain bliss, does not perform duties. Only he who obtains bliss, performs duties. This bliss, however, we must desire to understand.'

'Sir, I desire to understand it.'

TWENTY-THIRD KHAṆḌA

'The Infinite (bhūman) is bliss. There is no bliss in anything finite. Infinity only is bliss. This Infinity, however, we must desire to understand.

'Sir, I desire to understand it.'

TWENTY-FOURTH KHAṆḌA

1. 'Where one sees nothing else, hears nothing else, understands nothing else, that is the Infinite. Where one sees something else, hears something else, understands something else, that is the finite. The Infinite is immortal, the finite is mortal.'

'Sir, in what does the Infinite rest?'

'In its own greatness—or not even in greatness.

2. 'In the world they call cows and horses, elephants and gold, slaves, wives, fields, and houses greatness. I do not mean this,' thus he spoke; 'for in that case one being (the possessor) rests in something else (but the Infinite cannot rest in something different from itself).

TWENTY-FIFTH KHAṆḌA

1. 'The Infinite indeed is below, above, behind, before, right, and left—it is indeed all this.

'Now follows the explanation of the Infinite as the I: I am below, I am above, I am behind, before, right, and left—I am all this.

2. 'Next follows the explanation of the Infinite as the Self: Self is below, above, behind, before, right, and left—Self is all this.

'He who sees, perceives, and understands this, loves the Self, delights in the Self, revels in the Self, rejoices in the Self—he becomes a Svarāj (an autocrat or self-ruler); he is lord and master in all the worlds.

'But those who think differently from this, live in perishable worlds, and have other beings for their rulers.

TWENTY-SIXTH KHAṆḌA

1. 'To him who sees, perceives, and understands this, the spirit (prāṇa) springs from the Self, hope springs from the Self, memory springs from the Self; so do ether, fire, water, appearance and disappearance, food, power, understanding, reflection, consideration, will, mind, speech, names, sacred hymns, and sacrifices—aye, all this springs from the Self.

2. 'There is this verse, "He who sees this, does not see death, nor illness, nor pain; he who sees this, sees everything, and obtains everything everywhere.

'"He is one (before creation), he becomes three (fire, water, earth), he becomes five, he becomes seven, he becomes nine; then again he is called the eleventh, and hundred and ten and one thousand and twenty."

'When the intellectual aliment has been purified, the whole nature becomes purified. When the whole nature has been purified, the memory becomes firm. And when the memory (of the Highest Self) remains firm, then all the ties (which bind us to a belief in anything but the Self) are loosened.

'The venerable Sanatkumāra showed to Nārada, after his faults had been rubbed out, the other side of darkness. They call Sanatkumāra Skanda, yea, Skanda they call him.'

EIGHTH PRAPĀṬHAKA

IRST KHAṆḌA[1]

1. Hari, Om. There is this city of Brahman (the body), and in it the palace, the small lotus (of the heart), and in it that

[1] The eighth Prapāṭhaka seems to form a kind of appendix to the Upanishad. The highest point that can be reached by speculation had been reached in the seventh Prapāṭhaka, the identity of our Self and of everything else with the Highest Self. This speculative effort, however, is too much for ordinary people. They cannot conceive the Sat or Brahman as out of space and time, as free from all qualities, and in order to help them, they are taught to adore the Brahman, as it appears in space and time, an object endowed with certain qualities, living in nature and in the human heart.

small ether. Now what exists within that small ether, that is to be sought for, that is to be understood.

2. And if they should say to him: 'Now with regard to that city of Brahman, and the palace in it, i.e. the small lotus of the heart, and the small ether within the heart, what is there within it that deserves to be sought for, or that is to be understood?'

3. Then he should say: 'As large as this ether (all space) is, so large is that ether within the heart. Both heaven and earth are contained within it, both fire and air, both sun and moon, both lightning and stars; and whatever there is of him (the Self) here in the world, and whatever is not (i.e. whatever has been or will be), all that is contained within it.'

4. And if they should say to him: 'If everything that exists is contained in that city of Brahman, all beings and all desires (whatever can be imagined or desired), then what is left of it, when old age reaches it and scatters it, or when it falls to pieces?'

5. Then he should say: 'By the old age of the body, that (the ether, or Brahman within it) does not age; by the death of the body, that (the ether, or Brahman within it) is not killed. That (the Brahman) is the true Brahma-city (not the body). In it all desires are contained. It is the Self, free from sin, free from old age, from death and grief, from hunger and thirst, which desires nothing but what it ought to desire, and imagines nothing but what it ought to imagine. Now as here on earth people follow as they are commanded, and depend on the object which they are attached to, be it a country or a piece of land,

6. 'And as here on earth, whatever has been acquired by exertion, perishes, so perishes whatever is acquired for the next world by sacrifices and other good actions performed on earth. Those who depart from hence without having discovered the Self and those true desires, for them there is no freedom in all the worlds. But those who depart from hence, after having discovered the Self and those true desires, for them there is freedom in all the worlds.

SECOND KHAṆḌA

1. 'Thus he who desires the world of the fathers, by his mere will the fathers come to receive him, and having obtained the world of the fathers, he is happy.

2. 'And he who desires the world of the mothers, by his mere

will the mothers come to receive him, and having obtained the world of the mothers, he is happy.

3. 'And he who desires the world of the brothers, by his mere will the brothers come to receive him, and having obtained the world of the brothers, he is happy.

4. 'And he who desires the world of the sisters, by his mere will the sisters come to receive him, and having obtained the world of the sisters, he is happy.

5. 'And he who desires the world of the friends, by his mere will the friends come to receive him, and having obtained the world of the friends, he is happy.

6. 'And he who desires the world of perfumes and garlands (gandhamālya), by his mere will perfumes and garlands come to him, and having obtained the world of perfumes and garlands, he is happy.

7. 'And he who desires the world of food and drink, by his mere will food and drink come to him, and having obtained the world of food and drink, he is happy.

8. 'And he who desires the world of song and music, by his mere will song and music come to him, and having obtained the world of song and music, he is happy.

9. 'And he who desires the world of women, by his mere will women come to receive him, and having obtained the world of women, he is happy.

'Whatever object he is attached to, whatever object he desires, by his mere will it comes to him, and having obtained it, he is happy.

THIRD KHAṆḌA

1. 'These true desires, however, are hidden by what is false; though the desires be true, they have a covering which is false. Thus, whoever belonging to us has departed this life, him we cannot gain back, so that we should see him with our eyes.

2. 'Those who belong to us, whether living or departed, and whatever else there is which we wish for and do not obtain, all that we find there (if we descend into our heart, where Brahman dwells, in the ether of the heart). There are all our true desires, but hidden by what is false. As people who do not know the country, walk again and again over a gold treasure that has been hidden somewhere in the earth and do not discover it, thus do all these creatures day after day go into the Brahma-world (they are merged in Brahman, while asleep), and yet do not

discover it, because they are carried away by untruth (they do not come to themselves, i.e. they do not discover the true Self in Brahman, dwelling in the heart).

3. 'That Self abides in the heart. And this is the etymological explanation. The heart is called hṛidayam, instead of hṛidy-ayam, i.e. He who is in the heart. He who knows this, that he is in the heart, goes day by day (when in sushupti, deep sleep) into heaven (svarga), i.e. into the Brahman of the heart.

4. 'Now that serene being which, after having risen from out his earthly body, and having reached the highest light (self-knowledge), appears in its true form, that is the Self,' thus he spoke (when asked by his pupils). This is the immortal, the fearless, this is Brahman. And of that Brahman the name is the True, Satyam,

5. This name Sattyam consists of three syllables, sat-tī-yam. Sat signifies the immortal, ti the mortal, and with yam he binds both. Because he binds both, the immortal and the mortal, therefore it is yam. He who knows this goes day by day into heaven (svarga).

FOURTH KHAṆḌA

1. That Self is a bank, a boundary, so that these worlds may not be confounded. Day and night do not pass that bank, nor old age, death, and grief; neither good nor evil deeds. All evil-doers turn back from it, for the world of Brahman is free from all evil.

2. Therefore he who has crossed that bank, if blind, ceases to be blind; if wounded, ceases to be wounded; if afflicted, ceases to be afflicted. Therefore when that bank has been crossed, night becomes day indeed, for the world of Brahman is lighted up once for all.

3. And that world of Brahman belongs to those only who find it by abstinence—for them there is freedom in all the worlds.

FIFTH KHAṆḌA

1. What people call sacrifice (yajña), that is really abstinence (brahmacharya). For he who knows, obtains that (world of Brahman, which others obtain by sacrifice) by means of abstinence.

What people call sacrifice (ishṭa), that is really abstinence, for by abstinence, having searched (ishṭvā), he obtains the Self.

2. What people call sacrifice (sattrāyaṇa), that is really abstinence, for by abstinence he obtains from the Sat (the true), the safety (trāṇa) of the Self.

What people call the vow of silence (mauna), that is really abstinence, for he who by abstinence has found out the Self, meditates (manute).

3. What people call fasting (anāśakāyana), that is really abstinence, for that Self does not perish (na naśyati), which we find out by abstinence.

What people call a hermit's life (araṇyāyana), that is really abstinence. Ara and Ṇya are two lakes in the world of Brahman, in the third heaven from hence; and there is the lake Airammadīya, and the Aśvattha tree, showering down soma, and the city of Brahman (Hiraṇyagarbha) Aparājitā, and the golden Prabhuvimita (the hall built by Prabhu, Brahman).

Now that world of Brahman belongs to those who find the lakes Ara and Ṇya in the world of Brahman by means of abstinence; for them there is freedom in all the worlds.

SIXTH KHAṆḌA

1. Now those arteries of the heart consist of a brown substance, of a white, blue, yellow, and red substance, and so is the sun brown, white, blue, yellow, and red.

2. As a very long highway goes to two places, to one at the beginning, and to another at the end, so do the rays of the sun go to both worlds, to this one and to the other. They start from the sun, and enter into those arteries; they start from those arteries, and enter into the sun.

3. And when a man is asleep, reposing, and at perfect rest so that he sees no dream, then he has entered into those arteries. Then no evil touches him, for he has obtained the light (of the sun).

4. And when a man falls ill, then those who sit round him say, 'Do you know me? Do you know me?' As long as he has not departed from this body, he knows them.

5. But when he departs from this body, then he departs upwards by those very rays (towards the worlds which he has gained by merit, not by knowledge); or he goes out while meditating on Om (and thus securing an entrance into the Brahmaloka). And while his mind is failing, he is going to the sun. For the sun is the door of the world (of Brahman). Those

vho know, walk in; those who do not know, are shut out. There is this verse: ' There are a hundred and one arteries of the heart; one of them penetrates the crown of the head; moving upwards by it a man reaches the immortal; the others serve for departing in different directions, yea, in different directions.'

SEVENTH KHAṆḌA

1. Prajāpati said: ' The Self which is free from sin, free from old age, from death and grief, from hunger and thirst, which desires nothing but what it ought to desire, and imagines nothing but what it ought to imagine, that it is which we must search out, that it is which we must try to understand. He who has searched out that Self and understands it, obtains all worlds and all desires.'

2. The Devas (gods) and Asuras (demons) both heard these words, and said: ' Well, let us search for that Self by which, if one has searched it out, all worlds and all desires are obtained.'

Thus saying Indra went from the Devas, Virochana from the Asuras, and both, without having communicated with each other, approached Prajāpati, holding fuel in their hands, as is the custom for pupils approaching their master.

3. They dwelt there as pupils for thirty-two years. Then Prajāpati asked them: ' For what purpose have you both dwelt here?'

They replied: ' A saying of yours is being repeated, viz. " the Self which is free from sin, free from old age, from death and grief, from hunger and thirst, which desires nothing but what it ought to desire, and imagines nothing but what it ought to imagine, that it is which we must search out, that it is which we must try to understand. He who has searched out that Self and understands it, obtains all worlds and all desires." Now we both have dwelt here because we wish for that Self.'

Prajāpati said to them: ' The person that is seen in the eye, that is the Self. This is what I have said. This is the immortal, the fearless, this is Brahman.'

They asked: ' Sir, he who is perceived in the water, and he who is perceived in a mirror, who is he?'

He replied: ' He himself indeed is seen in all these.'

EIGHTH KHAṆḌA

1. ' Look at your Self in a pan of water, and whatever you do not understand of your Self, come and tell me.'

They looked in the water-pan. Then Prajāpati said to them: 'What do you see?'

They said: 'We both see the self thus altogether, a picture even to the very hairs and nails.'

2. Prajāpati said to them: 'After you have adorned yourselves, have put on your best clothes and cleaned yourselves, look again into the water-pan.'

They, after having adorned themselves, having put on their best clothes and cleaned themselves, looked into the water-pan.

Prajāpati said: 'What do you see?'

3. They said: 'Just as we are, well adorned, with our best clothes and clean, thus we are both there, Sir, well adorned, with our best clothes and clean.'

Prajāpati said: 'That is the Self, this is the immortal, the fearless, this is Brahman.'

Then both went away satisfied in their hearts.

4. And Prajāpati, looking after them, said: 'They both go away without having perceived and without having known the Self, and whoever of these two, whether Devas or Asuras, will follow this doctrine (upanishad), will perish.'

Now Virochana, satisfied in his heart, went to the Asuras and preached that doctrine to them, that the self (the body) alone is to be worshipped, that the self (the body) alone is to be served and that he who worships the self and serves the self, gains both worlds, this and the next.

5. Therefore they call even now a man who does not give alms here, who has no faith, and offers no sacrifices, an Āsura for this is the doctrine (upanishad) of the Asuras. They deck out the body of the dead with perfumes, flowers, and fine raiment by way of ornament, and think they will thus conquer that world.

NINTH KHAṆḌA

1. But Indra, before he had returned to the Devas, saw this difficulty. As this self (the shadow in the water) is well adorned when the body is well adorned, well dressed, when the body is well dressed, well cleaned, if the body is well cleaned, that self will also be blind, if the body is blind, lame, if the body is lame crippled, if the body is crippled, and will perish in fact as soon as the body perishes. Therefore I see no good in this (doctrine).

2. Taking fuel in his hand he came again as a pupil to Prajāpati. Prajāpati said to him: 'Maghavat (Indra), as you went

away with Virochana, satisfied in your heart, for what purpose did you come back?'

He said: 'Sir, as this self (the shadow) is well adorned, when the body is well adorned, well dressed, when the body is well dressed, well cleaned, if the body is well cleaned, that self will also be blind, if the body is blind, lame, if the body is lame, crippled, if the body is crippled, and will perish in fact as soon as the body perishes. Therefore I see no good in this (doctrine).'

3. 'So it is indeed, Maghavat,' replied Prajāpati; 'but I shall explain him (the true Self) further to you. Live with me another thirty-two years.'

He lived with him another thirty-two years, and then Prajāpati said:

TENTH KHAṆḌA

1. 'He who moves about happy in dreams, he is the Self, this is the immortal, the fearless, this is Brahman.'

Then Indra went away satisfied in his heart. But before he had returned to the Devas, he saw this difficulty. Although it is true that that self is not blind, even if the body is blind, nor lame, if the body is lame, though it is true that that self is not rendered faulty by the faults of it (the body),

2. Nor struck when it (the body) is struck, nor lamed when it is lamed, yet it is as if they struck him (the self) in dreams, as if they chased him. He becomes even conscious, as it were, of pain, and sheds tears. Therefore I see no good in this.

3. Taking fuel in his hands, he went again as pupil to Prajāpati. Prajāpati said to him: 'Maghavat, as you went away satisfied in your heart, for what purpose did you come back?'

He said: 'Sir, although it is true that that self is not blind even if the body is blind, nor lame, if the body is lame, though it is true that that self is not rendered faulty by the faults of it (the body),

4. 'Nor struck when it (the body) is struck, nor lamed when it is lamed, yet it is as if they struck him (the self) in dreams, as if they chased him. He becomes even conscious, as it were, of pain, and sheds tears. Therefore I see no good in this.'

'So it is indeed, Maghavat,' replied Prajāpati; 'but I shall explain him (the true Self) further to you. Live with me another thirty-two years.'

He lived with him another thirty-two years. Then Prajāpati said:

ELEVENTH KHAṆḌA

1. 'When a man being asleep, reposing, and at perfect rest, sees no dreams, that is the Self, this is the immortal, the fearless, this is Brahman.'

Then Indra went away satisfied in his heart. But before he had returned to the Devas, he saw this difficulty. In truth he thus does not know himself (his self) that he is I, nor does he know anything that exists. He is gone to utter annihilation. I see no good in this.

2. Taking fuel in his hand he went again as pupil to Prajāpati. Prajāpati said to him: 'Maghavat, as you went away satisfied in your heart, for what purpose did you come back?'

He said: 'Sir, in that way he does not know himself (his self) that he is I, nor does he know anything that exists. He is gone to utter annihilation. I see no good in this.'

3. 'So it is indeed, Maghavat,' replied Prajāpati; 'but I shall explain him (the true Self) further to you, and nothing more than this. Live here other five years.'

He lived there other five years. This made in all one hundred and one years, and therefore it is said that Indra Maghavat lived one hundred and one years as a pupil with Prajāpati. Prajāpati said to him:

TWELFTH KHAṆḌA

1. 'Maghavat, this body is mortal and always held by death. It is the abode of that Self which is immortal and without body. When in the body (by thinking this body is I and I am this body) the Self is held by pleasure and pain. So long as he is in the body, he cannot get free from pleasure and pain. But when he is free of the body (when he knows himself different from the body), then neither pleasure nor pain touches him.

2. 'The wind is without body, the cloud, lightning, and thunder are without body (without hands, feet, etc.). Now as these, arising from this heavenly ether (space), appear in their own form, as soon as they have approached the highest light,

3. 'Thus does that serene being, arising from this body, appear in its own form, as soon as it has approached the highest light (the knowledge of Self). He (in that state) is the highest person (uttama pūrusha). He moves about there laughing (or eating), playing, and rejoicing (in his mind), be it with women, carriages, or relatives, never minding that body into which he was born.

'Like as a horse attached to a cart, so is the spirit (prāṇa, ·ajñātman) attached to this body.

4. 'Now where the sight has entered into the void (the open ›ace, the black pupil of the eye), there is the person of the eye, ıe eye itself is the instrument of seeing. He who knows, let ıe smell this, he is the Self, the nose is the instrument of smell-ıg. He who knows, let me say this, he is the Self, the tongue the instrument of saying. He who knows, let me hear this, e is the Self, the ear is the instrument of hearing.

5. 'He who knows, let me think this, he is the Self, the mind his divine eye. He, the Self, seeing these pleasures (which to thers are hidden like a buried treasure of gold) through his ivine eye, i.e. the mind, rejoices.

'The Devas who are in the world of Brahman meditate on ıat Self (as taught by Prajāpati to Indra, and by Indra to the •evas). Therefore all worlds belong to them, and all desires. Ie who knows that Self and understands it, obtains all worlds nd all desires.' Thus said Prajāpati, yea, thus said Prajāpati.

THIRTEENTH KHAṆḌA

From the dark (the Brahman of the heart) I come to the ebulous (the world of Brahman), from the nebulous to the dark, ıaking off all evil, as a horse shakes his hairs, and as the moon ·ees herself from the mouth of Rāhu. Having shaken off the ody, I obtain, self made and satisfied, the uncreated world of Brahman, yea, I obtain it.

FOURTEENTH KHAṆḌA

He who is called ether (ākāśa) is the revealer of all forms nd names. That within which these forms and names are ontained is the Brahman, the Immortal, the Self.

I come to the hall of Prajāpati, to the house; I am the glorious mong Brāhmans, glorious among princes, glorious among men. obtained that glory, I am glorious among the glorious. May I ıever go to the white, toothless, yet devouring, white abode; ıay I never go to it.

FIFTEENTH KHAṆḌA

Brahmā (Hiraṇyagarbha or Parameśvara) told this to rajāpati (Kaśyapa), Prajāpati to Manu (his son), Manu to ıankind. He who has learnt the Veda from a family of teachers, according to the sacred rule, in the leisure time left from the duties to be performed for the Guru, who, after receiving his discharge, has settled in his own house, keeping up the memory of what he has learnt by repeating it regularly in some sacred spot, who has begotten virtuous sons, and concentrated all his senses on the Self, never giving pain to any creature, except at the tīrthas (sacrifices, etc.), he who behaves thus all his life, reaches the world of Brahman, and does not return, yea, he does not return.

KAṬHA UPANISHAD

First Adhyāya

FIRST VALLĪ

. Vājaśravasa, desirous (of heavenly rewards), surrendered at a sacrifice) all that he possessed. He had a son of the ame of Nachiketas.

2. When the (promised) presents were being given (to the riests), faith entered into the heart of Nachiketas, who was still boy, and he thought:

3. 'Unblessed, surely, are the worlds to which a man goes y giving (as his promised present at a sacrifice) cows which ave drunk water, eaten hay, given their milk, and are arren.'

4. He (knowing that his father had promised to give up all hat he possessed, and therefore his son also) said to his father: Dear father, to whom wilt thou give me?'

He said it a second and a third time. Then the father eplied (angrily):

'I shall give thee unto Death.'

(The father, having once said so, though in haste, had to be rue to his word and to sacrifice his son.)

5. The son said: 'I go as the first, at the head of many (who ave still to die); I go in the midst of many (who are now dying). Vhat will be the work of Yama (the ruler of the departed) hich to-day he has to do unto me?

6. 'Look back how it was with those who came before, look rward how it will be with those who come hereafter. A ortal ripens like corn, like corn he springs up again.'

(Nachiketas enters into the abode of Yama Vaivasvata, and here is no one to receive him. Thereupon one of the attendants f Yama is supposed to say:)

7. 'Fire enters into the houses, when a Brāhmaṇa enters as guest. That fire is quenched by this peace-offering—bring ater, O Vaivasvata!

8. 'A Brāhmaṇa that dwells in the house of a foolish man ithout receiving food to eat, destroys his hopes and expecta-

tions, his possessions, his righteousness, his sacred and his good deeds, and all his sons and cattle.'

(Yama, returning to his house after an absence of three nights, during which time Nachiketas had received no hospitality from him, says:)

9. 'O Brāhmaṇa, as thou, a venerable guest, hast dwelt in my house three nights without eating, therefore choose now three boons. Hail to thee! and welfare to me!'

10. Nachiketas said: 'O Death, as the first of the three boons I choose that Gautama, my father, be pacified, kind, and free from anger towards me; and that he may know me and greet me, when I shall have been dismissed by thee.'

11. Yama said: 'Through my favour Auddālaki Āruṇi, thy father, will know thee, and be again towards thee as he was before. He shall sleep peacefully through the night, and free from anger, after having seen thee freed from the mouth of death.'

12. Nachiketas said: 'In the heaven-world there is no fear; thou art not there, O Death, and no one is afraid on account of old age. Leaving behind both hunger and thirst, and out of the reach of sorrow, all rejoice in the world of heaven.

13. 'Thou knowest, O Death, the fire-sacrifice which leads us to heaven; tell it to me, for I am full of faith. Those who live in the heaven-world reach immortality—this I ask as my second boon.'

14. Yama said: 'I tell it thee, learn it from me, and when thou understandest that fire-sacrifice which leads to heaven, know, O Nachiketas, that it is the attainment of the endless worlds, and their firm support, hidden in darkness.'

15. Yama then told him that fire-sacrifice, the beginning of all the worlds, and what bricks are required for the altar, and how many, and how they are to be placed. And Nachiketas repeated all as it had been told to him. Then Mṛityu, being pleased with him, said again:

16. The generous, being satisfied, said to him: 'I give thee now another boon; that fire-sacrifice shall be named after thee; take also this many-coloured chain.

17. 'He who has three times performed this Nāchiketa rite, and has been united with the three (father, mother, and teacher), and has performed the three duties (study, sacrifice, almsgiving), overcomes birth and death. When he has learnt and understood this fire, which knows (or makes us know) all that is born

of Brahman, which is venerable and divine, then he obtains everlasting peace.

18. 'He who knows the three Nāchiketa fires, and knowing the three, piles up the Nāchiketa sacrifice, he, having first thrown off the chains of death, rejoices in the world of heaven, beyond the reach of grief.

19. 'This, O Nachiketas, is thy fire which leads to heaven, and which thou hast chosen as thy second boon. That fire all men will proclaim. Choose now, O Nachiketas, thy third boon.'

20. Nachiketas said: 'There is that doubt, when a man is dead—some saying, he is; others, he is not. This I should like to know, taught by thee; this is the third of my boons.'

21. Death said: 'On this point even the gods have doubted formerly; it is not easy to understand. That subject is subtle. Choose another boon, O Nachiketas, do not press me, and let me off that boon.'

22. Nachiketas said: 'On this point even the gods have doubted indeed, and thou, Death, hast declared it to be not easy to understand, and another teacher like thee is not to be found—surely no other boon is like unto this.'

23. Death said: 'Choose sons and grandsons who shall live a hundred years, herds of cattle, elephants, gold, and horses. Choose the wide abode of the earth, and live thyself as many harvests as thou desirest.

24. 'If you can think of any boon equal to that, choose wealth, and long life. Be (king), Nachiketas, on the wide earth. I make thee the enjoyer of all desires.

25. 'Whatever desires are difficult to attain among mortals, ask for them according to thy wish; these fair maidens with their chariots and musical instruments—such are indeed not to be obtained by men—be waited on by them whom I give to thee, but do not ask me about dying.'

26. Nachiketas said: 'These things last till to-morrow, O Death, for they wear out this vigour of all the senses. Even the whole of life is short. Keep thou thy horses, keep dance and song for thyself.

27. 'No man can be made happy by wealth. Shall we possess wealth, when we see thee? Shall we live, as long as thou rulest? Only that boon (which I have chosen) is to be chosen by me.

28. 'What mortal, slowly decaying here below, and knowing, after having approached them, the freedom from decay enjoyed

by the immortals, would delight in a long life, after he has pondered on the pleasures which arise from beauty and love?

29. 'No, that on which there is this doubt, O Death, tell us what there is in that great hereafter. Nachiketas does not choose another boon but that which enters into the hidden world.'

SECOND VALLĪ

1. Death said: 'The good is one thing, the pleasant another; these two, having different objects, chain a man. It is well with him who clings to the good; he who chooses the pleasant, misses his end.

2. 'The good and pleasant approach man: the wise goes round about them and distinguishes them. Yea, the wise prefers the good to the pleasant, but the fool chooses the pleasant through greed and avarice.

3. 'Thou, O Nachiketas, after pondering all pleasures that are or seem delightful, hast dismissed them all. Thou hast not gone into the road that leadeth to wealth, in which many men perish.

4. 'Wide apart and leading to different points are these two, ignorance, and what is known as wisdom. I believe Nachiketas to be one who desires knowledge, for even many pleasures did not tear thee away.

5. 'Fools dwelling in darkness, wise in their own conceit, and puffed up with vain knowledge, go round and round, staggering to and fro, like blind men led by the blind.

6. 'The hereafter never rises before the eyes of the careless child, deluded by the delusion of wealth. "This is the world," he thinks, "there is no other"—thus he falls again and again under my sway.

7. 'He (the Self) of whom many are not even able to hear, whom many, even when they hear of him, do not comprehend; wonderful is a man, when found, who is able to teach him (the Self); wonderful is he who comprehends him, when taught by an able teacher.

8. 'That (Self), when taught by an inferior man, is not easy to be known, even though often thought upon; unless it be taught by another, there is no way to it, for it is inconceivably smaller than what is small.

9. 'That doctrine is not to be obtained by argument, but when it is declared by another, then, O dearest, it is easy to

understand. Thou hast obtained it now; thou art truly a man of true resolve. May we have always an inquirer like thee!'

10. Nachiketas said: 'I know that what is called a treasure is transient, for that eternal is not obtained by things which are not eternal. Hence the Nāchiketa fire(-sacrifice) has been laid by me (first); then, by means of transient things, I have obtained what is not transient (the teaching of Yama).'

11. Yama said: 'Though thou hadst seen the fulfilment of all desires, the foundation of the world, the endless rewards of good deeds, the shore where there is no fear, that which is magnified by praise, the wide abode, the rest, yet being wise thou hast with firm resolve dismissed it all.

12. 'The wise who, by means of meditation on his Self, recognises the Ancient, who is difficult to be seen, who has entered into the dark, who is hidden in the cave, who dwells in the abyss, as God, he indeed leaves joy and sorrow far behind.

13. 'A mortal who has heard this and embraced it, who has separated from it all qualities, and has thus reached the subtle Being, rejoices, because he has obtained what is a cause for rejoicing. The house (of Brahman) is open, I believe, O Nachiketas.'

14. Nachiketas said: 'That which thou seest as neither this nor that, as neither effect nor cause, as neither past nor future, tell me that.'

15. Yama said: 'That word (or place) which all the Vedas record, which all penances proclaim, which men desire when they live as religious students, that word I tell thee briefly, it is Om.

16. 'That (imperishable) syllable means Brahman, that syllable means the highest (Brahman); he who knows that syllable, whatever he desires, is his.

17. 'This is the best support, this is the highest support; he who knows that support is magnified in the world of Brahmā.

18. 'The knowing (Self) is not born, it dies not; it sprang from nothing, nothing sprang from it. The Ancient is unborn, eternal, everlasting; he is not killed, though the body is killed.

19. 'If the killer thinks that he kills, if the killed think that he is killed, they do not understand; for this one does not kill, nor is that one killed.

20. 'The Self, smaller than small, greater than great, is hidden in the heart of that creature. A man who is free from

desires and free from grief, sees the majesty of the Self by the grace of the Creator.

21. 'Though sitting still, he walks far; though lying down, he goes everywhere. Who, save myself, is able to know that God who rejoices and rejoices not?

22. 'The wise who knows the Self as bodiless within the bodies, as unchanging among changing things, as great and omnipresent, does never grieve.

23. 'That Self cannot be gained by the Veda, nor by understanding, nor by much learning. He whom the Self chooses, by him the Self can be gained. The Self chooses him (his body) as his own.

24. 'But he who has not first turned away from his wickedness, who is not tranquil, and subdued, or whose mind is not at rest, he can never obtain the Self (even) by knowledge.

25. 'Who then knows where He is, He to whom the Brahmans and Kshatriyas are (as it were) but food, and death itself a condiment?

THIRD VALLĪ

1. 'There are the two,[1] drinking their reward in the world of their own works, entered into the cave (of the heart), dwelling on the highest summit (the ether in the heart). Those who know Brahman call them shade and light; likewise, those householders who perform the Triṇāchiketa sacrifice.

2. 'May we be able to master that Nāchiketa rite which is a bridge for sacrificers; also that which is the highest, imperishable Brahman for those who wish to cross over to the fearless shore.

3. 'Know the Self to be sitting in the chariot, the body to be the chariot, the intellect (buddhi) the charioteer, and the mind the reins.

4. 'The senses they call the horses, the objects of the senses their roads. When he (the Highest Self) is in union with the body, the senses, and the mind, then wise people call him the Enjoyer.

5. 'He who has no understanding and whose mind (the reins) is never firmly held, his senses (horses) are unmanageable, like vicious horses of a charioteer.

6. 'But he who has understanding and whose mind is always firmly held, his senses are under control, like good horses of a charioteer.

[1] The two are explained as the higher and lower Brahman, the former being the light, the latter the shadow.

7. 'He who has no understanding, who is unmindful and always impure, never reaches that place, but enters into the round of births.

8. 'But he who has understanding, who is mindful and always pure, reaches indeed that place, from whence he is not born again.

9. 'But he who has understanding for his charioteer, and who holds the reins of the mind, he reaches the end of his journey, and that is the highest place of Vishṇu.

10. 'Beyond the senses there are the objects, beyond the objects there is the mind, beyond the mind there is the intellect, the Great Self is beyond the intellect.

11. 'Beyond the Great there is the Undeveloped, beyond the Undeveloped there is the Person (purusha). Beyond the Person there is nothing—this is the goal, the highest road.

12. 'That Self is hidden in all beings and does not shine forth, but it is seen by subtle seers through their sharp and subtle intellect.

13. 'A wise man should keep down speech and mind; he should keep them within the Self which is knowledge; he should keep knowledge within the Self which is the Great; and he should keep that (the Great) within the Self which is the Quiet.

14. 'Rise, awake! having obtained your boons, understand them! The sharp edge of a razor is difficult to pass over; thus the wise say the path (to the Self) is hard.

15. 'He who has perceived that which is without sound, without touch, without form, without decay, without taste, eternal, without smell, without beginning, without end, beyond the Great, and unchangeable, is freed from the jaws of death.

16. 'A wise man who has repeated or heard the ancient story of Nachiketas told by Death, is magnified in the world of Brahman.

17. 'And he who repeats this greatest mystery in an assembly of Brāhmans, or full of devotion at the time of the Śrāddha sacrifice, obtains thereby infinite rewards.

Second Adhyāya

FOURTH VALLĪ

1. Death said: 'The Self-existent pierced the openings (of the senses) so that they turn forward: therefore man looks forward, not backward into himself. Some wise man, however, with

his eyes closed and wishing for immortality, saw the Self behind.

2. 'Children follow after outward pleasures, and fall into the snare of widespread death. Wise men only, knowing the nature of what is immortal, do not look for anything stable here among things unstable.

3. 'That by which we know form, taste, smell, sounds, and loving touches, by that also we know what exists besides. This is that (which thou hast asked for).

4. 'The wise, when he knows that that by which he perceives all objects in sleep or in waking is the great omnipresent Self, grieves no more.

5. 'He who knows this living soul which eats honey (perceives objects) as being the Self, always near, the Lord of the past and the future, henceforward fears no more. This is that.

6. 'He who (knows) him who was born first from the brooding heat (for he was born before the water), who, entering into the heart, abides therein, and was perceived from the elements. This is that.

7. '(He who knows) Aditi also, who is one with all deities, who arises with Prāṇa (breath or Hiraṇyagarbha), who, entering into the heart, abides therein, and was born from the elements. This is that.

8. 'There is Agni (fire), the all-seeing, hidden in the two fire-sticks, well-guarded like a child (in the womb) by the mother, day after day to be adored by men when they awake and bring oblations. This is that.

9. 'And that whence the sun rises and whither it goes to set, there all the Devas are contained, and no one goes beyond. This is that.

10. 'What is here (visible in the world), the same is there (invisible in Brahman); and what is there, the same is here. He who sees any difference here (between Brahman and the world), goes from death to death.

11. 'Even by the mind this (Brahman) is to be obtained, and then there is no difference whatsoever. He goes from death to death who sees any difference here.

12. 'The person (purusha), of the size of a thumb, stands in the middle of the Self (body ?), as lord of the past and the future, and henceforward fears no more. This is that.

13. 'That person, of the size of a thumb, is like a light without

smoke, lord of the past and the future, he is the same to-day and to-morrow. This is that.

14. 'As rain-water that has fallen on a mountain-ridge runs down the rocks on all sides, thus does he, who sees a difference between qualities, run after them on all sides.

15. 'As pure water poured into pure water remains the same, thus, O Gautama, is the Self of a thinker who knows.

FIFTH VALLĪ

1. 'There is a town with eleven gates belonging to the Unborn (Brahman), whose thoughts are never crooked. He who approaches it, grieves no more, and liberated (from all bonds of ignorance) becomes free. This is that.

2. 'He (Brahman) is the swan (sun), dwelling in the bright heaven; he is the Vasu (air), dwelling in the sky; he is the sacrificer (fire) ,dwelling on the hearth; he is the guest (Soma), dwelling in the sacrificial jar; he dwells in men, in gods (vara), in the sacrifice (ṛita), in heaven; he is born in the water, on earth, in the sacrifice (ṛita), on the mountains; he is the True and the Great.

3. 'He (Brahman) it is who sends up the breath (prāṇa), and who throws back the breath (apāna). All the Devas (senses) worship him, the adorable (or the dwarf), who sits in the centre.

4. 'When that incorporated (Brahman), who dwells in the body, is torn away and freed from the body, what remains then? This is that.

5. 'No mortal lives by the breath that goes up and by the breath that goes down. We live by another, in whom these two repose.

6. 'Well then, O Gautama, I shall tell thee this mystery, the old Brahman, and what happens to the Self, after reaching death.

7. 'Some enter the womb in order to have a body, as organic beings, others go into inorganic matter, according to their work and according to their knowledge.

8. 'He, the highest Person, who is awake in us while we are asleep, shaping one lovely sight after another, that indeed is the Bright, that is Brahman, that alone is called the Immortal. All worlds are contained in it, and no one goes beyond. This is that.

9. 'As the one fire, after it has entered the world, though one, becomes different according to whatever it burns, thus the one Self within all things becomes different, according to whatever it enters, and exists also without.

10. 'As the one air, after it has entered the world, though one, becomes different according to whatever it enters, thus the one Self within all things becomes different, according to whatever it enters, and exists also without.

11. 'As the sun, the eye of the whole world, is not contaminated by the external impurities seen by the eyes, thus the one Self within all things is never contaminated by the misery of the world, being himself without.

12. 'There is one ruler, the Self within all things, who makes the one form manifold. The wise who perceive him within their Self, to them belongs eternal happiness, not to others.

13. 'There is one eternal thinker, thinking non-eternal thoughts, who, though one, fulfils the desires of many. The wise who perceive him within their Self, to them belongs eternal peace, not to others.

14. 'They perceive that highest indescribable pleasure, saying, This is that. How then can I understand it? Has it its own light, or does it reflect light?

15. 'The sun does not shine there, nor the moon and the stars, nor these lightnings, and much less this fire. When he shines, everything shines after him; by his light all this is lighted.

SIXTH VALLĪ

1. 'There is that ancient tree,[1] whose roots grow upward and whose branches grown downward—that indeed is called the Bright, that is called Brahman, that alone is called the Immortal. All worlds are contained in it, and no one goes beyond. This is that.

2. 'Whatever there is, the whole world, when gone forth (from the Brahman), trembles in its breath. That Brahman is a great terror, like a drawn sword. Those who know it become immortal.

3. 'From terror of Brahman fire burns, from terror the sun burns, from terror Indra and Vāyu, and Death, as the fifth, run away.

4. 'If a man could not understand it before the falling

[1] The fig-tree which sends down its branches so that they strike root and form new stems, one tree growing into a complete forest.

asunder of his body, then he has to take body again in the worlds of creation.

5. 'As in a mirror, so (Brahman may be seen clearly) here in this body; as in a dream, in the world of the fathers; as in the water, he is seen about in the world of the Gandharvas; as in light and shade, in the world of Brahmā.

6. 'Having understood that the senses are distinct (from the Ātman), and that their rising and setting (their waking and sleeping) belongs to them in their distinct existence (and not to the Ātman), a wise man grieves no more.

7. 'Beyond the senses is the mind, beyond the mind is the highest (created) Being, higher than that Being is the Great Self, higher than the Great, the highest Undeveloped.

8. 'Beyond the Undeveloped is the Person, the all-pervading and entirely imperceptible. Every creature that knows him is liberated, and obtains immortality.

9. 'His form is not to be seen, no one beholds him with the eye. He is imagined by the heart, by wisdom, by the mind. Those who know this, are immortal.

10. 'When the five instruments of knowledge stand still together with the mind, and when the intellect does not move, that is called the highest state.

11. 'This, the firm holding back of the senses, is what is called Yoga. He must be free from thoughtlessness then, for Yoga comes and goes.

12. 'He (the Self) cannot be reached by speech, by mind, or by the eye. How can it be apprehended except by him who says: "He is"?

13. 'By the words "He is," is he to be apprehended, and by (admitting) the reality of both (the invisible Brahman and the visible world, as coming from Brahman). When he has been apprehended by the words "He is," then his reality reveals itself.

14. 'When all desires that dwell in his heart cease, then the mortal becomes immortal, and obtains Brahman.

15. 'When all the ties of the heart are severed here on earth, then the mortal becomes immortal—here ends the teaching.

16. 'There are a hundred and one arteries of the heart, one of them penetrates the crown of the head. Moving upwards by it, a man (at his death) reaches the Immortal; the other arteries serve for departing in different directions.

17. 'The Person not larger than a thumb, the inner Self, is

always settled in the heart of men. Let a man draw that Self forth from his body with steadiness, as one draws the pith from a reed. Let him know that Self as the Bright, as the Immortal; yes, as the Bright, as the Immortal.'

18. Having received this knowledge taught by Death and the whole rule of Yoga (meditation), Nachiketa became free from passion and death, and obtained Brahman. Thus it will be with another also who knows thus what relates to the Self.

19. May He protect us both! May He enjoy us both! May we acquire strength together! May our knowledge become bright! May we never quarrel! Om! Peace! peace! peace! Hari, Om!

ĪŚĀ UPANISHAD

SOMETIMES CALLED

Vājasaneyi-Saṁhitā Upanishad

1. All this, whatsoever moves on earth, is to be hidden in the Lord (the Self). When thou hast surrendered all this, then thou mayest enjoy. Do not covet the wealth of any man!

2. Though a man may wish to live a hundred years, performing works, it will be thus with him; but not in any other way: work will thus not cling to a man.

3. There are the worlds of the Asuras covered with blind darkness. Those who have destroyed their self (who perform works, without having arrived at a knowledge of the true Self), go after death to those worlds.

4. That one (the Self), though never stirring, is swifter than thought. The Devas (senses) never reached it, it walked before them. Though standing still, it overtakes the others who are running. Mātariśvan (the wind, the moving spirit) bestows powers on it.

5. It stirs and it stirs not; it is far, and likewise near. It is inside of all this, and it is outside of all this.

6. And he who beholds all beings in the Self, and the Self in all beings, he never turns away from it.

7. When to a man who understands, the Self has become all things, what sorrow, what trouble can there be to him who once beheld that unity?

8. He (the Self) encircled all, bright, incorporeal, scatheless, without muscles, pure, untouched by evil; a seer, wise, omnipresent, self-existent, he disposed all things rightly for eternal years.

9. All who worship what is not real knowledge (good works), enter into blind darkness: those who delight in real knowledge, enter, as it were, into greater darkness.

10. One thing, they say, is obtained from real knowledge; another, they say, from what is not knowledge. Thus we have heard from the wise who taught us this.

11. He who knows at the same time both knowledge and not-knowledge, overcomes death through not-knowledge, and obtains immortality through knowledge.

12. All who worship what is not the true cause, enter into blind darkness; those who delight in the true cause, enter, as it were, into greater darkness.

13. One thing, they say, is obtained from (knowledge of) the cause; another, they say, from (knowledge of) what is not the cause. Thus we have heard from the wise who taught us this.

14. He who knows at the same time both the cause and the destruction (the perishable body), overcomes death by destruction (the perishable body), and obtains immortality through (knowledge of) the true cause.

15. The door of the True is covered with a golden disk. Open that, O Pūshan, that we may see the nature of the True.

16. O Pūshan, only seer, Yama (judge), Sūrya (sun), son of Prajāpati, spread thy rays and gather them! The light which is thy fairest form, I see it. I am what He is (viz. the person in the sun).

17. Breath to air, and to the immortal! Then this my body ends in ashes. Om! Mind, remember! Remember thy deeds! Mind, remember! Remember thy deeds!

18. Agni, lead us on to wealth (beatitude) by a good path, thou, O God, who knowest all things! Keep far from us crooked evil, and we shall offer thee the fullest praise! (Rv. I, 189, 1.)

This Upanishad, though apparently simple and intelligible, is in reality one of the most difficult to understand properly. It begins by declaring that all has to be surrendered to the Lord. The name Īś, lord, is peculiar, as having a far more personal colouring than Ātman, Self, or Brahman, the usual names given by the Upanishads to what is the object of the highest knowledge.

Next follows a permission to continue the performance of sacrifices, provided that all desires have been surrendered. And here occurs our first difficulty, which has perplexed ancient as well as modern commentators.

I hold that the Upanishad wishes to teach the uselessness by themselves of all good works, whether we call them sacrificial, legal, or moral, and yet, at the same time, to recognize, if not the necessity, at least the harmlessness of good works, provided they are performed without any selfish motives, without any desire of reward, but simply as a preparation for higher knowledge, as a means, in fact, of subduing all passions, and producing that serenity of mind without which man is incapable of receiving the highest knowledge. From that point of view the Upanishad may well say, Let a man wish to live here his appointed time, let him even perform all works. If only he knows that all must be surrendered to the Lord, then the work done by him will not cling to him. It will not work on and produce effect after effect, nor will it involve him in a succession of new births in which to enjoy the reward of his works, but it will leave him free to enjoy the blessings of the highest knowledge. It will have served as a preparation for that higher knowledge which the Upanishad imparts, and which secures freedom from further births.

ŚVETĀŚVATARA UPANISHAD

First Adhyāya

1. The Brahma-students say: Is Brahman the cause? Whence are we born? Whereby do we live, and whither do we go? O ye who know Brahman, (tell us) at whose command we abide, whether in pain or in pleasure?

2. Should time, or nature, or necessity, or chance, or the elements be considered as the cause, or he who is called the person (purusha, vijñānātmā)? It cannot be their union either, because that is not self-dependent, and the self also is powerless, because there is (independent of him) a cause of good and evil.

3. The sages, devoted to meditation and concentration, have seen the power belonging to God himself, hidden in its own qualities (guṇa). He, being one, superintends all those causes, time, self, and the rest.

4. We meditate on him who (like a wheel) has one felly with three tires, sixteen ends, fifty spokes, with twenty counter-spokes, and six sets of eight; whose one rope is manifold, who proceeds on three different roads, and whose illusion arises from two causes.

5. We meditate on the river whose water consists of the five streams, which is wild and winding with its five springs, whose waves are the five vital breaths, whose fountain head is the mind, the course of the five kinds of perceptions. It has five whirlpools, its rapids are the five pains; it has fifty kinds of suffering, and five branches.

6. In that vast Brahma-wheel, in which all things live and rest, the bird flutters about, so long as he thinks that the self (in him) is different from the mover (the god, the lord). When he has been blessed by him, then he gains immortality.[1]

7. But what is praised (in the upanishads) is the Highest

[1] If he has been blessed by the Īśvara, i.e. when he has been accepted by the Lord, when he has discovered his own true self in the Lord. It must be remembered, however, that both the Īśvara, the Lord, and the purusha, the individual soul, are phenomenal only, and that the Brahma-wheel is meant for the prapañch, the manifest, but unreal world.

Brahman, and in it there is the triad. The Highest Brahman is the safe support, it is imperishable. The Brahma-students, when they have known what is within this (world), are devoted and merged in the Brahman, free from birth.

8. The Lord (īśa) supports all this together, the perishable and the imperishable, the developed and the undeveloped. The (living) self, not being a lord, is bound, because he has to enjoy (the fruits of works); but when he has known the god (deva), he is freed from all fetters.

9. There are two, one knowing (īśvara), the other not-knowing (jīva), both unborn, one strong, the other weak; there is she, the unborn, through whom each man receives the recompense of his works; and there is the infinite Self (appearing) under all forms, but himself inactive. When a man finds out these three, that is Brahma.[1]

10. That which is perishable is the Pradhāna (the first), the immortal and imperishable is Hara. The one god rules the perishable (the pradhāna) and the (living) self. From meditating on him, from joining him, from becoming one with him there is further cessation of all illusion in the end.

11. When that god is known, all fetters fall off, sufferings are destroyed, and birth and death cease. From meditating on him there arises, on the dissolution of the body, the third state, that of universal lordship; but he only who is alone, is satisfied.[2]

12. This, which rests eternally within the self, should be known; and beyond this not anything has to be known. By knowing the enjoyer, the enjoyed, and the ruler, everything has been declared to be threefold, and this is Brahman.

13. As the form of fire, while it exists in the under-wood, is not seen, nor is its seed destroyed, but it has to be seized again and again by means of the stick and the under-wood, so it is in both cases, and the Self has to be seized in the body by means of the praṇava (the syllable Om).

14. By making his body the under-wood, and the syllable Om the upper-wood, man, after repeating the drill of meditation, will perceive the bright god, like the spark hidden in the wood.

[1] The three are (1) the lord, the personal god, the creator and ruler; (2) the individual soul or souls; and (3) the power of creation, the devātmaśakti of verse 3. All three are contained in Brahman; see verses 7, 12.

[2] This alone-ness, kevalatvam, is produced by the knowledge that the individual self is one with the divine self, and that both the individual and the divine self are only phenomenal forms of the true Self, the Brahman.

15. As oil in seeds, as butter in cream, as water in (dry) river-beds, as fire in wood, so is the Self seized within the self, if man looks for him by truthfulness and penance;

16. (If he looks) for the Self that pervades everything, as butter is contained in milk, and the roots whereof are self-knowledge and penance. That is the Brahman taught by the upanishad.

Second Adhyāya

1.[1] Savitṛi (the sun), having first collected his mind and expanded his thoughts, brought Agni (fire), when he had discovered his light, above the earth.

2. With collected minds we are at the command of the divine Savitṛi, that we may obtain blessedness.

3. May Savitṛi, after he has reached with his mind the gods as they rise up to the sky, and with his thoughts (has reached) heaven, grant these gods to make a great light to shine.

4. The wise sages of the great sage collect their mind and collect their thoughts. He who alone knows the law (Savitṛi) has ordered the invocations; great is the praise of the divine Savitṛi.

5. Your old prayer has to be joined with praises. Let my song go forth like the path of the sun! May all the sons of the Immortal listen, they who have reached their heavenly homes.

6. Where the fire is rubbed, where the wind is checked, where the soma flows over, there the mind is born.

7. Let us love the old Brahman by the grace of Savitṛi; if thou make thy dwelling there, the path will not hurt thee.

8. If a wise man hold his body with its three erect parts (chest, neck, and head) even, and turn his senses with the mind towards the heart, he will then in the boat of Brahman cross all the torrents which cause fear.

9. Compressing his breathings let him, who has subdued all motions, breathe forth through the nose with gentle breath. Let the wise man without fail restrain his mind, that chariot yoked with vicious horses.

10. Let him perform his exercises in a place level, pure, free from pebbles, fire, and dust, delightful by its sounds, its water, and bowers, not painful to the eye, and full of shelters and caves.

[1] The seven introductory verses are taken from hymns addressed to Savitṛi as the rising sun.

11. When Yoga is being performed, the forms which come first, producing apparitions in Brahman, are those of misty smoke, sun, fire, wind, fire-flies, lightnings, and a crystal moon.

12. When, as earth, water, light, heat, and ether arise, the fivefold quality of Yoga takes place; then there is no longer illness, old age, or pain for him who has obtained a body, produced by the fire of Yoga.

13. The first results of Yoga they call lightness, healthiness, steadiness, a good complexion, an easy pronunciation, a sweet odour, and slight excretions.

14. As a metal disk (mirror), tarnished by dust, shines bright again after it has been cleaned, so is the one incarnate person satisfied and free from grief, after he has seen the real nature of the self.

15. And when by means of the real nature of his self he sees, as by a lamp, the real nature of Brahman, then having known the unborn, eternal god, who is beyond all natures, he is freed from all fetters.

16. He indeed is the god who pervades all regions: he is the first-born (as Hiraṇyagarbha), and he is in the womb. He has been born, and he will be born. He stands behind all persons, looking everywhere.

17. The god who is in the fire, the god who is in the water, the god who has entered into the whole world, the god who is in plants, the god who is in trees, adoration be to that god, adoration!

THIRD ADHYĀYA [1]

1. The snarer who rules alone by his powers, who rules all the worlds by his powers, who is one and the same, while things arise and exist—they who know this are immortal.

2. For there is one Rudra only, they do not allow a second, who rules all the worlds by his powers. He stands behind all persons, and after having created all worlds he, the protector, rolls it up at the end of time.

3. That one god, having his eyes, his face, his arms, and his feet in every place, when producing heaven and earth, forges them together with his arms and his wings.

[1] This Adhyāya represents the Highest Self as the personified deity, as the lord, Īśa, or Rudra, under the sway of his own creative power, prakṛiti or māyā.

4. He, the creator and supporter of the gods, Rudra, the great seer, the lord of all, he who formerly gave birth to Hiraṇyagarbha, may he endow us with good thoughts.

5. O Rudra, thou dweller in the mountains, look upon us with that most blessed form of thine which is auspicious, not terrible, and reveals no evil!

6. O lord of the mountains, make lucky that arrow which thou, a dweller in the mountains, holdest in thy hand to shoot. Do not hurt man or beast!

7. Those who know beyond this the High Brahman, the vast, hidden in the bodies of all creatures, and alone enveloping everything, as the Lord, they become immortal.

8. I know that great person (purusha) of sunlike lustre beyond the darkness. A man who knows him truly, passes over death; there is no other path to go.

9. This whole universe is filled by this person (purusha), to whom there is nothing superior, from whom there is nothing different, than whom there is nothing smaller or larger, who stands alone, fixed like a tree in the sky.

10. That which is beyond this world is without form and without suffering. They who know it, become immortal, but others suffer pain indeed.

11. That Bhagavat exists in the faces, the heads, the necks of all, he dwells in the cave (of the heart) of all beings, he is all-pervading, therefore he is the omnipresent Śiva.

12. That person (purusha) is the great lord; he is the mover of existence, he possesses that purest power of reaching everything; he is light, he is undecaying.

13. The person (purusha), not larger than a thumb, dwelling within, always dwelling in the heart of man, is perceived by the heart, the thought, the mind; they who know it become immortal.

14. The person (purusha) with a thousand heads, a thousand eyes, a thousand feet, having compassed the earth on every side, extends beyond it by ten fingers' breadth.

15. That person alone (purusha) is all this, what has been and what will be; he is also the lord of immortality; he is whatever grows by food.

16. Its hands and feet are everywhere, its eyes and head are everywhere, its ears are everywhere, it stands encompassing all in the world.

17. Separate from all the senses, yet reflecting the qualities

of all the senses, it is the lord and ruler of all, it is the great refuge of all.

18. The embodied spirit within the town with nine gates, the bird, flutters outwards, the ruler of the whole world, of all that rests and of all that moves.

19. Grasping without hands, hasting without feet, he sees without eyes, he hears without ears. He knows what can be known, but no one knows him; they call him the first, the great person (purusha).

20. The Self, smaller than small, greater than great, is hidden in the heart of the creature. A man who has left all grief behind, sees the majesty, the Lord, the passionless, by the grace of the creator (the Lord).

21. I know this undecaying, ancient one, the self of all things, being infinite and omnipresent. They declare that in him all birth is stopped, for the Brahma-students proclaim him to be eternal.

Fourth Adhyāya

1. He, the sun, without any colour, who with set purpose by means of his power (śakti) produces endless colours, in whom all this comes together in the beginning, and comes asunder in the end—may he, the god, endow us with good thoughts.

2. That (Self) indeed is Agni (fire), it is Āditya (sun), it is Vāyu (wind), it is Chandramas (moon); the same also is the starry firmament, it is Brahman (Hiraṇyagarbha), it is water, it is Prajāpati (Virāj).

3. Thou art woman, thou art man; thou art youth, thou art maiden; thou, as an old man, totterest along on thy staff; thou art born with thy face turned everywhere.

4. Thou art the dark-blue bee, thou art the green parrot with red eyes, thou art the thunder-cloud, the seasons, the seas. Thou art without beginning,[1] because thou art infinite, thou from whom all worlds are born.

5.[2] There is one unborn being (female), red, white, and

[1] We see throughout the constant change from the masculine to the neuter gender, in addressing either the lord or his true essence.

[2] This is again one of the famous verses of our Upanishad, because it formed for a long time a bone of contention between Vedāntaand Sāṃkhya philosophers. The Sāṃkhyas admit two principles, the Purusha, the absolute subject, and the Prakṛiti, generally translated by nature. The Vedānta philosophers admit nothing but the one absolute subject, and

black, uniform, but producing manifold offspring. There is one unborn being (male) who loves her and lies by her; there is another who leaves her, while she is eating what has to be eaten.

6. Two birds, inseparable friends, cling to the same tree. One of them eats the sweet fruit; the other looks on without eating.

7. On the same tree man sits grieving, immersed, bewildered, by his own impotence (an-īśā). But when he sees the other lord (īśa) contented, and knows his glory, then his grief passes away.

8. He who does not know that indestructible being of the Ṛigveda, that highest ether-like (Self) wherein all the gods reside, of what use is the Ṛigveda to him? Those only who know it, rest contented.

9. That from which the maker (māyin) sends forth all this—the sacred verses, the offerings, the sacrifices, the panaceas, the past, the future, and all that the Vedas declare—in that the other is bound up through that māyā.

10. Know then Prakṛiti (nature) is Māyā (art), and the great Lord the Māyin (maker); the whole world is filled with what are his members.

11. If a man has discerned him, who being one only, rules over every germ (cause), in whom all this comes together and comes asunder again, who is the lord, the bestower of blessing, the adorable god, then he passes for ever into that peace.

12. He, the creator and supporter of the gods, Rudra, the great seer, the lord of all, who saw Hiraṇyagarbha being born, may he endow us with good thoughts.

13. He who is the sovereign of the gods, he in whom all the worlds rest, he who rules over all two-footed and four-footed beings, to that god let us sacrifice an oblation.

14. He who has known him who is more subtile than subtile, in the midst of chaos, creating all things, having many forms, alone enveloping everything, the happy one (Śiva), passes into peace for ever.

15. He also was in time the guardian of this world, the lord of all, hidden in all beings. In him the Brahmarshis and the

look upon nature as due to a power inherent in that subject. The later Sāṃkhyas therefore, who are as anxious as the Vedāntins to find authoritative passages in the Veda, confirming their opinions, appeal to this and other passages, to show that their view of Prakṛiti, as an independent power, is supported by the Veda.

deities are united, and he who knows him cuts the fetters of death asunder.

16. He who knows Śiva (the blessed) hidden in all beings, like the subtile film that rises from out the clarified butter, alone enveloping everything—he who knows the god, is freed from all fetters.

17. That god, the maker of all things, the great Self, always dwelling in the heart of man, is perceived by the heart, the soul, the mind;—they who know it become immortal.

18. When the light has risen, there is no day, no night, neither existence nor non-existence; Śiva (the blessed) alone is there. That is the eternal, the adorable light of Savitṛi—and the ancient wisdom proceeded thence.

19. No one has grasped him above, or across, or in the middle. There is no image of him whose name is Great Glory.

20. His form cannot be seen, no one perceives him with the eye. Those who through heart and mind know him thus abiding in the heart, become immortal.

21. 'Thou art unborn,' with these words some one comes near to thee, trembling. O Rudra, let thy gracious face protect me for ever!

22. O Rudra! hurt us not in our offspring and descendants, hurt us not in our own lives, nor in our cows, nor in our horses! Do not slay our men in thy wrath, for, holding oblations, we call on thee always.

Fifth Adhyāya

1. In the imperishable and infinite Highest Brahman, wherein the two, knowledge and ignorance, are hidden, the one, ignorance, perishes, the other, knowledge, is immortal; but he who controls both, knowledge and ignorance, is another.

2. It is he who, being one only, rules over every germ (cause), over all forms, and over all germs; it is he who, in the beginning, bears in his thoughts the wise son, the fiery, whom he wishes to look on while he is born.

3. In that field in which the god, after spreading out one net after another in various ways, draws it together again, the Lord, the great Self, having further created the lords, thus carries on his lordship over all.

4. As the car (of the sun) shines, lighting up all quarters, above, below, and across, thus does that god, the holy, the

adorable, being one, rule over all that has the nature of a germ.

5. He, being one, rules over all and everything, so that the universal germ ripens its nature, diversifies all natures that can be ripened, and determines all qualities.

6. Brahmā (Hiraṇyagarbha) knows this, which is hidden in the upanishads, which are hidden in the Vedas, as the Brahma-germ. The ancient gods and poets who knew it, they became it and were immortal.

7.[1] But he who is endowed with qualities, and performs works that are to bear fruit, and enjoys the reward of whatever he has done, migrates through his own works, the lord of life, assuming all forms, led by the three Guṇas, and following the three paths.

8. That lower one also, not larger than a thumb, but brilliant like the sun, who is endowed with personality and thoughts, with the quality of mind and the quality of body, is seen small even like the point of a goad.

9. That living soul is to be known as part of the hundredth part of the point of a hair, divided a hundred times, and yet it is to be infinite.

10. It is not woman, it is not man, nor is it neuter; whatever body it takes, with that it is joined (only).

11. By means of thoughts, touching, seeing, and passions the incarnate Self assumes successively in various places various forms, in accordance with his deeds, just as the body grows when food and drink are poured into it.

12. That incarnate Self, according to his own qualities, chooses (assumes) many shapes, coarse or subtile, and having himself caused his union with them, he is seen as another and another, through the qualities of his acts, and through the qualities of his body.

13. He who knows him who has no beginning and no end, in the midst of chaos, creating all things, having many forms, alone enveloping everything, is freed from all fetters.

14. Those who know him who is to be grasped by the mind, who is not to be called the nest (the body), who makes existence and non-existence, the happy one (Śiva), who also creates the elements, they have left the body.

[1] Here begins the description of what is called the tvam (thou), as opposed to the tat (that), i.e. the living soul, as opposed to the Highest Brahman.

SIXTH ADHYĀYA

1. Some wise men, deluded, speak of Nature, and others of Time (as the cause of everything); but it is the greatness of God by which this Brahma-wheel is made to turn.

2. It is at the command of him who always covers this world, the knower, the time of time, who assumes qualities and all knowledge, it is at his command that this work (creation) unfolds itself, which is called earth, water, fire, air, and ether;

3. He who, after he has done that work and rested again, and after he has brought together one essence (the self) with the other (matter), with one, two, three, or eight, with time also and with the subtile qualities of the mind,

4. Who, after starting the works endowed with (the three) qualities, can order all things, yet when, in the absence of all these, he has caused the destruction of the work, goes on, being in truth different (from all he has produced);

5. He is the beginning, producing the causes which unite (the soul with the body), and, being above the three kinds of time (past, present, future), he is seen as without parts, after we have first worshipped that adorable god, who has many forms, and who is the true source (of all things), as dwelling in our own mind.

6. He is beyond all the forms of the tree (of the world) and of time, he is the other, from whom this world moves round, when one has known him who brings good and removes evil, the lord of bliss, as dwelling within the self, the immortal, the support of all.

7. Let us know that highest great lord of lords, the highest deity of deities, the master of masters, the highest above, as god, the lord of the world, the adorable.

8. There is no effect and no cause known of him, no one is seen like unto him or better; his high power is revealed as manifold, as inherent, acting as force and knowledge.

9. There is no master of his in the world, no ruler of his, not even a sign of him. He is the cause, the lord of the lords of the organs, and there is of him neither parent nor lord.

10. That only god who spontaneously covered himself, like a spider, with threads drawn from the first cause (pradhāna), grant us entrance into Brahman.

11. He is the one God, hidden in all beings, all-pervading, the self within all beings, watching over all works, dwelling in

all beings, the witness, the perceiver, the only one, free from qualities.

12. He is the one ruler of many who (seem to act, but really) do not act; he makes the one seed manifold. The wise who perceive him within their self, to them belongs eternal happiness, not to others.

13. He is the eternal among eternals, the thinker among thinkers, who, though one, fulfils the desires of many. He who has known that cause which is to be apprehended by Sāṃkhya (philosophy) and Yoga (religious discipline), he is freed from all fetters.

14. The sun does not shine there, nor the moon and the stars, nor these lightnings, and much less this fire. When he shines, everything shines after him; by his light all this is lightened.

15. He is the one bird in the midst of the world; he is also (like) the fire (of the sun) that has set in the ocean. A man who knows him truly, passes over death; there is no other path to go.

16. He makes all, he knows all, the self-caused, the knower, the time of time (destroyer of time), who assumes qualities and knows everything, the master of nature and of man, the lord of the three qualities (guṇa), the cause of the bondage, the existence, and the liberation of the world.

17. He who has become that, he is the immortal, remaining the lord, the knower, the ever-present guardian of this world, who rules this world for ever, for no one else is able to rule it.

18. Seeking for freedom I go for refuge to that God who is the light of his own thoughts, he who first creates Brahman (m.) and delivers the Vedas to him;

19. Who is without parts, without actions, tranquil, without fault, without taint, the highest bridge to immortality—like a fire that has consumed its fuel.

20. Only when men shall roll up the sky like a hide, will there be an end of misery, unless God has first been known.

21. Through the power of his penance and through the grace of God has the wise Śvetāśvatara truly proclaimed Brahman, the highest and holiest, to the best of ascetics, as approved by the company of Ṛishis.

22. This highest mystery in the Vedānta, delivered in a former age, should not be given to one whose passions have not been subdued, nor to one who is not a son, or who is not a pupil.

23. If these truths have been told to a high-minded man, who

feels the highest devotion for God, and for his Guru as for God, then they will shine forth—then they will shine forth indeed.[1]

[1] 'What is really peculiar in the Śvetāśvatara Upanishad is the strong stress that it lays on the personality of the Lord, the Īśvara. . . . It is God as creator and ruler of the world, as Īśvara, lord, but not as Paramātman, or the Highest Self. The Paramātman constitutes, no doubt, his real essence, but creation and creator have a phenomenal character only. The creation is māyā, in its original sense of work, then of phenomenal work, then of illusion. The creator is māyīn, in its original sense of worker as maker, but again, in that character phenomenal only.'

(From the Introduction to the Upanishad.)

PART III

BHAGAVADGÎTÂ

THE LORD'S SONG

LESSON THE FIRST

King Dhṛitarāshṭra's charioteer Sanjaya tells Dhṛitarāshṭra what has happened on the field. Before battle was joined, the leader of the Kurus, Duryodhana, discoursed with Droṇa; then Bhīshma sounded a trumpet-blast, which was answered by the musical instruments of both armies. Thereupon the Pāndava prince Arjuna bade his charioteer, the god Kṛishṇa (Vāsudeva), drive his car forward. There he was overcome by remorse at the thought of the fratricidal struggle into which he and his brothers were about to cast the two armies in order to win their kingdom.

DHṚITARĀSHṬRA SPAKE:—

1. Meeting for strife in the Field of the Law,[1] the Kuru-field, what did my men and Pāṇḍu's folk, O Sanjaya?

SANJAYA SPAKE:—

2. In sooth, King Duryodhana, when he beheld the marshalled host of Pāṇḍu's folk, went unto his master and spake this word:—

3. 'Look, Master, upon this mighty host of Pāṇḍu's sons marshalled by Drupada's son, thy wise disciple.

4. Therein are men of valour, mighty archers like to Bhīma and Arjuna in the fray—Yuyudhāna, Virāṭa, Drupada lord of the great chariot,

5. Dhṛishṭaketu, Chekitāna, the stout king of Kāśī, Purujit, Kuntibhoja, and the lord of the Śibis, mighty among men;

6. Yudhāmanyu the bold, stout Uttamaujas, Subhadrā's son, Draupadī's sons, all lords of great chariots.

7. But mark, O noblest of Brahmans, the captains of my host who most excel; I speak to recall their names to thee:—

8. Thou, and Bhīshma, Karṇa, Kṛipa the war-winner, Aśvatthāman, Vikarṇa, and Somadatta's son,

[1] The word *Dharma*, which here and elsewhere may be translated as 'law,' properly includes the whole sphere of moral and religious duty connoted by the term 'caste.'

9. Also many other mighty men there be that have offered up their lives for me, wielding many sorts of weapons, all right cunning in the fight.

10. Guarded by Bhīshma, this our host cannot be coped with; guarded by Bhīma, yonder host of theirs can be coped with.

11. So stand ye all in due order, each in his place, and guard Bhīshma.'

12. Arousing in him joy, the Kuru elder, the grandsire majestic, blew his conch, ringing a high blast of lion-roar.

13. Thereupon conchs, drums, tambours, gongs, and trumpets straightway struck up; and wild was the sound that rose.

14. Then Madhu's lord and Pāṇḍu's son, standing in a great car yoked with white steeds, blew each his glorious conch.

15. The high-haired one blew 'Pānchajanya,' the wealth-winner blew 'God's gift'; the doer of grim deeds, wolf-bowel, blew the great conch 'Pauṇḍra.'

16. Kuntī's son, King Yudhishṭhira, blew 'eternal-victory'; Nakula and Sahadeva blew 'sweet-sound' and 'gem-blossom,'

17. The Kāśī-king, peerless bowman, and Śikhaṇḍin lord of the great car, Dhṛishṭadyumna, Virāṭa, and Sātyaki the unconquered,

18. Drupada and Draupadī's sons together, O lord of earth, and Subhadrā's stout-armed son blew each his conch.

19. The wild roar cleft the hearts of Dhṛitarāshṭra's folk, and made the heavens and the earth ring.

20. Then the lord of the ape-banner, Pāṇḍu's son, seeing Dhṛitarāshṭra's folk standing in array with all weapons set forth, took up his bow,

And then, O lord of earth, he spake this word to the high-haired one.

ARJUNA SPAKE:—

21. 'Set thou my chariot, O never-falling, midway between the two armies,

22. Whiles I behold these that stand in array wishful for battle, with whom I must strive in this toil of war,

23. And I mark them that are come together here for battle, to do the pleasure of Dhṛitarāshṭra's ill-judging son.'

SANJAYA SPAKE:—

24. Thus bidden by the wearer of the hair-knot, O thou of Bharata's race, the high-haired one set the peerless chariot midway between the two armies,

25. Before Bhīshma, Droṇa, and all the princes of the earth, and thus he spake: 'Behold these Kurus come together, O Pṛithā's son.'

26. There Pṛithā's son saw standing fathers, grandsires, teachers, uncles, brethren, sons, grandsons, and comrades,

27. Fathers-in-law and friends, in either host. Beholding all these kinsfolk in counter-array,

Kuntī's son was stricken with exceeding compassion, and in despair spake thus:

Arjuna spake:—

28. 'As I look, O Kṛishṇa, upon these kinsfolk meeting for battle,

29. My limbs fail and my face withers. Trembling comes upon my body, and upstanding of the hair;

30. Gāṇḍīva falls from my hand, and my skin burns. I cannot stand in my place; my mind is as if awhirl.

31. Contrary are the omens that I behold, O long-haired one. I see no blessing from slaying of kinsfolk in strife;

32. I desire not victory, O Kṛishṇa, nor kingship, nor delights. What shall avail me kingship, O lord of the herds, or pleasures, or life?

33. They for whose sake I desired kingship, pleasures, and delights stand here in battle-array, offering up their lives and substance—

34. Teachers, fathers, sons, likewise grandsires, uncles, fathers-in-law, grandsons, brothers-in-law, kinsmen also.

35. These though they smite me I would not smite, O Madhu-slayer, even for the sake of empire over the three worlds, much less for the sake of the earth.

36. What pleasure can there be to us, O troubler of the folk, from slaughter of Dhṛitarāshṭra's folk? Guilt in sooth will lodge with us for doing these to death with armed hand.

37. Therefore it is not meet that we slay Dhṛitarāshṭra's folk, our kinsmen; for if we do to death our own kith how can we walk in joy, O lord of Madhu?

38. Albeit they, whose wits are stopped by greed, mark not the guilt of destroying a stock and the sin of treason to friends,

39. Yet how, O troubler of the folk, shall not we with clear sight see the sin of destroying a stock, so that we be stayed from this guilt?

40. In the destruction of a stock perish the ancient laws of the

stock; when law perishes, lawlessness falls upon the whole stock.

41. When lawlessness comes upon it, O Kṛishṇa, the women of the stock fall to sin; and from the women's sinning, O thou of Vṛishṇi's race, castes become confounded.

42. Confounding of caste brings to hell alike the stock's slayers and the stock; for their fathers fall when the offerings of the cake and the water to them fail.

43. By this guilt of the destroyers of a stock, which makes castes to be confounded, the everlasting laws of race and laws of stock are overthrown.

44. For men the laws of whose stock are overthrown, O troubler of the folk, a dwelling is ordained in hell; thus have we heard.

45. Ah me! a heavy sin have we resolved to do, that we strive to slay our kin from lust after the sweets of kingship!

46. It were more comfortable to me if Dhṛitarāshṭra's folk with armed hand should slay me in the strife unresisting and weaponless.'

SANJAYA SPAKE:—

47. So spake Arjuna, and sate down on the seat of his chariot in the field of war; and he let fall his bow and arrows, for his heart was heavy with sorrow.

Thus ends the First Lesson, intituled 'The Rule of Arjuna's Despair,' in the Communion of the Blest Kṛishṇa and Arjuna, which is the Teaching-Book of the Rule, the Knowledge of Brahma, the Discourses of the Blest Bhagavadgītā.

NOTE.—Dr. L. D. Barnett, in his Introduction to the translation of the Gītā, here reproduced, summarizes the whole teaching of the poem in a paragraph which will be of assistance to the student.

'Kṛishṇa's argument in sum is as follows. Every class of men has *dharma*, a code of social-religious works (*karma*) incumbent upon it. On the other hand, the paramount religious duty of man is to "save his soul," to bring the conditioned self or individual soul into unity with the Supreme Self or Vāsudeva, who is represented in incarnate form by Kṛishṇa himself and the way to this consummation lies through *knowledge* of the fundamental distinction between self and not-self (soul and matter), and through devotion to the Supreme, *bhakti*. Now, such enlightenment can be reached, according to our author, by two roads. One is that of *sannyāsa*, the purely intellectual course of the Sāṃkhyan *sannyāsin*, or recluse who has cast off all social ties and dwells alone in a forest or wilderness strictly meditating upon the nature of the two opposite categories of soul and matter. The other is the " Rule of Works," *karma-yoga*, the performance of all the social and religious duties of caste and class in a spirit of absolute selflessness, solely for the love of God, and without the least regard for the direct or indirect results that may accrue from them. This is the more natural and convenient way, and it is infallible; therefore it should be followed by Arjuna. The corollary is that, as Arjuna's caste-duty is to be a fighting man, he ought now to fight without repining, but to fight in a spirit of perfect selflessness.'

Lesson the Second

To comfort Arjuna and encourage him to battle, Kṛishṇa sets forth his doctrine. The Self (soul, essential reality in each being) is indestructible, unchangeable, unaffected by physical experience in the cycle of births, a phase of the unchanging universal soul; it passes from body to body under the law of predestination, but bodily experiences nowise modify its essence. Therefore it is wrong to regret the sufferings of mortality (*vv.* 1–30). *Besides, a knight must fulfil his caste-duty, and fight; if slain he will win the joys of Paradise, if victorious the joys of earth* (*vv.* 31–37). *Let Arjuna then fight, but with unselfishness of purpose* (*v.* 38). *This doctrine* (*namely, vv.* 11–30) *is Sāṃkhya; now follows the principle of the Yoga* (*v.* 39). *The latter cannot appeal to those who are selfishly attached to Vedic rituals and the worldly benefits that result thence, and fetter them to mortality* (*vv.* 40–46). *Let Arjuna do religious and social works, but with no thought of gaining benefit thence; this indifference is Yoga, a moral elevation above one's works while doing them, which prepares the soul for redemption from the flesh* (*vv.* 47–53). *Next is described the condition of profound apathy of body and mind, culminating in understanding of the Divine, which arises from the preliminary exercises of the Yoga* [*the* Kriyā-yoga], *and forms the essential or superior Yoga* [Rāja-yoga]. *Death in such a condition is immediately followed by everlasting emancipation of the soul and its union with the Divine* (*vv.* 54–72).

Sanjaya spake:—

1. So was he stricken by compassion and despair, with clouded eyes full of tears; and the slayer of Madhu spake to him this word.

THE LORD SPAKE:—

2. 'Wherefore, O Arjuna, hath come upon thee in thy straits this defilement, such as is felt by the ignoble, making not for heaven, begetting dishonour?

3. Fall not into unmanliness, O Pṛithā's son; it is unmeet for thee. Cease from this base faintness of heart and rise up, O affrighter of the foe!'

ARJUNA SPAKE:—

4. 'O Madhu's slayer, how shall I contend in the strife with my arrows against Bhīshma and Droṇa, who are meet for honour, O smiter of foes?

5. Verily it were more blest to eat even the food of beggary in this world, without slaughter of noble masters; were I to slay my masters, I should enjoy here but wealth and loves—delights sullied with blood.

6. We know not which is the better for us, whether we should overcome them or they overcome us; before us stand arrayed Dhṛitarāshṭra's folk, whom if we slay we shall have no wish for life.

7. My soul stricken with the stain of unmanliness, my mind all unsure of the law, I ask thee—tell me clearly what will be the more blest way. I am thy disciple; teach me, who am come to thee for refuge.

8. I behold naught that can cast out the sorrow that makes my limbs to wither, though I win to wide lordship without rival on earth and even to empire over the gods.'

9. So spake to the high-haired one the wearer of the hair-knot, affrighter of foes; 'I will not war,' he said to the lord of the herds, and made an end of speaking.

10. And as he sate despairing between the two hosts, O thou of Bharata's race, the high-haired one with seeming smile spake to him this word.

THE LORD SPAKE:—

11. 'Thou hast grieved over them for whom grief is unmeet, though thou speakest words of understanding. The learned grieve not for them whose lives are fled nor for them whose lives are not fled.

12. Never have I not been, never hast thou and never have

these princes of men not been; and never shall time yet come when we shall not all be.

13. As the body's tenant goes through childhood and manhood and old age in this body, so does it pass to other bodies; the wise man is not confounded therein.

14. It is the touchings of the senses' instruments, O Kuntī's son, that beget cold and heat, pleasure and pain; it is they that come and go, that abide not; bear with them, O thou of Bharata's race.

15. Verily the man whom these disturb not, indifferent alike to pain and to pleasure, and wise, is meet for immortality, O chief of men.

16. Of what is not there cannot be being; of what is there cannot be aught but being. The bounds of these twain have been beheld by them that behold the Verity.

17. But know that That which pervades this universe is imperishable; there is none can make to perish that changeless being.

18. It is these bodies of the everlasting, unperishing, incomprehensible body-dweller that have an end, as it is said. Therefore fight, O thou of Bharata's race.

19. He who deems This to be a slayer, and he who thinks This to be slain, are alike without discernment; This slays not, neither is it slain.

20. This never is born, and never dies, nor may it after being come again to be not; this unborn, everlasting, abiding ancient is not slain when the body is slain.

21. Knowing This to be imperishable, everlasting, unborn, changeless, O son of Pṛithā, how and whom can a man make to be slain, or slay?

22. As a man lays aside outworn garments and takes others that are new, so the body-dweller puts away outworn bodies and goes to others that are new.

23. Weapons cleave not This, fire burns not This, waters wet not This, wind dries it not.

24. Not to be cleft is This, not to be burned, nor to be wetted, nor likewise to be dried; everlasting is This, dwelling in all things, firm, motionless, ancient of days.

25. Unshown is This called, unthinkable This, unalterable This; therefore, knowing it in this wise, thou dost not well to grieve.

26. So though thou deemest it everlastingly to pass through

births and everlastingly through deaths, nevertheless, O strong of arm, thou shouldst not grieve thus.

27. For to the born sure is death, to the dead sure is birth; so for an issue that may not be escaped thou dost not well to sorrow.

28. Born beings have for their beginning the unshown state, for their midway the shown, O thou of Bharata's race, and for their ending the unshown; what lament is there for this?

29. As a marvel one looks upon This; as a marvel another tells thereof; and as a marvel another hears of it; but though he hear of This none knows it.

30. This body's tenant for all time may not be wounded, O thou of Bharata's stock, in the bodies of any beings. Therefore thou dost not well to sorrow for any born beings.

31. Looking likewise on thine own law, thou shouldst not be dismayed; for to a knight there is no thing more blest than a lawful strife.

32. Happy the knights, O son of Pṛithā, who find such a strife coming unsought to them as an open door to Paradise.

33. But if thou wilt not wage this lawful battle, then wilt thou fail thine own law and thine honour, and get sin.

34. Also born beings will tell of thee a tale of unchanging dishonour; and to a man of repute dishonour is more than death.

35. The lords of great chariots will deem thee to have held back from the strife through fear; and thou wilt come to be lightly esteemed of those by whom thou wert erstwhile deemed of much worth.

36. They that seek thy hurt will say many words of ill speech, crying out upon thee for thy faintness; now what is more grievous than this?

37. If thou be slain, thou wilt win Paradise; if thou conquer, thou wilt have the joys of the earth; therefore rise up resolute for the fray, O son of Kuntī.

38. Holding in indifference alike pleasure and pain, gain and loss, conquest and defeat, so make thyself ready for the fight; thus shalt thou get no sin.

39. This understanding has been told to thee according to the School of the Count[1]; now hear of that understanding according

[1] *The Sāṃkhya:* 'The object of the Sāṃkhya is to win for the sou[l] deliverance from the cycle of birth and sorrow (saṃsāra) by the savin[g] grace of knowledge and knowledge alone by which all castes and condition[s] of men may be redeemed.'—L. D. Barnett.

to the School of the Rule,[1] by rule of which, O son of Pṛithā, thou shalt cast off the bond of works.

40. Herein there is no failing of enterprise, nor backsliding. Even a very little of this law saves from the great dread.

41. One and sure is the understanding that is herein, O son of the Kurus; but many-branched and endless are the understandings of the unsure.

42. That flowery speech, O son of Pṛithā, which is spoken by the undiscerning, who hold fast to the words of the Veda, and say " There is naught else,"

43. Whose spirit is all lust, whose supreme end is Paradise—(speech) appointing births as meed of works, and dwelling much on various rites for reaching pleasure and empire—

44. That (speech) steals away the wit of such lusters after pleasure and empire, and their understanding, being not sure, cannot be brought to concent.

45. The Vedas' realm is the three moods (guṇas). Be thou not of the three moods, O Arjuua, be without the pairs, abiding in everlasting goodness, neither winning nor hoarding, possessed of Self.

46. As much profit as is in a pool of waters gathered from all sides lies in all the Vedas, for the discerning Brahman.

47. In works be thine office; in their fruits must it never be. Be not moved by the fruits of works; but let not attachment to worklessness dwell in thee.

48. Abiding under the Rule and casting off attachment, O wealth-winner, so do thy works, indifferent alike whether thou gain or gain not. Indifference is called the Rule.

49. For work is far lower than the Rule of the understanding, O wealth-winner. Seek refuge in the understanding; base are they who are moved by fruits.

50. Under the Rule of the understanding a man leaves behind him here alike good deeds and ill. Therefore set thyself to the Rule; skill in works is the Rule.

51. For under the Rule of the understanding prudent men regard not fruits of works, and loose themselves from the bond of birth, and go to a land where no sickness is.

52. When thine understanding shall have passed through the

[1] *Yoga:* The Bhagavadgītā 'seeks not to establish the individual soul in a lonely empire of superhuman power and final isolation, but to bring it straightway into the bosom of the Divine Love. . . . In the main it seeks, not very successfully, to distinguish two forms of Yoga or " Rule." These are the " Rule of Knowledge " (Jnāna-yoga) and the " Rule of Works " (Karma-yoga).'—L. D. BARNETT.

broil of confusion, then thou wilt come into discontent with the things that thou shalt hear and hast heard.

53. When thine understanding, that erstwhile swayed unbalanced by reason of what thou hast heard, shall stand firm and moveless in concent, then shalt thou come into the Rule.'

ARJUNA SPAKE:—

54. 'What are the words for the man of abiding wisdom who stays in concent, O long-haired one? What will the man of abiding wisdom say? How shall he sit or walk?'

THE LORD SPAKE:—

55. 'When one leaves all the loves that dwell in the mind, O son of Pṛithā, and is gladdened only in his Self by his Self, then he is said to be of abiding wisdom.

56. He whose mind is undismayed in pain, who is freed from longings for pleasure, from whom passion, fear, and wrath have fled, is called a man of abiding prudence, a saintly man.

57. He who is without affection for aught, and whatever fair or foul fortune may betide neither rejoices in it nor loathes it, has wisdom abidingly set.

58. When such a one draws in his sense-instruments altogether from the objects of the sense-instruments, as a tortoise draws in its limbs, he has wisdom abidingly set.

59. The ranges of sense vanish away from a body-dweller who haunts them not, save only relish; and at sight of the Supreme the relish likewise passes away from him.

60. For though the prudent man strive, O son of Kuntī, his froward instruments of sense carry away his mind perforce.

61. Let him hold all these in constraint and sit under the Rule, given over to me; for he who has his sense-instruments under his sway has wisdom abidingly set.

62. In the man whose thoughts dwell on the ranges of sense arises attachment to them; from attachment is born love; from love springs wrath.

63. From wrath is confusion born; from confusion wandering of memory; from breaking of memory wreck of understanding; from wreck of understanding a man is lost.

64. But he who walks through the ranges of sense with sense-instruments severed from passion and hatred and obedient to the Self, and possesses his Self in due order, comes to clearness.

65. In clearness it comes about that all pains in him vanish away; for in them whose minds are clear the understanding is utterly steadfast.

66. In him who is not under the Rule is no understanding; in him who is not under the Rule is no inspiration; in him who feels no inspiration peace is not; in him who has not peace whence can there be joy?

67. For if a man's mind move under the sway of errant sense-instruments, it sweeps away his enlightenment, as the wind a ship on the waters.

68. Therefore he only who utterly holds back his sense-instruments from sense-objects, O mighty-armed one, has wisdom abidingly set.

69. In the night of all born beings the austere man is awake; the time when born beings are awake is night to the saintly man who has vision.

70. He whom all loves enter as waters enter the full and immovably established ocean wins to peace; not so the lover of loves.

71. The man who casts off all desires and walks without desire, with no thought of a *Mine* and of an *I*, comes unto peace.

72. This is the state of abiding in Brahma, O son of Pṛithā. He that has come therein is not confounded; if even at his last hours he dwell in it, he passes to extinction in Brahma.'

Thus ends the Second Lesson, intituled 'The Rule of the School of the Count,' in the Communion of the Blest Kṛishṇa and Arjuna, which is the Teaching-Book of the Rule, the Knowledge of Brahma, the Discourses of the Blest Bhagavadgītā.

Lesson the Third

The sheer inaction (akarma) *which the Sāṃkhyas prescribe is not a true casting-off* (sannyāsa) *of works, or worklessness* (naishkarmya), *and cannot release soul from body; for it is physically impossible to carry inaction to its logical extreme. The right course is the Yoga—doing works in the spirit of utter unselfishness that renders them no-works* (*vv.* 1–8). *To such*

Yoga-work belongs especially the duty of sacrifice, for on this depends the welfare of living things (*vv.* 9–16). *Such works and such a spirit are meet for aspirants to salvation, even the noblest; for thus is set up a good example for the daily life of common men* (*vv.* 17–21). *The Almighty himself does such work* (*vv.* 22–4). *The sage performs the same work as worldly men, but in the Yoga-spirit of combined knowledge, selflessness, and devotion* (*vv.* 25–35). *Selfish and sinful activity in the world arises from the spirit of desire, which must be suppressed in order that the soul be cleansed and enlightened to its own selfhood* (*vv.* 36–43).

ARJUNA SPAKE:—

1. 'If thou deemest understanding more excellent than works, O troubler of the folk, then wherefore dost thou engage me in a grim work, O long-haired one?

2. Thou confoundest my understanding with seemingly tangled utterance; tell me surely the one thing whereby I shall win to bliss.'

THE LORD SPAKE:—

3. 'In this world is a twofold foundation declared of old by me, O sinless one, in the knowledge-rule of the School of the Count and the work-rule of the School of the Rule.

4. Without undertaking works no man may possess worklessness, nor can he come to adeptship by mere casting-off of works.

5. For no man ever, even for a moment, abides workless; everyone is perforce made to do work by the moods[1] born of nature.

6. He who sits with his sense-instruments of action restrained but with his mind dwelling on the objects of the sense-instruments is said to be a deluded soul, a walker in vain ways.

7. But he is more excellent who, having the sense-instruments under control of the mind, engages his sense-instruments of action on the Rule of works, free from attachment, O Arjuna.

8. Do thine ordained work; for work is more excellent than no-work. Even the subsistence of thy body cannot be won from no-work.

[1] *Gunas*: 'The phases into which matter or nature by its own essence is determined for the fulfilment of its immanent activities without losing thereby its ultimate unity. . . . The Guṇas are called *Sattva* ("goodness" or "truth" or "real being"), *Rajas* ("fieriness" or "passion"), and *Tamas* ("gloom").'—L. D. BARNETT.

9. This world is fettered by works, save in the work that has for its end the sacrifice. Work to this end do thou fulfil, O son of Kuntī, freed from attachment.

10. The lord of beings aforetime, creating beings together with the sacrifice, spake thus: "By this increase your kind; be this the milch-cow of your desires.

11. With this comfort ye the gods, and let the gods comfort you; comforting one another, ye shall get supreme bliss.

12. For the gods, comforted by the sacrifice, shall give to you the pleasures of your desire. He that enjoys these their gifts without giving to them is a thief.

13. Good folk that eat what is left over from the sacrifice are released from all defilements; but they that dress food only for themselves are evildoers, and eat sin."

14. From food are born beings; from rain arises food; from sacrifice comes rain; and from works does sacrifice arise.

15. Know that works arise from Brahma; Brahma is born of the imperishable; therefore Brahma, the everlasting, who abides in all things, has his seat in the sacrifice.

16. Thus is the cycle made to revolve, and he who joins not in its course here, O son of Pṛithā, lives in vain, his life being sin and his delight being from the sense-instruments.

17. But for the man whose delight is in Self, who is contented with Self, and is glad of Self, there is naught for which he should work.

18. He has indeed no object here either in work or no-work, nor do his purposes lie with any of born beings.

19. Therefore fulfil ever without attachment the work that thou hast to do; for the man that does his work without attachment wins to the supreme.

20. For it was with works that Janaka and others came unto adeptship; thou too shouldst do them, considering the order of the world.

21. Whatsoever the noble man does, that same the other folk do; whatever he makes his standard, that the world obeys.

22. There is naught in the three worlds, O son of Pṛithā, that I must needs do, naught that I have not gotten or that I shall not get; yet do I abide in work.

23. For if I should not abide ever unwearying in work, O son of Pṛithā, men would altogether follow in my way;

24. These worlds would perish, if I should not do works; I should make confusion, and bring these beings to harm.

25. As do the unwise, attached to works, O thou of Bharata's race, so should the wise do, but without attachment, seeking to establish order in the world.

26. He should not bring about a rift in the understanding of the unwise who are attached to works; the sage should approve all works, fulfilling them under the Rule.

27. Works are done altogether by the moods of nature; but he whose Self is confounded by the thought of an *I* imagines "*I* am the doer thereof."

28. But he that knows the verity of the two orders of moods and works, O mighty-armed one, judges that moods dwell in moods, and has no attachment.

29. Confounded by the moods of nature, men are attached to the works of the moods; the man of perfect knowledge should not shake these dull men of imperfect knowledge.

30. Casting off all thy works upon me with thy mind on the One over Self,[1] be thou without craving and without thought of a *mine*, and put away thy fever and fight.

31. The men who ever fulfil this my teaching, possessed of faith and unmurmuring, are released from works.

32. But know that they who murmur at this my teaching and fulfil it not are confounded in all knowledges, mindless, and lost.

33. Even the man of knowledge does acts like to his own nature; all born beings follow nature; what can repression do?

34. Passion and loathing are appointed to the object of each several sense-instrument; one should not come under the sway of these twain, for they are foes in his path.

35. There is more happiness in doing one's own law without excellence than in doing another's law well. It is happier to die in one's own law; another's law brings dread.'

ARJUNA SPAKE:—

36. 'Then what stirs this or that man to walk in sin, moved even against his will as though by violence, O thou of Vṛishṇi's race?'

THE LORD SPAKE:—

37. 'It is love, it is wrath, sprung from the fiery mood, mighty to devour, mighty to sin; know this to be the foe here.

[1] *Adhyātma*: 'The phase of the universal soul which constitutes the individual self.'—L. D. BARNETT.

38. As fire is covered over by smoke, as a mirror by foulness, as a germ by a membrane, so is this world covered over thereby.

39. The knowledge of the wise man, O son of Kuntī, is covered over by this his everlasting changeling foe, unquenchable and insatiable.

40. The sense-instruments, mind, and understanding, they say, are its seat; by these it confounds the body's tenant, covering over knowledge.

41. Therefore do thou first by constraint of the sense-instruments, O Bharata-prince, loose thyself from this sinful one that destroys knowledge and discernment.

42. The sense-instruments, they say, are high; higher than the sense-instruments is the mind; higher than the mind is understanding; but higher than understanding is This.

43. Thus, knowing Self to be higher than understanding, and supporting by Self thy Self, O mighty-armed one, slay this changeling foe so hard to reach.'

Thus ends the Third Lesson, intituled 'The Rule of Works,' in the Communion of the Blest Kṛishṇa and Arjuna, which is the Teaching-book of the Rule, the Knowledge of Brahma, the Discourses of the Blest Bhagavadgītā.

Lesson the Fourth

This doctrine has been revealed in divers times to divers friends of God (vv. 1–3). Vāsudeva from time to time incarnates himself to guide the world to righteousness and knowledge; he maintains the religious and social orders, dispensing worldly weal for worldly righteousness and salvation for enlightened devotion (vv. 4–12). These his works are no-works, no fetters of soul, for they are done in divine unselfishness; the wise imitate them (vv. 13–15), doing their works of caste and religion in the Yogic spirit of utter selflessness and devotion that renders them no-works (vv. 16–22). Chief among these works is sacrifice. This is performed in many ways, literally and symbolically, according to the worshipper's condition; but if done in the Yogic spirit, it always leads to salvation (vv. 23–32). Highest is the sacrifice of knowledge, where the soul in the enlightenment of perfect wisdom surrenders itself to the supreme wisdom and love. Knowledge is the surest way to salvation; and it arises from observing the Yoga with loving faith (*vv.* 33–42).

THE LORD SPAKE:—

1. 'This unaltering Rule I declared to Vivasvat; Vivasvat declared it to Manu, and Manu told it to Ikshvāku.

2. Thus was this Rule passed down in order, and kingly sages learned it; but by length of time, O affrighter of the foe, it has been lost here.

3. Now is this ancient Rule declared by me to thee, for that thou art devoted to me and friend to me; for it is a most high mystery.'

ARJUNA SPAKE:—

4. 'Near was thy birth, and far-off was the birth of Vivasvat. How may I understand that thou didst declare it in the beginning?'

THE LORD SPAKE:—

5. 'Many births of me and thee have passed, O Arjuna. I know them all; but thou knowest them not, O affrighter of the foe.

6. Though birthless and unchanging of essence, and though lord of born beings, yet in my sway over the Nature that is mine own I come into birth by my own magic.

7. For whensoever the law fails and lawlessness uprises, O thou of Bharata's race, then do I bring myself to bodied birth.

8. To guard the righteous, to destroy evildoers, to establish the law, I come into birth age after age.[1]

9. He who knows in verity my divine birth and works comes not again to birth when he has left the body; he comes to me, O Arjuna.

10. Many, freed from passion, fear, and wrath, instinct with me, making their home in me, and cleansed by the mortifications of knowledge, have come into my Being.

11. With them that seek me I deal in like measure; mortals altogether follow in my path, O son of Pṛithā.

12. In desire for their works to bear fruit do men here offer

[1] There are ten incarnations or avatāras of Vishṇu-Vāsudeva, of which the best known are those as Rāma and Kṛishṇa.

sacrifice to gods; for speedily is fruit born of works in the world of mortality.

13. The four castes were created by me according to the orders of moods and works; know that I am indeed the doer of that work, yet no worker, unchanging.

14. Works defile me not; in me is no longing for fruit of works. He who recognizes me as such is not fettered by works.

15. With such knowledge works were done by former seekers after deliverance; therefore do thou likewise works as were done by former men in former days.

16. What is work, what no-work? Herein even seers are bewildered. That work I will declare to thee, by knowledge whereof thou shalt be delivered from ill.

17. For of work there should be heed, and of ill-work there should be heed, and of no-work there should be heed; devious is the course of work.

18. He who beholds in work no-work, and in no-work work, is the man of understanding among mortals; he is in the Rule, a doer of perfect work.

19. The man whose every motion is void of love and purpose, whose works are burned away by the fire of knowledge, the enlightened call "learned."

20. Free from attachment to fruit of works, everlastingly contented, unconfined, even though he be engaged in work he does not work at all.

21. Whoso, being without craving, restrained of mind, surrendering all possessions, does but work of the body's office, gets no defilement.

22. Happy in what chance brings him, beyond the pairs, void of envy, indifferent alike whether he gain or gain not, even in working he becomes not fettered.

23. In one who, being void of attachment, delivered, and possessing a mind established in knowledge, yet fulfils the sacrifice, all works vanish away.

24. Brahma is the deed of sacrifice; Brahma is the oblation, by Brahma offered in the fire that is Brahma; and to Brahma shall he go who dwells in concent with the works that are Brahma.

25. Some there be, men of the Rule, that worship the sacrifice to the gods; some with the sacrifice offer sacrifice in the fire which is Brahma.

26. Some offer the ear and other sense-instruments in the

fires of constraint; others offer sound and other ranges of sense in the fires of the sense-instruments.

27. Others offer the works of all sense-instruments and works of breath in the knowledge-kindled fire of the Rule that is constraint in Self.

28. Other anchorites there are, strict of vows, who make offering of substance, or of mortification, or of the Rule, or of the knowledge of their scripture-reading.

29. Others offer the outward breath in the inward breath, or the inward breath in the outward breath; or they set themselves to constraint of breath by staying the course alike of outward and inward breath.

30. Others, restricting their food, offer breaths in breaths. All these, knowers of sacrifice, cleanse away their defilements by sacrifice.

31. Feeding on the ambrosial remains of sacrifice, they come to the ancient Brahma. This world is not for him who offers no sacrifice; how then should another be for him, O best of Kurus?

32. Thus manifold are the sacrifices set forth in the mouth of Brahma. Know that they are all born of works; with this knowledge shalt thou be delivered.

33. There is more bliss in sacrifice of knowledge than in sacrifice of substance, O wealth-winner; all works without limit, O son of Pṛithā, are contained in knowledge.

34. Know thou that for reverence, for asking, and for service men of knowledge who behold the verity will teach thee this knowledge.

35. Knowing that, thou wilt never again fall into such bewilderment, O son of Pāṇḍu; by that thou wilt see born beings altogether in thy self, and likewise in me.

36. Even though thou shouldst be of all sinners the greatest evildoer, thou shalt be by the boat of knowledge carried over all evil.

37. As a kindled fire makes its fuel into ashes, O Arjuna, so the fire of knowledge makes into ashes all works.

38. For there is naught here that is like in power of cleansing to knowledge; this the adept of the Rule himself finds after many days in his Self.

39. Knowledge he wins who has faith, who is devoted, who restrains the instruments of sense; having won knowledge, he speedily comes to supreme peace.

40. He perishes who has not knowledge or faith, who is all unbelief; neither this world nor the world beyond nor pleasantness is for him who is unbelieving.

41. But works fetter not him who has cast off works under the Rule, who has cleft unbelief by knowledge, and possesses his Self, O wealth-winner.

42. Therefore arise, O thou of Bharata's race, and set thyself to the Rule, cleaving with the sword of knowledge this unbelief in Self, born of ignorance, that lodges in thy heart.'

Thus ends the Fourth Lesson, intituled 'The Rule of Knowledge and Casting-off of Works,' in the Communion of the Blest Kṛishṇa and Arjuna, which is the Teaching-Book of the Rule, the Knowledge of Brahma, the Discourses of the Blest Bhagavadgītā.

Lesson the Fifth

The Sāṃkhyas, seeking salvation in inaction, and the Yogins, seeking it in works, both attain it, and thus they are really of the same school. But the way of the Yogin is the nobler and easier (vv. 1–6). He discharges the duties of caste and religion as a service of God, in perfect selflessness; and thus [*as* Kriyā-yoga] *they purify his soul and bring him to knowledge and peace* [Rāja-yoga], *and thence to immediate redemption after death (vv. 7–29).*

Arjuna spake:—

1. 'Thou tellest, O Kṛishṇa, of casting-off of works and again of the Rule; declare to me surely which of these is the happier.'

The Lord spake:—

2. 'Casting-off of works and Rule of works both lead to bliss; but of these the Rule of works is higher than casting-off of works.

3. He who hates not and desires not should be deemed to have everlastingly cast off works; for he who knows not the pairs, O mighty-armed one, is easily delivered from the fetter.

4. The simple speak of the School of the Count and the

School of the Rule as diverse, but not so the learned; he that has meetly set himself thereto finds the same fruit from either.

5. The place won by the men of the Count is likewise reached by the Rule-men; he who sees the School of the Count and the School of the Rule to be one sees indeed.

6. But it is hard to win to casting-off of works without the Rule, O mighty-armed one. The holy man who follows the Rule speedily comes to Brahma.

7. Following the Rule, cleansed of spirit, victorious over himself, holding the sense-instruments under his sway, his Self become the Self of all born beings, he is not defiled though he do works.

8. The knower of the verity following the Rule will wot well that he does not works at all, though he see, hear, touch, smell, eat, walk, sleep, breathe,

9. Speak, loose, seize, open or close his eyes; or he bears in mind that the sense-instruments dwell in the objects of the sense-instruments.

10. He who in doing works lays his works on Brahma and puts away attachment is not defiled, as the lotus-leaf is unsullied by the water.

11. With body, mind, understanding, and bare sense-instruments, the men of the Rule do their works to purify the Self, putting away attachment.

12. Following the Rule, putting aside the fruit of works, one wins to fundamental peace; following not the Rule, attached by the workings of desire to fruits, one becomes bound.

13. When one has cast off by power of mind all works, the body-dweller abides in pleasantness and mastery in the nine-gated city, neither working nor moving to work.

14. The lord creates not for the world either power of work, or works, or union of fruit with works; it is its own nature that moves.

15. The supreme takes unto himself no sin of any man, and likewise no good deed. Knowledge is covered over by ignorance, whereby creatures are confounded.

16. But to them in whom this ignorance of Self is by knowledge dispelled, knowledge sun-like reveals the supreme verity.

17. With understanding set on That, with Self at one with That, with heart in That, with That for their supreme path, cleansed of defilement by knowledge, they return never again.

18. The learned look with indifference alike upon a wise and

courteous Brahman, a cow, an elephant, a dog, or an outcast man.

19. They are victorious over birth in this world whose minds abide in indifference; for Brahma is stainless and indifferent, and therefore they abide in Brahma.

20. Firm of understanding, unbewildered, the knower of Brahma, who abides in Brahma, will not rejoice when pleasant things befall nor be dismayed when things unpleasing betide him.

21. His spirit unattached to outward touch, he finds in his Self pleasantness; his spirit following the Brahma-Rule, he is fed with undying pleasantness.

22. For the delights born of touch, having beginning and end, are in truth founts of pain, O son of Kuntī; the enlightened man has no joy in them.

23. He who has strength to bear here ere release from the body the passion born of love and wrath, is of the Rule, he is a happy man.

24. The man of the Rule that has joy within, pleasance within, and light within becomes Brahma and wins to extinction in Brahma.

25. Extinction in Brahma do saints win in whom impurity is destroyed, that have cleft unbelief, strict of soul, delighting in the weal of all born beings.

26. Strict-minded saintly men, who have cast away love and wrath, and know the Self, are compassed around by extinction in Brahma.

27. Putting outward touchings without and the eyes in the midst of the brows, making the outward and the inward breaths equal in their course within the nostrils,

28. The saintly man subdued in sense-instruments, mind, and understanding, who has made deliverance his supreme goal and is ever void of desire, fear, and wrath, is in truth delivered.

29. Knowing that I am he whom sacrifice and austerity touch, the great lord of all worlds, the friend of all born beings, he wins to peace.'

Thus ends the Fifth Lesson, intituled 'The Rule of Casting-Off,' in the Communion of the Blest Kṛishṇa and Arjuna, which is the Teaching-Book of the Rule, the Knowledge of Brahma, the Discourses of the Blest Bhagavadgītā.

Lesson the Sixth

To do works of caste and religion in the Yogic spirit [as Kriyā-yoga], *is really to be workless, and is a truer 'casting-off of works' than the inaction of the Sāṃkhya* (*vv.* 1–2). *Such works, by rendering a man perfectly selfless, lift him to a higher sphere of thought and action* [*the state of* Rāja-yoga], *where he abides in full realization of the unity of his personal Self with the absolute Self, utterly indifferent to the world and the flesh* (*vv.* 3–9), *constantly performing in seclusion the ascetic practices of the Rāja-yoga, and thus attaining to the stillness of divine peace* (*vv.* 10–32). *This way is not easy; but it is quite feasible* (*vv.* 33–36). *And though one should fail through weakness to win to the end of it in his present life, the merit of his effort will abide with him after death, so that after many years of heavenly bliss he shall in future births go through the same course of Yogic progress and advance ever farther in each life, until at length he comes to the end, and is redeemed* (*vv.* 37–47).

The Lord spake:—

1. 'One that does his appointed works without heed to fruit of works is both a caster-off of works and a man of the Rule; not so the fireless, workless man.

2. Know thou, O son of Pāṇḍu, that what men call casting-off is the Rule; for none becomes a man of the Rule without he cast off purpose.

3. For the saintly man who seeks to rise on the Rule, works are said to be the means; after he has risen on the Rule, calm is said to be the means.

4. For when one clings not to the objects of the sense-instruments and to works, and has cast off all purposes, then is he said to have *risen on the Rule*.

5. He shall by Self lift up himself, nor let himself sink; for a man's self has no friend but Self, no foe but Self.

6. The Self is friend to that self that has by self conquered self; but Self will be a very foe warring against him who possesses not his self.

7. In him that has conquered self and come to peace, the supreme Self abides in concent, alike in cold and heat, in joy and sorrow, in honour and dishonour.

8. With spirit contented in knowledge and discernment, set on high, victorious over the sense-instruments, the man of the

Rule to whom clods, stones, and gold are alike is said to be *under the Rule.*

9. Most excellent is he whose understanding is indifferent alike to the friend, the lover, the enemy, the indifferent, the one facing both ways, the hateful, and the kinsman, alike to the good and the evil.

10. The man of the Rule shall ever hold himself under the Rule, abiding alone in a secret place, utterly subdued in mind, without craving and without possessions.

11. On a pure spot he shall set for himself a firm seat, neither over-high nor over-low, and having over it a cloth, a deer's skin, and *kuśa* grass.

12. On this couch he shall seat himself with thought intent and the workings of mind and sense-instruments restrained, and shall for purification of spirit labour on the Rule.

13. Firm, holding body, head, and neck in unmoving equipoise, gazing on the end of his nose, and looking not round about him,

14. Calm of spirit, void of fear, abiding under the vow of chastity, with mind restrained and thought set on me, so shall he sit that is under the Rule, given over to me.

15. In this wise holding himself ever under the Rule, the strict-minded man of the Rule comes to the peace that ends in extinction and that abides with me.

16. The Rule is not with him that eats overmuch nor with him that eats not at all, not with him that is given to overmuch leep nor with him that sleeps not, O Arjuna.

17. The sorrow-slaying Rule is with him whose eating and walking are by rule, whose action in works is by rule, whose leeping and waking are by rule.

18. When he, void of longing for any loves, sets his restrained mind upon his Self, then is he said to be *under the Rule.*

19. As a lamp in a windless spot flickers not, such is the like-ness that is told of the strict-minded man of the Rule who abours upon the Rule of the Self.

20. When the mind, held in check by service of the Rule, omes to stillness, and when from beholding Self by Self he has oy in Self,

21. And when he knows the boundless happiness that lies eyond sense-instruments and is grasped by understanding, nd in steadfastness swerves not from the verity,

22. Than which, once gotten, he deems no other boon better; therein he abides, and is not shaken even by sore pain ;

23. This severance from union with pain, be it known to him, bears the name of the *Rule*; on this Rule he should resolutely labour, with unwearied mind.

24. Putting away utterly all the loves born of purpose, by force of mind compassing with restraint the group of sense-instruments,

25. Little by little he shall win stillness by understanding ruled in firmness; making his mind abide in the Self, he shall ponder upon nothing whatsoever.

26. Wheresoever the fickle and unsteady mind wanders off, there he shall check it and bring it into obedience to the Self.

27. For to this peaceful-minded man of the Rule, who has stilled the mood of fieriness, who is stainless, one with Brahma, there comes exceeding joy.

28. Thus the man of the Rule, void of stain, who ever labours upon the Self, has easy enjoyment of boundless happiness in touch with Brahma.

29. With spirit following the Rule, with vision indifferent towards all things, he beholds the Self dwelling in all born beings and all born beings in the Self.

30. If one sees me in all things and all things in me, I am not lost to him nor is he lost to me.

31. The man of the Rule, who, setting himself to union, worships me as dwelling in all born beings, abides in me, wheresoever he may abide.

32. He who sees indifferently all things in the likeness o Self, O Arjuna, whether joy or sorrow betide, is deemed th supreme Man of the Rule.'

ARJUNA SPAKE:—

33. 'Thou hast declared this Rule to be of indifference, C Madhu-slayer; but I see not how it may be firmly established by reason of fickleness.

34. For fickle is the mind, O Kṛishṇa, froward, forceful, anc stiff; I deem it as hard to check as is the wind.'

THE LORD SPAKE:—

35. 'Doubtless the mind is ill to check and fickle, O mighty armed one; but by constant labour and passionlessness, O so of Kuntī, it may be held.

36. For one of unrestrained spirit the Rule is hard of attai ment, I trow; but by one of obedient spirit who strives it ma be won by the means thereto.'

ARJUNA SPAKE:—

37. 'If one possessed of faith mortify himself not, and his mind swerve from the Rule, so that he wins not to accomplishment of the Rule, into what ways comes he, O Kṛishṇa?

38. Falls he not from both paths, and perishes he not like a riven cloud, O mighty-armed one, unestablished and bewildered in the road to Brahma?

39. This is my doubt, O Kṛishṇa, it is meet for thee to resolve altogether; there is no resolver of this doubt beside thee.'

THE LORD SPAKE:—

40. 'Son of Pṛithā, neither here nor in the other world is there destruction for him; for none that does righteousness, beloved, comes to evil estate.

41. He that is fallen from the Rule wins to the worlds of them that do godly deeds, and dwells there changeless years; then he is born in the house of pure and prosperous folk.

42. Or haply he may be born in the race of wise men of the Rule; but such birth as this is very hard to win in the world.

43. There he is given that Rule of the understanding which he had in his former body, O child of the Kurus, and therefore he strives further for adeptship.

44. For he is led onward, without will of his own, by that former striving; if he have even the wish to know the Rule, he passes beyond the Word-Brahma.

45. But the man of the Rule who labours stoutly, when cleansed of defilements and brought to adeptship through many births, goes thence by the way supreme.

46. Greater than mortifiers of the flesh is deemed the man of the Rule, greater also than men of knowledge, and greater than doers of works; therefore be thou a man of the Rule, O Arjuna.

47. Of all men of the Rule I deem him who worships me in faith with his inward Self dwelling in me to be most utterly under the Rule.'

Thus ends the Sixth Lesson, intituled 'The Rule of Meditation,' in the Communion of the Blest Kṛishṇa and Arjuna, which is the Teaching-Book of the Rule, the Knowledge of Brahma, the Discourses of the Blest Bhagavadgītā.

Lesson the Seventh

The supreme being creates the universe from himself by assuming a twofold nature or phase of qualified existence; the lower of these natures is matter (Prakṛiti) *in all its grades as analysed in the Sāṃkhya, the higher is the 'Elemental soul'* (Jīva-bhūta) *or world-spirit, the Self informing the universe* (*vv.* 1–6). *Thus the supreme is the essence of all things, their material and mental substrate* (*vv.* 7–12). *Misguided souls, understanding not this mystery, remain in low incarnations* (*vv.* 13–15). *The perfectly enlightened worshipper of Vāsudeva follows the Yoga in knowledge and love, and wins eternal redemption; worshippers of other gods Vāsudeva allows to rise in later births to incarnation as gods, whence in time they return to mortal birth* (*vv.* 16–23). *Few understand the triple character of Vāsudeva as absolute being, world-soul, and world-substance* (*vv.* 24–30).

The Lord spake:—

1. 'Hear, son of Pṛithā, how, if thou labourest upon the Rule with mind clinging to me and with me for thy dwelling-place, thou shalt surely know me in my fullness.

2. I will tell thee of the knowledge and discernment which if thou possessest there shall remain naught else to know.

3. Of thousands of men, but few strive for adeptship; of the adepts that strive, but few know me in verity.

4. A nature have I of eight orders—Earth, Water, Fire, Wind, Ether, Mind, Understanding, and Thought of an *I*.

5. This is the lower. But know that I have another and higher nature than this, one of Elemental Soul, O mighty-armed one, and thereby is upheld this universe.

6. Learn that from these twain are sprung all born beings; the source of the whole universe and its dissolution am I.

7. There is naught higher than I, O wealth-winner; all this universe is strung upon me, as rows of gems upon a thread.

8. I am the taste in water, O son of Kuntī; I am the light in moon and sun, the Om in all the Vedas, sound in the ether, manhood in men.

9. The pure scent in earth am I, and the light in fire; the life in all born beings am I, and the mortification of them that mortify the flesh.

10. Know me to be the ancient seed of all born beings, O son

of Pṛithā; I am the understanding of them that understand, the splendour of the splendid.

11. The might of the mighty am I, void of love and passion; I am the desire in born beings which the law bars not, O Bharata-prince.

12. Know that from me are the existences alike of the goodness-mood, the fiery-mood, and the gloom-mood; I am not in them, but they are in me.

13. Bewildered by these three existences of mood, this whole universe perceives not that I am higher than they, and changeless.

14. For this my divine magic of mood is hard to fathom; but they who make their refuge in me pass beyond this magic.

15. But not to me come for refuge besotted workers of evil, basest of men; being through the magic bereft of knowledge, they come into dæmonic existence.

16. Four orders of doers of righteousness worship me, O Arjuna—the afflicted, the seeker after knowledge, the desirer of substance, and the man of knowledge, O Bharata-prince.

17. Of these most excellent is the man of knowledge, everlastingly under the Rule, worshipping me alone; for exceeding dear am I to the man of knowledge, and he to me.

18. High in rank are all these, but the man of knowledge I deem to be my very Self; for he with spirit under the Rule sets himself to the supreme way—and that am I.

19. At the end of many births, the man of knowledge finds refuge in me, knowing Vāsudeva to be the all; very rare is such a great-hearted man.

20. But they whose knowledge is swept away by this and that love make other gods their refuge, holding by this and that rule, and bound by their own nature.

21. If any worshipper whatsoever seeks with faith to reverence any body whatsoever, that same faith in him I make steadfast.

22. Ruled by that faith, he seeks to do reverence thereto, and wins thence his desires, dispensed by me.

23. But there is an end to this fruit that comes to these men of little wit. They that make offering to gods go to gods; worshippers of me come to me.

24. Men of no understanding deem me to have come from the unshown to the shown state, knowing not my higher being to be changeless, supreme.

25. Veiled by the magic of my Rule, I am not light to all the world; this world is bewildered, and recognizes me not as birthless and unchanging.

26. I know the born beings that have gone before, and that are now, and that shall be, O Arjuna; but me no one knows.

27. By the delusion of the pairs that springs from desire and hatred, O thou of Bharata's race, all born beings at birth fall into bewilderment, O affrighter of the foe.

28. But the folk whose sin is come to an end and who do righteousness are delivered from the delusion of the pairs and worship me, steadfast in their vows.

29. They who strive for deliverance from age and death and turn to me know me to be That Brahma, the universal One over Self, and the whole of works.

30. Men with minds under the Rule, that know how in me are alike the One over born beings, the One over gods, and the One over sacrifice, even in the hour of going hence, know me.'

Thus ends the Seventh Lesson, intituled 'The Rule of Knowledge and Discernment,' in the Communion of the Blest Kṛishṇa and Arjuna, which is the Teaching-Book of the Rule, the Knowledge of Brahma, the Discourses of the Blest Bhagavadgītā.

Lesson the Eighth

Vāsudeva is (1) *the absolute* (' *That Brahma* '), (2) *the* ' *One over Self* ' (Adhyātma) *or individual soul,* (3) *the power of* ' *works* ' (Karma), (4) *the* ' *One over born beings* ' (Adhibhūta) *or principle of matter,* (5) *the* ' *One over gods* ' (Adhidaivata) *or cosmic spirit, and* (6) *the* ' *One over sacrifice* ' (Adhiyajna) *or the supreme incarnate in bodily form. The observer of Yoga comes at once after death to the supreme Vāsudeva* (*vv.* 5–16). *In each cosmic period material existences issue from and return to the mass of primal matter; but beyond this is a higher being, the absolute spirit of Vāsudeva* (*vv.* 17–22). *The two ways of the passage of the Yogin's soul are described* (*vv.* 23–28).

ARJUNA SPAKE:—

1. 'What is "That Brahma," what the "One over Self," what are "Works," O male-supreme; what is that called "One over born beings," what that hight "One over Gods"?

2. Who is the "One over sacrifice" here in this body, and how may it be, O Madhu-slayer; and how at the hour of their going hence mayst thou be known by men of strict spirit?'

THE LORD SPAKE:—

3. 'Brahma is the imperishable, the supreme; the nature of each is called the One over Self; the creative force that makes born beings arise into existence bears the name of works.

4. The One over born beings is perishable existence; the One over gods is the male; the One over sacrifice am I in this body, O best of men.

5. He who at his last hour, when he casts off the body, goes hence remembering me, goes assuredly into my being.

6. Whatsoever being a man at his end in leaving the body remembers, to that same he always goes, O son of Kuntī, inspired to being therein.

7. Therefore at all times remember me, and fight; if thy mind and understanding are devoted to me, thou wilt assuredly come to me.

8. With mind guided by rule of constant labour, and turning to naught else, O son of Pṛithā, one goes to the heavenly supreme male on whom the thought dwells.

9. Whoso shall remember the ancient seer, the guide, the one subtler than an atom, creator of the all, inconceivable of form, sun-hued, beyond the dark,

10. At time of going hence, with steadfast understanding, guided by devotion and force of the Rule, setting the breath aright midway between the brows, he comes to the heavenly supreme male.

11. I will tell thee briefly of that abode which Veda-knowers call the imperishable, whereinto strict men void of passion enter, and in desire whereof men observe chastity.

12. Closing all doors, shutting the mind within the heart, bringing the breath of Self into the head, set upon maintenance of the Rule,

13. Uttering Om, the one-syllabled Brahma, and remembering

me—whoso in this wise goes hence, goes on leaving the body into the supreme way.

14. To the man of the Rule everlastingly under the Rule, who always and everlastingly with undivided mind remembers me, I am easy to win, O son of Pṛithā.

15. After coming to me the great-hearted that have reached supreme adeptship light never again upon birth, the inconstant home of sorrows.

16. The worlds, even to the Brahman-realm, O Arjuna, come and go; but for them that have come to me, O son of Kuntī, there is no birth again.

17. They that know the day of Brahman to endure for a thousand ages and the night thereof to endure for a thousand ages are the knowers of night and day.

18. At coming of the day spring from the unshown state all shown existences, at coming of the night they dissolve into this same unshown state, as men call it.

19. This same sum of born beings, rising to birth after birth, dissolves away without will of its own at the coming of the night, O son of Pṛithā, and springs forth again at coming of the day.

20. But there is another existence beyond this, an unshown beyond this unshown, an ancient, which is in all born beings, but perishes not with them.

21. "The imperishable" is this unshown called; this, they tell, is the way supreme, which once won men return not; and this is my supreme abode.

22. This is the supreme male, O son of Pṛithā, to be won by undivided devotion, wherein born beings abide, wherewith this whole universe is filled.

23. I will declare the times wherein the men of the Rule go hence, going either to return no more or to return, O prince of Bharata's race.

24. Fire, light, day, the waxing half of the month, the six moons of the northern course—in these go hence the knowers of Brahma, and come to Brahma.

25. Smoke, night, the waning half of the month, the six moons of the southern course—in these the man of the Rule attains to the light of the moon, and returns.

26. These are deemed the two everlasting ways, light and dark, of the world; by the one a man comes back never again, by the other he returns.

27. No man of the Rule, O son of Pṛithā, is bewildered if he
now these two paths; therefore be thou at all times guided by
ıe Rule, Arjuna.
28. The man of the Rule, knowing the fruits of righteousness
rdained for scriptures, offerings, mortifications, and alms-
iving, passes beyond this present universe, and reaches the
ıpreme, primal sphere.'[1]

Thus ends the Eighth Lesson, intituled 'The Saving Brahma-Rule,' in the Communion of the Blest Kṛishṇa and Arjuna, which is the Teaching-Book of the Rule, the Knowledge of Brahma, the Discourses of the Blest Bhagavadgītā.

Lesson the Ninth

Vāsudeva is the absolute spiritual substrate of all existence, moulding the universe of physical nature or matter and from time to time incarnating himself in human shape (vv. 1–10). The misguided know him not, and sink in the cycle of birth. The wise worship him in divers ways, and rise to union with him, knowing him to be the essence of universal life (vv. 11–19). They who to win their desires observe Vedic rituals, rise to Paradise, and in time sink again to mortal birth; but worshippers of Vāsudeva never lapse thus, but rise higher and higher in their births (vv. 20–25). To him the humblest offering of faith is acceptable; every deed of social and religious life should be dedicated to him; thus salvation is to be won, even by the basest (vv. 26–34).

ıe Lord spake:—

1. 'Now will I declare to thee, who murmurest not, this most
:ret knowledge, together with discernment, knowing which
ou shalt be delivered from ill.
2. A royal knowledge, a royal mystery is this, pure and most
;h, patent to understanding, lawful, very easy to work,
angeless.

[1] For what is set forth in vv. 23–28 see Chhāndogya Upanishad, IV, 5 f., V, x, and Bṛihadāraṇyaka Upanishad, VI, ii, 15 f.

3. Men without faith in this law, O affrighter of the foe, wir not to me, and return on the path of deathly wandering.

4. By me, unshown of form, is this whole universe filled; ir me abide all born beings, but I am not lodged in them.

5. Yet not in me do born beings abide. Behold my kingly rule; bearer of born beings, but not abiding in born beings, i my Self, creating born beings.

6. Know that as the mighty wind everlastingly abides in th ether and goes everywhere, in such wise do all born beings abid in me.

7. When an age dissolves away, O son of Kuntī, all bor beings enter into my nature; when an age begins again I re mould them.

8. Holding under my sway mine own nature, I remoul again and again the whole of this subject mass of born being by power of nature.

9. But these works fetter me not, O wealth-winner, for abide as one indifferent and unattached to these works.

10. Under my control nature gives birth to the world moving and unmoving things; by reason thereof, O son of Kunt the world goes round on its course.

11. Misguided men despise me when I enter a mortal fram not knowing my higher being as the great lord of born beings

12. Vain of hope, vain of works, vain of knowledge, void mind, they fall into a wildering devilish or dæmonic nature.

13. But into a godlike nature, O son of Pṛithā, enter grea hearted men who worship me with undivided mind, knowi me to be the beginning of born beings, the unchanging;

14. Ever singing my praises, labouring firm in their vow devoutly doing homage, everlastingly under the Rule, men wa on me.

15. Others again there are that wait on me, offering t sacrifice of knowledge, according to my unity, or my severalt or my manifold aspects that face all ways.[1]

16. The sacrifice am I, the offering am I, the father's oblati

[1] *vv.* 13–15. 'The idea is apparently that enlightened worshippers Vāsudeva assume at least the same physical refinement as the g (by predominance of the mood of *Sattva*), and at the end of their prese lives most of them rise at least to the paradise of the gods, whilst the m exalted of them are at once united with Vāsudeva himself (xvi. 1 Those of them that rise to paradise never lapse, but advance in success births until they also reach Vāsudeva.'—L. D. Barnett.

am I, the herb am I, the spell am I, the butter-libation am I, the fire am I, the rite of oblation am I;

17. Father of this universe am I, mother, ordainer, grandsire, the thing that is known and the being that makes clean, the word Om, the Ṛich, the Sāma, and the Yajus;

18. The way, the supporter, the lord, the witness, the dwelling, the refuge, the friend, the origin, the dissolution, the abiding-place, the house of ward, the changeless seed.

19. I give heat; I arrest and let loose the rain; I am likewise power of immortality and death, being and no-being, O Arjuna.

20. Men of the threefold lore that drink the soma and are cleansed of sin, worshipping me with sacrifices, pray for the way to paradise; winning as meed of righteousness the world of the lord of gods, they taste in heaven the heavenly delights of the gods.

21. When they have enjoyed that wide world of paradise and their wage of righteousness is spent, they enter into the world of mortals; thus the lovers of loves who follow the Law of the Three Books win but a going and a coming.

22. But to the men everlastingly under the Rule, who in undivided service think and wait on me, I bring power to win and to maintain.

23. They also who worship other gods and make offering to them with faith, O son of Kuntī, do verily make offering to me, though not according to ordinance.

24. For I am he that has enjoyment and lordship of all sacrifices; but they recognize me not in verity, and therefore they fall.

25. They whose vows are to the gods go to the gods, they whose vows are to the fathers go to the fathers; they who offer to ghosts go to ghosts; but they that offer to me go to me.

26. If one of earnest spirit set before me with devotion a leaf, flower, fruit, or water, I enjoy this offering of devotion.

27. Whatever be thy work, thine eating, thy sacrifice, thy gift, thy mortification, make thou it an offering to me, O son of Kuntī.

28. Thus shalt thou be released from the bonds of works, fair or foul of fruit; thy spirit inspired by casting-off of works and following the Rule, thou shalt be delivered and come unto me.

29. I am indifferent to all born beings; there is none whom I hate, none whom I love. But they that worship me with devotion dwell in me, and I in them.

30. Even though he should be a doer of exceeding evil that worships me with undivided worship, he shall be deemed good; for he is of right purpose.

31. Speedily he becomes righteous of soul, and comes to lasting peace. O son of Kuntī, be assured that none who is devoted to me is lost.

32. For even they that be born of sin, O son of Pṛithā—women, traffickers, and serfs—if they turn to me, come to the supreme path;

33. How much more then shall righteous Brahmans and devout kingly sages? As thou hast come into this unstable and joyless world, worship me.

34. Have thy mind on me, thy devotion toward me, thy sacrifice to me, do homage to me. Thus guiding thyself, given over to me, so to me shalt thou come.'

Thus ends the Ninth Lesson, intituled 'The Rule of the Royal Knowledge and the Royal Secret,' in the Communion of the Blest Kṛishṇa and Arjuna, which is the Teaching-Book of the Rule, the Knowledge of Brahma, the Discourses of the Blest Bhagavadgītā.

Lesson the Tenth

The supreme primal, changeless, and adorable being, the source of all phases of determinate existence, is worshipped by the enlightened with the Yoga in love and joyous self-surrender, and brings them to union with himself (*vv.* 1–11). *Kṛishṇa-Vāsudeva enumerates his powers or manifestations as the highest or most essential of the various phases of existence* (*vv.* 12–42).

The Lord spake:—

1. 'Again, O strong-armed one, hearken to my sublime tale which in desire for thy weal I will recite to thy delighted ear.

2. The ranks of the gods and the saints know not my origin for I am altogether the beginning of gods and saints.

3. He who unbewildered knows me to be the unborn, the one without beginning, great lord of worlds, is released from all sins amidst mortals.

4. Understanding, knowledge, unconfounded vision, patience, ruth, restraint of sense and spirit, joy and sorrow, origination and not-being, fear and fearlessness,

5. Harmlessness, indifference, delight, mortification, almsgiving, fame, and infamy—these are the forms of born beings' existence severally dispensed by me.

6. The seven great saints, the four ancients, and the Manus had their spirit of me, and were born of my mind; of them are these living creatures in the world.

7. He that knows in verity my power and rule is assuredly uled by unwavering Rule.

8. I am the origin of the All; from me the All proceeds; with his belief the enlightened, possessed of the spirit, pay worship o me.

9. With mind on me, with life-breath in me instructing one nother and telling of me, they are in everlasting delight and ontent.

10. On these, who are ever under the Rule, worshipping me vith love, I bestow the Rule of understanding, whereby they ome to me.

11. Present in their spirit's mood, I for pity's sake dissipate vith the radiant lamp of knowledge the darkness born in them f ignorance.'

ARJUNA SPAKE:—

12. 'Supreme Brahma, supreme glory, power of highest urity art thou. The male, unchanging, heavenly, primal of ods, unborn, all-pervading—

13. Thus have all the saints named thee, and the god-saint Nārada, Asita, Devala, and Vyāsa, and so thou tellest me hyself.

14. All this that thou tellest me, O long-haired one, I believe rue; for neither gods nor Dānavas, O lord, know thine apparition.

15. Thou of thyself knowest Self by Self, O male supreme, nspirer of born beings, lord of born beings, god of gods, master f the universe.

16. So I pray thee to tell to me fully thine own divine powers, wherewith thou abidest pervading these worlds.

17. How, O ruler, may I know thee in constant meditation; nd in what forms of existence art thou to be conceived, my ord, by me?

18. Relate again to me in fullness thy Rule and powers, O troubler of the folk; for I am not sated with hearing that immortal tale.'

THE LORD SPAKE:—

19. 'Lo, I will tell thee of mine own divine powers, best of Kurus, in their chiefness; for there is no bound to my fullness.

20. I am the Self inwardly dwelling in all born beings, O wearer of the hair-knot; the beginning, and the midst, and the end of born beings am I.

21. Of the Âdityas I am Vishṇu, of lights the radiant sun; of the Maruts I am Marichi, of the nightly luminaries the moon.

22. Of Vedas I am the Sāma-veda, of gods Indra; of sense-instruments I am the mind, of born beings I am intelligence.

23. Of the Rudras I am Śankara, of elves and goblins the lord of wealth; of the Vasus I am fire, of mountains Meru.

24. Of priests, O son of Pṛithā, know me to be the first, Bṛihaspati; of captains of hosts I am Skaṇda, of waters the ocean.

25. Of the great saints I am Bhṛigu, of words the one syllable; of sacrifices I am the offering of murmured prayer, of rigid things the Himālaya.

26. Of all trees I am the sacred fig-tree, of god-saints Nārada, of Gandharvas Chitraratha, of adepts the saintly Kapila.

27. Of horses know me to be Uchchaiḥśravas, born of the essence of immortality; of royal elephants Airāvata; of men the king.

28. Of weapons I am the thunderbolt, of cows the Kāma-dhuk; the begetter Kandarpa am I; of serpents I am Vāsuki.

29. Of Nāgas I am Ananta, of ocean-creatures Varuṇa; of the fathers I am Aryaman, of chastisers I am Yama.

30. Of Daityas I am Prahlāda, of them that make count I am time; of beasts I am the king of beasts, of birds Garuḍa.

31. Of cleansing things I am the wind, of weapon-wielders Rāma; of fishes I am the Makara, of rivers the Ganges.

32. Of creations I am the beginning and the end and likewise the midst, O Arjuna, of sciences the science of the one over-Self, of speakers the speech.

33. Of letters I am the syllable a, of compounded speech the pair-word; I am imperishable time, I am the ordainer facing all ways.

34. I am death that ravishes all, and the source of all thing

to be; of female names glory, fortune, and speech, memory, wisdom, constancy, patience.

35. Of the Sāmas I am also the Bṛihat-sāma, of verse-forms the Gāyatrī, of months Mārgaśirsha, of seasons the spring.

36. Of the guileful I am the dice-play, of the splendid the splendour; I am victory, I am resolution, I am the goodness of those possessed of the goodness-mood.

37. Of the Vṛishṇis I am Vāsudeva, of the Pāṇḍavas the wealth-winner, of saintly men Vyāsa, of seers the seer Uśanas.

38. Of them that subdue I am the rod, of them that seek victory I am policy; of secret things also I am silence, of them that know the knowledge.

39. The seed of all born beings likewise am I, O Arjuna; there is naught that can be in existence, moving or unmoving, without me.

40. There is no bound to my divine powers, O affrighter of the foe; but in part have I declared this fullness of my power.

41. Whatsoever thing is potent, prosperous, or forceful, know that this same springs from a portion of my splendour.

42. But wherefore this long lesson for thee, Arjuna? It is I that with one portion of me have established this whole universe.'

Thus ends the Tenth Lesson, intituled 'The Rule of Powers,' in the Communion of the Blest Kṛishṇa and Arjuna, which is the Teaching-Book of the Rule, the Knowledge of Brahma, the Discourses of the Blest Bhagavadgītā.

Lesson the Eleventh

At the prayer of Arjuna, Vāsudeva reveals himself in all his diverse aspects of godhead at once (*vv.* 1–13). *Overcome with awe, Arjuna bows before him, describes the divine vision, and salutes the supreme in a hymn* (*vv.* 14–46). *Vāsudeva then reassumes his form as Kṛishṇa* (*vv.* 47–55).

ARJUNA SPAKE:—

1. 'Of thy grace to me hast thou related the supreme mystic tale hight *the One over Self*, and thereby my bewilderment is dispelled.

2. For I have heard from thee in fullness, O thou whose eyes are as lotus-leaves, the origin and dissolution of born beings and thy changeless majesty.

3. So I am fain, O supreme lord, to look upon thy sovran form even as thou sayest that thou art, O male supreme.

4. If thou deemest, lord, that it may be beheld by me, then show to me thy changeless self, sovran of the Rule.'

THE LORD SPAKE:—

5. 'Behold, son of Pṛithā, the hundreds and thousands of my forms, diverse, divine, various of colour and shape.

6. Behold the Ādityas, Vasus, Rudras, Aśvins, and Maruts; behold, O thou of Bharata's race, many marvels erstwhile unseen.

7. Behold now, O wearer of the hair-knot, the whole universe, moving and unmoving, solely lodged in this my body, and all else that thou art fain to see.

8. But for that thou canst not see me with this thine own eye, I give thee a divine eye; behold my sovran Rule.'

SANJAYA SPAKE:—

9. Thus speaking, Hari, the great lord of the Rule, O king, then showed to Pṛithā's son his sovran form supreme,

10. Of many mouths and eyes, of many marvellous aspects, of many divine ornaments, with uplifted weapons many and divine;

11. Wearing divine flower-chaplets and robes, with anointment of divine perfumes, compound of all marvels, the boundless god facing all ways.

12. If the light of a thousand suns should of a sudden rise in the heavens, it would be like to the light of that mighty being.

13. There the son of Pāṇḍu beheld the whole universe in its manifold divisions solely lodged in that body of the god of gods

14. Thereupon the wealth-winner, smitten with amazement with hair standing on end, bowed his head, and with clasped hands spake to the god.

ARJUNA SPAKE:—

15. 'I behold in thy body, O god, all the gods and hosts of the orders of born beings, lord Brahman sitting on the lotus throne, and all the saints and heavenly serpents.

16. I behold thee of many arms, bellies, faces, and eyes, on all sides endless; I behold in thee no end nor midst nor beginning, O all-sovran of all forms;

17. I behold thee bearing diadem, mace, and disk, massed in radiance, on all sides glistening, hardly discernible, shining round about as gleaming fire and sun, immeasurable.

18. Thou art to my thought the supreme imperishable, the one to be known; thou art this universe's supreme place of ward; thou art the warden of everlasting law, thou art the ancient male.

19. I see thee without beginning or midst or end, boundless in potency, boundless of arms, with mouth of gleaming fire, giving of thine own radiance heat to this All.

20. For this mid-space between heaven and earth and all the quarters of the sky are filled with thee alone. Seeing this thy fearful and wonderful form, O great-hearted one, the threefold world quakes.

21. These hosts of Suras come unto thee; some, affrighted, praise with clasped hands. With cries of "Hail!" the hosts of great saints and adepts sing to thee hymns of abounding praise.

22. Rudras, Ādityas, Vasus, and Sādhyas all, the Aśvins, Maruts, drinkers of the warm draught, the hosts of Gandharvas, fairies, Asuras, and adepts all gaze on thee in amazement.

23. Looking upon thy mighty form of many mouths and eyes, of many arms and thighs and feet, of many bellies, and grim with many teeth, O mighty-armed one, the worlds and I quake.

24. For as I behold thee touching the heavens, glittering, many-hued, with yawning mouths, with wide eyes agleam, my inward soul trembles, and I find not constancy nor peace, O Vishṇu.

25. Seeing thy mouths grim with teeth, like to the fire of the Last Day, I recognize not the quarters of the heavens, and take no joy; lord of gods, home of the universe, be gracious!

26. These sons of Dhṛitarāshṭra all with the hosts of kings, Bhīshma, Droṇa, and the charioteer's son yonder, and likewise the chief of our warriors

27. Hasting enter into thy mouths grim with fangs and terrible; some, caught between the teeth, appear with crushed heads.

28. As many currents of rivers flow to meet the sea, so these warriors of the world of mankind pass into thy blazing mouths.

29. As moths with exceeding speed pass into a lighted fire

to perish, so pass the worlds with exceeding speed into thy mouths to perish.

30. Thou devourest and lickest up all the worlds around with flaming mouths; filling the whole universe with radiance, grim glow thy splendours, O Vishṇu.

31. Relate to me who thou art in this grim form. Homage to thee, chief of gods; be gracious! I would fain know thee as first being, for I understand not thy way of action.'

The Lord spake:—

32. 'I am time that makes worlds to perish away, waxed full and working here to compass the worlds' destruction. Even without thee, there shall live none of all the warriors that are arrayed in confronting ranks.

33. Therefore rise up and get thee glory; by conquest of thy foes enjoy ample empire. By me have they already been given to death; be thou the mere occasion thereto, O left-handed archer.

34. Droṇa, Bhīshma, Jayadratha, Karṇa, and other mighty men of war smite thou, for I have smitten them. Quail not, but fight; thou shalt overcome thine adversaries in the fray.'

Sanjaya spake:—

35. Hearing this word of the long-haired one, the diadem-wearer trembling clasped his hands, and with obeisance again spake thus bowing to Kṛishṇa, faltering in voice, and all afraid.

Arjuna spake:—

36. 'Meetly, O high-haired one, is the world at thy praise moved to delight and love; goblins in terror flee on all sides; and all the hosts of the adepts do homage.

31. And wherefore shall they not bow to thee, O great-hearted one, most reverend first creator even of Brahman? O boundless lord of gods, dwelling-place of the universe! thou art the imperishable, being and no-being, the supreme verity.

38. Thou art the first of gods, the ancient male; thou art the universe's supreme place of ward; thou art the knower and the known, the supreme abode; by thee, O boundless of form, is the all filled.

39. Thou art wind, yama, fire, moon, lord of beings, and the grandsire's sire. Homage, homage to thee a thousand times, and yet again homage, homage to thee!

40. Homage before and after thee, homage be to thee on all

ides, O all-being! Thou art of boundless potency and immeasurable prowess; thou fillest all, therefore art thou the all-eing.

41. Whatever rude word I have spoken, thinking of thee as friend, and hailing thee as "Kṛishṇa," "Yādava," or "comade" in ignorance of this thy majesty, through heedlessness or ffection,

42. And whatever deed of unkindness for the sake of mirth as been done to thee, whether alone or in sight of men, in anging abroad, lying, sitting, or eating—for these, O never-alling, I crave mercy of thee, who art immeasurable.

43. Thou art the father of this world, moving and unmoving, nd its worshipful and most reverend teacher. There is no eer to thee; how should there be a greater in all the three orlds, O being of power beyond likeness?

44. Therefore with obeisance and prostration of body I crave race of thee, the adorable lord; as father with son, as comrade ith comrade, as lover with mistress, mayst thou bear with ne, O god!

45. I am rejoiced with seeing what none before has seen. But my mind is quaking with fear; show me the same form [as efore]; be gracious, O lord of gods, home of the universe!

46. I would fain see thee in the same guise [as erstwhile], ith diadem, with mace, with disk in hand; assume that same our-armed shape, O thousand-armed universal-bodied being.'

HE LORD SPAKE:—

47. 'In grace to thee, Arjuna, have I shown thee of mine own ile this my supreme form, framed of radiance, universal, oundless, primal, which none save thee has yet beheld.

48. Not for study of Vedas and of sacrifices, not for alms-iving, not for works, not for grim mortifications may I be beheld such shape in the world of men by any but thee, O mighty an of the Kurus.

49. Let not trembling nor a spirit of bewilderment be thine in oking upon this so awful form. With fear cast off, with mind laddened, behold once more that same shape of mine [as rstwhile].'

ANJAYA SPAKE:—

50. Thus having spoken to Arjuna, Vāsudeva once more displayed his own form; and the great-hearted one, again assuming pleasant shape, comforted him in his terror.

ARJUNA SPAKE:—

51. 'Beholding now this thy pleasant manlike shape, O troubler of the folk, I am come to my senses and returned to my natural state.'

THE LORD SPAKE:—

52. 'That shape of mine that thou hast seen is very hard to behold; even the gods are everlastingly fain to see that form.

53. Not for the Vedas, not for mortifications, not for almsgiving, and not for sacrifice may I be seen in such guise as thou hast seen me.

54. But through undivided devotion, Arjuna, I may be known and seen in verity, and entered, O affrighter of the foe.

55. He who does my work, who is given over to me, who is devoted to me, void of attachment, without hatred to any born being, O son of Pāṇḍu, comes to me.'

Thus ends the Eleventh Lesson, intituled 'The Sight of the Universal Form,' in the Communion of the Blest Kṛishṇa and Arjuna, which is the Teaching-Book of the Rule, the Knowledge of Brahma, the Discourses of the Blest Bhagavadgītā.

LESSON THE TWELFTH

Which are the better servants of the Yoga—they that worship in complete devotion of spirit and works the deity as ruling in many forms the created universe, or they that with complete abandonment of works and strict mortification meditate upon him as absolute being and so win to him? (vv. 1–4). *The way of the latter is too hard for most men to follow* (v. 5). *The former way leads surely to salvation* (vv. 6–8) *; it may be followed according to a man's powers, by practising the exercises of the Yogic 'meditation with object'* (samprajnāta samādhi), *or by doing works on behalf of religion, or even works for one's own behoof, if they be done in the spirit of selflessness* (vv. 9–12). *The indifference, selflessness, and other virtues of the Yogin given over to worship and meditation are described* (vv. 13–20).

ARJUNA SPAKE:—

1. 'Of them that in everlasting obedience to the Rule worship thee with devotion and of them that worship thee as the imperishable and unshown, which know best the Rule?'

THE LORD SPAKE:—

2. 'I deem them to be right well under the Rule who lay their minds on me and do service to me everlastingly under the Rule, possessed of supreme faith.

3. But they who worship the imperishable, indefinable, unshown, that is everywhere present, inconceivable, set on high, unmovable, steadfast,

4. And who by suppression of the group of sense-instruments hold everywhere their understanding in indifference—they, rejoicing in the weal of all born beings, win to me.

5. Exceeding great is the toil of these whose mind is attached to the unshown; for the unshown way is painfully won by them hat wear the body.

6. But as for them who, having cast all works on me and given themselves over to me, worship me in meditation with undivided Rule,

7. I lift them up speedily from the ocean of deathly life-wanderings, O son of Pṛithā, as their mind is laid on me.

8. On me then set thy mind, in me let thine understanding dwell; so shalt thou assuredly abide afterward in me.

9. If so thou canst not set thy mind on me in steadfastness, then with rule of constant labour seek to win to me, O wealth-winner.

10. If thou hast not strength even for constant labour, give thyself over to works for me; if thou doest even works for my sake, thou shalt win to adeptship.

11. If likewise thou hast not strength to do this, then come thou unto my Rule and with restrained spirit surrender the fruit of all works.

12. For knowledge has more happiness than constant labour; meditation is more excellent than knowledge, surrender of fruits of works than meditation; after surrender, peace comes straight-ay.

13. Hateless toward all born beings, friendly, and pitiful, void of the thought of a *Mine* and an *I*, bearing indifferently pain and pleasure, patient.

14. Ever content, the man of the Rule subdued of spirit and steadfast of purpose, who has set mind and understanding on me and worships me, is dear to me.

15. He before whom the world is not dismayed and who is not dismayed before the world, who is void of joy, impatience, fear, and dismay,

16. Desireless, pure, skilful, impartial, free from terrors, who renounces all undertakings and worships me, is dear to me.

17. He who rejoices not, hates not, grieves not, desires not, who renounces alike fair and foul, and has devotion, is dear to me.

18. One indifferent to foe and to friend, indifferent in honour and in dishonour, in heat and in cold, in joy and in pain, free of attachment,

19. Who holds in equal account blame and praise, silent, content with whatsoever befall, homeless, firm of judgment possessed of devotion, is a man dear to me.

20. Truly the worshippers possessed of faith and given over to me, who do service to this lawful power of immortality whereof I have told, are exceedingly dear to me.'

Thus ends the Twelfth Lesson, intituled 'The Rule of Devotion,' in the Communion of the Blest Kṛishṇa and Arjuna, which is the Teaching-Book of the Rule, the Knowledge of Brahma, the Discourses of the Blest Bhagavadgītā.

Lesson the Thirteenth

Matter, as physical universe and as individual body, is the dwelling of the spirit (*vv.* 1–6). *Knowledge is defined* (*vv.* 7–11), *likewise the object of knowledge, which is the supreme being without condition, indwelling in all the conditions of the universe* (*vv.* 12–18). *In the union of spirit and matter constituting a living universe, matter only is active; spirit, dwelling in matter, is passively conscious of it, and in proportion as this consciousness begets attachment to matter, spirit sinks deeper into it; knowledge of this distinction brings salvation* (*vv.* 19–34).

THE LORD SPAKE:—

1. 'This body, O son of Kuntī, is hight the *dwelling*; the knower of it is called the *dwelling-knower* by them that have knowledge thereof.

2. Know, O thou of Bharata's race, that the dwelling-knower am I in all dwellings; the knowledge of dwelling and dwelling-knower is my doctrine.

3. What this dwelling is, of what sort, of what mutations, whence and what, and who is he and of what powers, hear from me in summary.

4. The saints have chanted it in manifold wise with divers psalms severally, and likewise with Brahma-aphorisms bearing reason and conviction.

5. The great-born things, the thought of an *I*, the understanding, the unshown, the ten sense-instruments, the one, and the five ranges of the sense-instruments,

6. Desire, hate, pleasure, pain, the bodily whole, intelligence, and constancy—these are declared in summary to be the dwelling, with its mutations.

7. Pridelessness, guilelessness, harmlessness, patience, uprightness, service of the master, purity, steadfastness, self-suppression,

8. Passionlessness towards the objects of the sense-instruments, lack of the thought of an *I*, perception of the frailties of birth, death, age, sickness, and pain,

9. Unattachment, independence of child, wife, home, and the like, everlasting indifference of mind whether fair or foul befall him,

10. Unswerving devotion towards me with undivided Rule, haunting of solitary places, lack of delight in the gatherings of men,

11. Ceaseless dwelling in the knowledge of the one over Self, vision of the goal of the knowledge of the verity—these are declared to be knowledge. Ignorance is otherwise than this.

12. The thing to be known will I declare, by understanding whereof one enjoys the essence of immortality—the beginningless supreme Brahma, which is called neither being nor no-being.

13. This has everywhere its hands and feet, everywhere its eyes, heads, and mouths, everywhere its hearing in the world, and abides enveloping the All;

14. Wearing the semblance of the functions of all sense-

instruments, yet void of all sense-instruments; unattached, yet supporting all; moodless, yet feeling the moods.

15. Within and without born beings, unmoving and moving, indiscernible is this from its subtleness, far away and yet near is this.

16. Undivided, yet as it were dwelling in division within born beings, this thing to be known is supporter, devourer, and begetter of born beings.

17. This is said to be the light even of lights, and above darkness—the knowledge, the thing to be known, and the goal of knowledge, established in the heart of all.

18. Thus have been told in sum the dwelling, the knowledge, and the thing to be known; discerning this, the worshipper of me attains to my being.

19. Know that nature and the male are both beginningless; know that mutations and moods spring from nature.

20. The motive-force for the making of effects and agencies thereof is called *nature*; the motive-force for feeling pleasure and pain is called the *male*.

21. For the male, dwelling in nature, feels the moods born of nature; his attachment to the moods is cause of birth in good or evil wombs.

22. Onlooker, approver, supporter, feeler, great sovereign, and highest self is the supreme male in this body called.

23. He who knows thus the male and nature with the moods, however he may be placed, never again comes to birth.

24. Some behold the Self in self by Self through contemplation, some through the Rule of the School of Count, and others through the Rule of Works.

25. Some again, that have not such knowledge, do worship according as they have heard from others; they likewise, though having hearsay for their highest way, pass beyond death.

26. Whatsoever living thing is born, whether motionless or moving, know that it is from the union of the dwelling-knower with the dwelling, O Bharata-prince.

27. He who sees the supreme lord abiding indifferently in all born beings and perishing not as they perish, does indeed see.

28. For seeing the lord indifferently lodging everywhere, he harms not the Self by self; therefore he goes to the supreme way.

29. He who sees that works are altogether worked by nature and that the Self works not, does indeed see.

30. When he perceives that the several existences of born

beings abide in one, and thence traces their manifoldness, then he wins to Brahma.

31. Inasmuch as it is without beginning and without moods, this supreme Self is unchanging; though dwelling in the body, O son of Kuntī, it works not, gets no defilement.

32. As by reason of its subtleness the ether, everywhere present, is not defiled, so the Self, dwelling everywhere, is not defiled in the body.

33. As the one sun illumines this whole world, so the dweller illumines the whole dwelling, O thou of Bharata's race.

34. They who perceive with the eye of knowledge the difference between dwelling and dwelling-knower, and the deliverance from the nature of born beings, come to the supreme.'

Thus ends the Thirteenth Lesson, intituled 'The Rule of the Discrimination of Nature and the Male,' in the Communion of the Blest Kṛishṇa and Arjuna, which is the Teaching-Book of the Rule, the Knowledge of Brahma, the Discourse of the Blest Bhagavadgītā.

Lesson the Fourteenth

Material nature and its activities are explained. To primal matter, which itself issues from him, the supreme being communicates the force which thence generates the forms of the physical universe (vv. 1–4). The three phases of energizing matter —'goodness,' 'fieriness,' and 'gloom'—are described in their nature and influence upon the associated Soul (vv. 5–20). The sage is described whose soul has risen superior to all these influences and is prepared for immediate redemption after death (vv. 21–27).

The Lord spake :—

1. 'Again I will declare the supreme knowledge, highest of knowledges, by understanding which all saintly men have passed hence to supreme adeptship.

2. Coming unto this knowledge, they become one in quality with me; in the creations they enter not upon birth, and in the dissolutions they are not disturbed.

3. The great Brahma is a womb for me; therein I set the germ; thence spring forth all born beings, O thou of Bharata's race.

4. Of the forms arising in all wombs, O son of Kuntī, the great Brahma is the womb, I the father that gives the seed.

5. *Goodness*, *fieriness*, and *gloom*, the moods arising from nature, O great-armed one, fetter in the body the body's changeless tenant.

6. Of these, *goodness*, because it is pellucid, is luminous and untroubled, and fetters by the attachment of pleasantness and the attachment of knowledge, O faultless one.

7. *Fieriness*, know thou, is in essence passion, and is sprung from yearnings and clingings; son of Kuntī, it fetters the body's tenant with the attachment of works.

8. *Gloom*, know thou, is born of ignorance, and bewilders all dwellers of body; it fetters by heedlessness, sloth, and sleep, O thou of Bharata's race.

9. *Goodness* binds to pleasure, *fieriness* to works, O thou of Bharata's race; but *gloom*, veiling knowledge, binds to heedlessness.

10. *Goodness* arises by prevailing over fieriness and gloom, O thou of Bharata's race, *fieriness* by prevailing over goodness and gloom, *gloom* by prevailing over goodness and fieriness.

11. When the light of knowledge springs forth in this body at all its gates, then one may know that *goodness* has waxed full.

12. Greed, activity, undertaking of works, restlessness, yearning, these arise when *fieriness* has waxed full, O Bharata-prince.

13. Uncleanness, inaction, heedlessness, and bewilderment arise when *gloom* has waxed full, O son of the Kurus.

14. When after full waxing of *goodness* the body-bearer comes to dissolution, it then wins to the pure worlds of most exalted sages.

15. If in *fieriness* it come to dissolution, it is born in men attached to works; and if dissolved in *gloom*, it is born in wombs of dullness.

16. Of a well-done work, they say, pure and " goodly " is the fruit; of fieriness the fruit is pain; of gloom the fruit is ignorance.

17. From goodness springs knowledge, from fieriness greed, from gloom heedlessness, bewilderment, and likewise ignorance.

18. They that abide in goodness go upward; they who are possessed of fieriness stay in the midway; they that are of gloom

dwelling under the influences of the lowest mood, go downward.

19. When the beholder discerns that there is none that works save the moods and that there is a higher than the moods, he enters into my existence.

20. Passing beyond these three moods, whence body has its rise, the body's dweller, delivered from birth, death, age, and pain, enjoys immortality.'

ARJUNA SPAKE:—

21. 'By what tokens is a man past these three moods, O lord? of what conduct is he, and how does he pass these three moods?'

THE LORD SPAKE:—

22. 'He who hates not illumination, activity, and bewilderment when they are at work, and desires them not when they have ceased;

23. He who, abiding as one indifferent, is not shaken by the moods, who stands unswaying, with the knowledge that it is the moods which move;

24. To whom pain and pleasure are alike; who abides in himself; to whom clods, stones, or gold are alike; to whom things sweet and things not sweet are equal; who is wise; to whom blame and praise of himself are equal;

25. Who is indifferent to honour and dishonour, indifferent to the interests of friend or foe; who renounces all undertakings —he is said to have passed beyond the moods.

26. He who serves me with unswerving rule of devotion becomes by passage beyond the moods fit for Brahmahood.

27. For I am the foundation of Brahma, of changeless immortality, of the everlasting law, and of absolute joy.'

Thus ends the Fourteenth Lesson, intituled 'The Rule of the Division of the Three Moods,' in the Communion of the Blest Kṛishṇa and Arjuna, which is the Teaching-Book of the Rule, the Knowledge of Brahma, the Discourses of the Blest Bhagavadgītā.

Lesson the Fifteenth

Under the parable of the Fig-tree is described conditioned existence in the material universe, from which the renunciation of enlightenment conveys the soul to the supreme, the primal absolute (*vv.* 1–6). *From the latter has issued the world-soul, the essential light of the cosmos, manifested in divers phases associated with divers bodies, and passing from one to the other* (*vv.* 7–12) *; it is the vivifying force of physical and mental life* (*vv.* 13–15). *Thus the supreme is at once absolute, world-soul, and essential of cosmic matter* (*vv.* 16–20).

The Lord spake:—

1. 'The changeless fig-tree, they say, has roots rising aloft and branches bending downwards; its leaves are the Psalms; he that knows it is a Veda-knower.

2. Upward and downward spread forth its branches, swollen by the moods and having the ranges of sense for their twigs; and downward do the roots stretch forth in succession of works, amid the world of men.

3. Its shape is not beheld here, nor its bound, nor its beginning, nor its foundation. When this fig-tree of swollen root has been cut down with the stout axe of unattachment,

4. Then may one seek out that region where once come men return never again. To this, the primal male, does one attain, whence has streamed forth the ancient energy.

5. They that are without pride and bewilderment, that have overcome the taint of attachment, that are constant to the one over self, that have their loves stilled, that are freed from the pairs called *pleasure* and *pain,* come unconfounded to this changeless region.

6. That supreme abode of mine, where once come men return not, the sun illumines not, nor the moon, nor fire.

7. A portion of me is the ancient elemental soul in the world of souls, which draws the five sense-instruments and mind lying in nature.

8. When the sovran reaches a body, and when he uprises thence, he carries with him these, as the wind carries perfumes from their seat.

9. Presiding over hearing, sight, touch, taste, smell, and mind, he waits upon the ranges of sense,

10. Whether he be uprising, or staying, or suffering, the bewildered perceive him not in his union with the moods; they that have the vision of knowledge behold him.

11. Men of the Rule who strive behold him lodged in their Self; men of imperfect spirit and vain of mind, though they strive, behold him not.

12. The radiance in the sun, in the moon, and in fire, that illumines the whole universe, know thou to be mine.

13. Entering the earth, I support with might born beings; as the soma, essential sap, I foster all herbs.

14. As the Vaiśvānara fire, I lodge in the bodies of breathing beings; and in union with the outward and inward breath I digest the four kinds of food.

15. I am seated in the heart of all; from me are memory, knowledge, and their negation. I am to be known by all the Vedas; I am the framer of the Veda's ends, the knower of the Vedas.

16. Two males there are in the world, a perishable and an imperishable. The perishable is all born beings; the imperishable is called the *One set on High*.

17. But there is another and highest male, called the *Supreme Self*, the changeless sovran who enters and supports the threefold world.

18. For that I am beyond the perishable and likewise higher than the imperishable, therefore I am famed in the world and in the Veda by the name of *Male-Supreme*.

19. He that unbewildered knows me thus as male-supreme is the knower of all, and worships me with his whole spirit, O thou of Bharata's race.

20. Such is this most deep teaching that I have told thee, O faultless one; by understanding thereof one will become a man of understanding and of fulfilled duty.'

Thus ends the Fifteenth Lesson, intituled 'The Rule of the Male-Supreme,' in the Communion of the Blest Kṛishṇa and Arjuna, which is the Teaching-Book of the Rule, the Knowledge of Brahma, the Discourses of the Blest Bhagavadgītā.

Lesson the Sixteenth

The moral qualities are described which appear in men qualified to rise higher in the cycle of birth and finally win redemption; likewise their opposites (*vv.* 1–5). *The former are the godlike order, their opposite the dæmonic; the latter are fully described* (*vv.* 6–24).

The Lord spake:—

1. 'Fearlessness, purity of the goodness-mood, abiding in knowledge and the Rule, almsgiving, restraint of sense, sacrifice, scripture-reading, mortification, uprightness,

2. Harmlessness, truth, wrathlessness, renunciation, restraint of spirit, lack of malice, pity towards born beings, unwantoning sense, tenderness, modesty, steadfastness,

3. Heroic temper, patience, constancy, purity, innocence, and lack of overweening spirit are in him that is born to gods' estate, O thou of Bharata's race.

4. Hypocrisy, haughtiness, overweening spirit, wrath, rudeness, and ignorance are in him that is born to dæmons' estate, O son of Pṛithā.

5. The gods' estate is deemed to lead to deliverance, the dæmons' estate to bondage. Grieve not; thou art born to gods' estate, O son of Pāṇḍu.

6. Two orders of born beings there are in this world, the godlike and the dæmonic. The godlike order has been fully declared; hear from me touching the dæmonic, O son of Prithā.

7. Dæmonic men have understanding neither of action nor of inaction; in them are found not purity, right conduct, or truth.

8. They say the universe is without truth, without foundation, without sovran, arising in no serial order, with nothing but desire for its motive force.

9. Perverted in spirit, mean of understanding, cruel in works, they that uphold this creed arise as foes for the destruction of the world.

10. Turned to insatiable desire, possessed of hypocrisy, pride, and lust, they seize in bewilderment upon false convictions and walk in foul rites.

11. Turned to unbounded imaginations issuing in ruin, given over to enjoyment of desires, assured that this is all,

12. Bound by hundreds of the bonds of hope, given over to desire and wrath, they seek to gather substance unrighteously for the enjoyment of their desires.

13. "This desire to-day have I won; this will I attain; this wealth is mine, this likewise shall afterward be mine.

14. This foe have I slain; others likewise will I slay. I am sovran; I am in enjoyment; I am successful, strong, happy.

15. I am wealthy, noble; what other man is like to me? I will make offerings and give alms; I will rejoice"—thus they say, bewildered by ignorance.

16. Erring in many imaginations, covered over with the mesh of bewilderment, attached to the enjoyments of desire, they fall into a foul hell.

17. Self-conceited, stiff, possessed of pride and lust from their wealth, they make sacrifices that are sacrifices but in name, with hypocrisy and not in accord with ordinance.

18. Turned to thought of an *I*, to force, pride, desire, and wrath, they jealously bear hate against me in their own and in others' bodies.

19. These that hate me, cruel, basest of men and foul, I unceasingly hurl as they wander through life into dæmonic wombs.

20. Falling into dæmonic wombs and bewildered in birth after birth, they win never to me, O son of Kuntī, and thence they come to the lowest way.

21. Desire, wrath, and greed, these are the triple gate of hell that destroys the Self; therefore should one forsake these three.

22. Released from these three gates of darkness, O son of Kuntī, a man works bliss for his Self; thence he goes to the supreme way.

23. He who walks under the guidance of desire, forsaking the ordinance of teaching-books, wins not to adeptship, nor to happiness, nor to the supreme way.

24. Therefore thou shouldst know the teaching-book to be the standard for determining right and wrong, and do here the works whereof the ordinance of the teaching-book tells.'

Thus ends the Sixteenth Lesson, intituled 'The Rule of Godlike and Dæmonic Estate,' in the Communion of the Blest Kṛishṇa and Arjuna, which is the Teaching-Book of the Rule, the Knowledge of Brahma, the Discourses of the Blest Bhagavadgītā.

Lesson the Seventeenth

The religious principle or faith of persons that perform rituals without orthodox authority is classified according to the three Guṇas (vv. 1–6). Descriptions are given of the favourite food (vv. 7–10), the sacrifices (vv. 11–13), the ascetic practices (vv. 14–19), and the almsgiving (vv. 20–22) of men characterized by predominance of each of the Guṇas. The mystic words Om Tat Sat *are expounded in their relation to works of religion (vv. 23–28).*

Arjuna spake:—

1. 'Now what, O Kṛishṇa, is the foundation of them that leave aside the ordinance of teaching-books and sacrifice in faith? is it the mood of goodness, or fieriness, or gloom?'

The Lord spake:—

2. 'Threefold is faith in body-dwellers; it is born of their natures, and is of the mood of goodness, or of fieriness, or of gloom. As such, hear it.

3. The faith of everyone is according to his condition, O thou of Bharata's race. Man is composed of faith; he is indeed as that wherein he has faith.

4. Men of the goodness-mood sacrifice to gods, they of the fiery mood to elves and goblins; men of the gloom-mood make offerings to the spirits of the dead and the ghostly bands.

5. The folk who rack themselves with grim mortifications not ordained by teaching-books, who are inspired by hypocrisy and thought of the *I*, possessed by the forces of desire and passion,

6. Mindless, wasting away the sum of born things dwelling in their bodies and me likewise that dwell within their bodies—these, know thou, are of dæmonic conviction.

7. Now threefold is the food that is dear to each, also the sacrifice, the mortification, and the gift. Hearken to this their distinction.

8. The foods that are dear to men of the goodness-mood are moist, oily, firm, and cordial, such as foster vitality, life, strength, health, comfort, and pleasure.

9. The foods dear to men of the mood of fieriness are bitter,

sour, salty, overhot, sharp, rough, and scorching, such as bring pain, grief, and sickness.

10. The fare dear to men of the gloom-mood is such as has been spoilt, which has lost its moisture and is stinking and stale, also food left from meals or unfit for sacrifice.

11. The sacrifice is of the goodness-mood that is observed according to ordinance and offered by men desiring not fruit thereof, whose mind is set in concent, in the knowledge that sacrifice must be done.

12. But know, O noblest of Bharatas, that the sacrifice is of the mood of fieriness which is offered with a purpose to get fruit therefrom, or because of hypocrisy.

13. The sacrifice is declared to be of the gloom-mood, which is without ordinance, without gift of food, lacking the spell and the fee, and void of faith.

14. Reverence to gods, Brahmans, elders, and sages, purity, uprightness, chastity, and harmlessness are called the mortification of the body.

15. Speech that gives no pain, true, pleasant, and wholesome, likewise practice of scripture-reading, are called the mortification of speech.

16. Clearness of the mind, pleasantness, silence, suppression of self, and cleanness of spirit, these are called the mortification of the mind.

17. This triple mortification fulfilled in supreme faith by men under the Rule, who desire not fruit, they declare to be of the goodness-mood.

18. Mortification done for the sake of entertainment, honour, and reverence, and in hypocrisy, is said here to be of the mood of fieriness, and is unstable and unsure.

19. Mortification done from a crazed conviction, with self-torment, or for the sake of destroying another, is pronounced to be of the gloom-mood.

20. The gift that is given as a duty to one who cannot make return, with fitness of place, time, and person, is known as a gift of the goodness-mood.

21. But that which is for the sake of reward or in view of fruit hereafter, or is grudged in the giving, is known as a gift of the mood of fieriness.

22. That which is given in an unfit place or time, or to unfit persons, or is given without entertainment or with disdain, is pronounced to be of the gloom-mood.

23. *Om Tat Sat* is known as the triune definition of Brahma; by it were ordained aforetime Brahmans, Vedas, and sacrifices.

24. Therefore it is with utterance of *Om* that the works of sacrifice, almsgiving, and mortification by expounders of Brahma are ever carried on, as declared by ordinance.

25. With *Tat* and with no heed of fruit are divers works of sacrifice and mortification and works of almsgiving done by seekers after deliverance.

26. The word *Sat* is applied to existence and goodness; moreover, the word *Sat* is used for a felicitous work, O son of Pṛithā.

27. Engagement in sacrifice, mortification, and almsgiving is likewise called *Sat*; and also works with these purposes are said to be *Sat*.

28. Libations offered, almsgiving bestowed, and mortification exercised without faith are called *Asat*, O son of Pṛithā, and avail neither hereafter nor here.'

Thus ends the Seventeenth Lesson, intituled ' The Rule of the Division of the Three Faiths,' in the Communion of the Blest Kṛishṇa and Arjuna, which is the Teaching-Book of the Rule, the Knowledge of Brahma, the Discourses of the Blest Bhagavadgītā.

Lesson the Eighteenth

Should the sage abandon religious rites performed to win certain objects of selfish desire ('Casting-off,' sannyāsa), *or should he perform rites, but with unselfish disregard of their fruits ('Surrender,'* tyāga)*?* [*Desire is altogether wrong; so rites inspired by it must not be done.*] *Rites prescribed for constant or occasional performance should be observed, but with disregard of their fruits, in faith and dutifulness; such works are of the Sattva Guṇa, a 'surrender,' and bind not the soul* (*vv.* 1–12). *The instrumental causes* (*vv.* 13–17) *and the motives of action* (*v.* 18) *are described. Knowledge, act, and agent are classified according to the three Guṇas* (*vv.* 19–28) *likewise understanding and constancy* (*vv.* 29–35), *likewise pleasure* (*vv.* 36–39). *The activities of the castes, as determined by the Guṇas, are detailed; each of these, if performed well and with discerning piety, raises the agent farther towards redemption* (*vv.* 40–48). *In the highest stage of fulfilled duty, perfectly restrained and mortified in sense and spirit, in utter surrender of soul and body, one attains the 'state of Brahma,' communion with the Absolute; then the supreme enlightenment of the Divine Love comes to him, and he enters for ever into union with the Supreme* (*vv.* 49–56). *Kṛishṇa exhorts Arjuna to follow his law, with a promise of salvation; Arjuna vows obedience* (*vv.* 57–73). *Sanjaya concludes his tale* (*vv.* 74–78).

ARJUNA SPAKE:—

1. 'I am fain, O mighty-armed one, to know the verity of *casting-off* and of *surrender* severally, O high-haired one, Keśin's slayer.'

THE LORD SPAKE:—

2. 'The putting aside of the works of desire seers know to be *casting-off*; surrender of the fruit of all works is what the wise call *surrender*.

3. Some sages say that works should be surrendered as a fault; others declare that works of sacrifice, almsgiving, and mortification should not be surrendered.

4. Hear from me the decision on this surrender, O best of Bharatas; for surrender, O tiger among men, is averred to be of three kinds.

5. Sacrifice, almsgiving, and mortification should not be surrendered, but should verily be done; sacrifice, almsgiving, and mortification purify sages.

6. But these very works must be done with surrender of attachment and fruits; such is the decision of my most high doctrine, O son of Pṛithā.

7. But to cast off a binding work is not fitting; surrender thereof by reason of bewilderment is declared to be of the gloom-mood.

8. If by reason of its painfulness one surrenders a work from fear of bodily distress, he performs a surrender of the fiery mood, and wins not the fruit of his surrender.

9. If a binding work be done as a duty, O Arjuna, with surrender of attachment and fruit, that surrender is deemed to be of the goodness-mood.

10. The surrenderer, enveloped in goodness, enlightened, with unbelief shattered, hates not the unbecoming work and clings not to the fitting work.

11. For the bearer of the body is not able to surrender works altogether; but he that surrenders fruit of works is called the *surrenderer*.

12. Threefold is the fruit of works—unpleasing, pleasing, and mixed—that comes after death to them that surrender not; but it comes not in any place to them that have cast off works.

13. Learn from me, O mighty-armed one, the five causes declared in the decisive School of the Count for the accomplishment of all works.

14. The seat, the agent, the several agencies, the various forms of several activity, and, fifth of these, providence—

15. These five are the causes of every work, rightful or the contrary, that a man sets himself to do, whether with body, or with speech, or with mind.

16. This being so, he who from imperfect understanding sees his pure Self to be an agent, in his foolishness sees not.

17. He whose spirit is not brought to thought of an *I*, whose understanding is not defiled, does no slaughter though he slay these worlds, and is not fettered.

18. The Knowledge, the Thing to be known, and the Knower are the threefold impulse to Work; the agency, the act, and the agent are the threefold union of Work.

19. Knowledge, work, and worker are declared in the count of moods to be of three kinds, according to the distinction of moods; hearken duly to these likewise.

20. Know that the knowledge whereby a man beholds in all born beings one changeless existence, in the divided an undivided, is of the goodness-mood.

21. But know that the knowledge whereby one severally perceives diverse and various existences in all born beings is knowledge of the fiery mood.

22. But that which clings to a single effect as though to the whole, looking not to the cause, seeing not the veritable significance, and mean, is pronounced to be of the gloom-mood.

23. The work that is binding, void of attachment, and done

without passion or hatred by one seeking not fruit, is said to be of the goodness-mood.

24. But the work that is done by one seeking to win his desires, or again by one having thought of an *I*, and that is of great labour, is pronounced to be of the fiery mood.

25. The work that is undertaken from bewilderment, without heed to future issue, destruction, harm, or one's own powers, is said to be of the gloom-mood.

26. A worker is said to be of goodness who is free from attachment, speaks not of an *I*, is possessed of constancy and vigour, and is unmoved whether he gain or gain not.

27. A worker is declared to be of fieriness who is passionate, wishful for fruits of works, greedy, essentially a doer of harm, impure, possessed by joy and grief.

28. A worker is said to be of gloom who is uncontrolled, unrefined, stiff, guileful, malign, idle, despondent, and given to delay.

29. Hear, O wealth-winner, the threefold division of understanding and constancy according to the moods, set forth fully and severally.

30. That understanding, O son of Pṛithā, is of the goodness-mood which knows action and inaction, the thing to be done and the thing to be not done, the thing to be feared and the thing to be not feared, bondage and deliverance.

31. That understanding, O son of Pṛithā, is of the fiery mood by which one has imperfect knowledge of law and lawlessness, of the thing to be done and the thing to be not done.

32. That understanding, O son of Pṛithā, is of the gloom-mood which, enveloped in gloom, deems lawlessness to be law and all objects to be their contraries.

33. That constancy, O son of Pṛithā, is of the goodness-mood by which, as it flags never, one holds to the actions of mind, breath, and sense-instruments under the Rule.

34. That constancy, O Arjuna, is of the fiery mood by which one holds to law, desire, and substance in obstinate desire of fruit, O son of Pṛithā.

35. That constancy is deemed to be of the gloom-mood whereby a man of ill wit puts never aside slumber, fear, sorrow, despair, and wantonness.

36. Now hear from me the threefold pleasure, O Bharata-prince, wherein a man has delight with constant use and comes to an end of pain.

37. That which at first is as poison and in its ripening is like ambrosia is said to be pleasure of goodness, born of the clearness of one's own understanding.

38. That which, coming from union of the sense-instruments with the ranges of sense, is at first as ambrosia and in its ripening like poison is known as pleasure of fieriness.

39. That pleasure which in its beginning and in its sequence bewilders the Self, being sprung from slumber, idleness, and heedlessness, is pronounced to be of gloom.

40. There is not either on earth nor again in heaven among the gods anything that is free from these three nature-born moods.

41. The works of Brahmans, knights, traffickers, and serfs, O affrighter of the foe, are severally distinguished by the moods sprung from nature.

42. Restraint of spirit and sense, mortification, purity, patience, uprightness, knowledge, discernment, and belief are the natural Brahma-works.

43. Valour, heroic temper, constancy, skill, steadfastness in strife, largesse, and princeliness are the natural knightly works.

44. Tilling the ground, herding kine, and trading are the natural works of traffickers; and the natural work of the serf is service.

45. According as each man devotes himself to his own proper work does he attain to consummation. Hear how by devotion to his proper work he wins consummation.

46. A mortal wins consummation by worshipping with his proper work him whence comes the energy of born beings and by whom this universe is filled.

47. There is more happiness in doing one's own law without excellence than in doing another's law well. In doing the work assigned by nature one gets no stain.

48. The work to which one is born he should not forsake, O son of Kuntī, faulty though it be; for all undertakings are involved in faultiness, as fire in smoke.

49. He whose understanding is without attachment, who has wholly conquered self, and from whom longings have passed away, wins by casting-off [of works] to the supreme consummation of worklessness.

50. Learn from me briefly, O son of Kuntī, how he that has won consummation wins to Brahma, which is the supreme foundation of knowledge.

51. Possessed of purified understanding, restraining self by constancy, forsaking sound and other ranges of sense, and casting aside passion and hatred,

52. Haunting the wilderness, eating little, restraining speech, body, and mind, given over to the Rule of meditation, turned everlastingly to passionlessness,

53. Free from thought of an *I*, from force, pride, desire, wrath, and possession, without thought of a *Mine*, and at peace, one becomes fit for Brahmahood.

54. Becoming Brahma, he is clear of spirit, he grieves not and desires not; indifferent towards all born beings, he wins to supreme devotion toward me.

55. By devotion he recognizes in verity who and what I am; then, knowing me in verity, he speedily enters into me.

56. Doing always all works, making his home in me, one attains by my grace to the everlasting changeless region.

57. Casting off with thy mind all works upon me, be thou given over to me; turned to Rule of the understanding, keep thy thought ever on me.

58. If thou hast thy thought on me, thou shalt by my grace pass over all hard ways; but if from thought of the *I* thou hearken not, thou shalt be lost.

59. Turned to thought of the *I*, thou art minded to fight not; but this thy resolve is vain, nature will drive thee.

60. Bound by thine own nature-born works, O son of Kuntī, that which from bewilderment thou seekest not to do thou shalt do perforce.

61. The lord dwells in the heart of all born beings, O Arjuna, and with magic makes all born beings spin about as though set upon a whirligig.

62. In him seek refuge with thy whole soul, O thou of Bharata's race; by his grace thou shalt win supreme peace, the everlasting realm.

63. Thus have I set forth to thee deepest of deep knowledge; ponder upon it in its fullness, and do as thou wilt.

64. Hear again my supreme word, deepest of all; for that thou art exceedingly beloved of me, therefore I will say what is for thy weal.

65. Have thy mind on me, thy devotion toward me, thy sacrifice to me, do homage to me. To me shalt thou come. I make thee a truthful promise; thou art dear to me.

66. Surrendering all the laws, come for refuge to me alone. I will deliver thee from all sins; grieve not.[1]

67. This thou mayst never tell to one doing not mortification, to one without devotion, to one that obeys not, or to one that murmurs against me.

68. He who in supreme devotion toward me shall recite this supreme secret among my worshippers shall assuredly come to me.

69. None of men shall be to me more acceptable of works than he; none shall be dearer to me on earth than he.

70. And by him that shall read this lawful communion of us twain I shall be worshipped with the offering of knowledge; thus is my thought.

71. The believing and unmurmuring man that shall but hear it shall be delivered, and win to the happy worlds of the workers of holiness.

72. Hast thou heard this, O son of Pṛithā, with wholly intent mind? has thy bewilderment of ignorance vanished away, O wealth-winner?'

ARJUNA SPAKE:—

73. 'My bewilderment has vanished away; I have gotten remembrance by thy grace, O never-falling. I stand freed from doubt; I will do thy word.'

SANJAYA SPAKE:—

74. Thus was this wondrous, hair-stirring communion of Vāsudeva and the great-hearted son of Pṛithā that I heard.

75. By the grace of Vyāsa I heard this supreme secret from Kṛishṇa, the lord of the Rule, himself reciting his Rule.

76. O king, as often as I remember this wondrous and holy communion of the long-haired one and Arjuna, I rejoice time after time.

77. And as often as I remember the exceedingly wondrous form of Hari, great astonishment comes upon me, O king, and I rejoice again and again.

78. Whereso is Kṛishṇa the lord of the Rule, whereso is the

[1] *V*. 66 is known as the *charama-śloka* ('final verse') and regarded as a summary of the whole poem in the school of Rāmānuja. It refers to the idea of 'surrender' expounded in xviii. 2 ff., and means that the devotee of Vāsudeva should in act perform the whole of *dharma*, religious and social law, while in spirit renouncing their fruit.

archer, Pṛithā's son, there, I trow, are fortune, victory, sure weal, and policy.

Thus ends the Eighteenth Lesson, intituled 'The Rule of Casting-off and Deliverance,' in the Communion of the Blest Kṛishṇa and Arjuna, which is the Teaching-Book of the Rule, the Knowledge of Brahma, the Discourses of the Blest Bhagavadgītā.

GLOSSARY

GLOSSARY

Aditi, 'the earliest name invented to express the Infinite' (Max Müller).

Ādityas, the, sons of Aditi, especially Varuṇa and the sun.

Agni, the god of fire and light.

Agnihotra, a sacrifice to fire.

Aṅgiras, a name sometimes given to Agni: also a race of semi-divine beings.

Asat, the negation of *sat* (being, hence the true).

Asura, a divine being—*later* a demon.

Aśvamedha-sacrifice, the horse-sacrifice, an important animal sacrifice in ancient India.

Aśvins, the twin horsemen, heralds of dawn.

Ativādin, one who declares something beyond what has gone before.

Bhaga, god of good fortune.

Bhagavat, name of a deity: also holy.

Bhāratī, goddess of speech.

Brahmachārin, a student of sacred knowledge, who has taken vows and lives an austere life.

Brahmaṇaspati (or *Bṛihaspati*), the lord of prayer.

Chaṇḍāla, an outcaste (son of a Śūdra father and a Brāhman mother).

Dānavas, demons.

Dānu, said to be the mother of Vṛitra.

Dāsas (or *Dasyus*), evil beings or demons: also applied to non-Āryan inhabitants of ancient India.

Devas, gods.

Dragon, the, Vṛitra or Ahi, the rain-storm that Indra with his thunderbolt 'slays.'

Fervour, tapas, literally, heat: hence austerity.

Gandharvas, demigods, celestia musicians.

Gāthā, song.

Guṇas, qualities, distinctions: translated in the *Bhagavadgītā* as moods.

Guru, a spiritual preceptor.

Hiraṇyagarbha, the golden germ, the sun-god.

Homa, a sacrificial rite or offering.

Hotar, an invoking priest who calls the gods to enjoy the offering.

Hotrā, invocation personified.

Indra, the favourite national deity in the Vedic age. He reigns in the atmosphere and conquers demons with his thunderbolt.

Īś or *Īśa*, Lord, a more personal name for the highest Being than Brahman.

Jātavedas, omniscient, an epithet of Agni.

Karma, an act which brings fruit in the present or a future birth.

Kavyas, a class of spirits of an ancient race.

Lambara, a musical instrument.

Maghavan, lord of bounty (Indra).
Mantra, hymn, incantation.
Manu, the generic name for the mythical father of the human race.
Maruts, storm-gods.
Māyā, 'Māyā means making or art, but . . . conveys at the same time the sense of illusion' (Max Müller).
Māyin, 'the maker, the artist, but also the magician or juggler' (Max Müller).
Mṛityu, Death.
Muni, saint, anchorite.

Nivid, formula of incantation.

Om, a sacred syllable, which had to be pronounced at the beginning of each Veda and of every recitation of Vedic Hymns.

Paulkasa, an outcaste (son of a Śūdra father and a Kshatriya mother).
Prajāpati, lord of creatures.
Prastotṛi, the priest who chants praise.
Purusha, man regarded as the soul and original source of the universe: also simply the soul.
Pūshan, a sun-god.
Pavamāna, an epithet of Soma, meaning purifying.

Rājanya, a king or prince: also the second or Kshatriya caste.

Rasā, the mythical river of the firmament.
Rātri, the goddess of night.
Rauhina, a demon of drought.
Ṛishi, a seer.
Ṛishis, the seven, the seven stars of the constellation, Ursa Major.
Rivers, the seven, said to include the five rivers of the Punjab and the Sarasvati.

Sādhyas, celestial beings.
Sat, existing: hence true, good, happy.
Savitar, the sun.
Sindhu, the Indus or any great river.
Śloka, a verse.
Sisters, the, day and night.
Śiva, name of a deity: also propitious, happy.
Soma, the fermented juice of a plant used in Vedic ritual, and also deified. 'Soma is the child of heaven, is the milk of heaven and is purified in heaven: he is the lord of heaven' (A. A. Macdonell).
Śrāddha, funeral ceremony.
Śramaṇa, a mendicant.
Śūdra, the fourth caste, that of labourers.
Sūrya, the sun.
Svadhā, the sacrificial exclamation 'Svadhā, or, their allotted portion' (R. T. H. Griffith).
Svāhā, a salutation, 'hail.'

Tāpasa, one who performs penances.
Tat, 'That Brahman,' that is, the Absolute.
Trita, an ancient god, identified in one place with Varuṇa.
Tvashṭar, the divine artificer.

Udgātṛi, the Sama-veda priest.
Udgītha, ritual chant.

Unborn, the, the primæval divine being.

Ūrmyā, an epithet of night.

Vaiśvānara fire, fire as pervading the universe.

Vaiśya, the third caste, that of traders.

Vallī, literally 'creeper,' used in the sense of 'chapter.'

Varuṇa, king of the air and sea, one of the Ādityas.

Vārutrīs, guardian goddesses.

Vāsishtha, a famous Vedic seer.

Vāyu, the wind.

Virāj, one of the sources of existence: also a metre of ten syllables and a name of food.

Viśvakarman, the creator of the universe.

Yajña, sacrifice.

Yama, king of the dead.

Yoga, 'the firm holding back of the senses is what is called Yoga' (*Kaṭha Upan.*, ii, 6, 11). The word is translated in the *Bhagavadgītā* as Rule.

Printed in the United Kingdom by
Lightning Source UK Ltd., Milton Keynes
141153UK00001B/160/A

9 781408 631393